THE EVIDENCE FOR QUALITY

E. Grady Bogue
Robert L. Saunders

THE EVIDENCE FOR QUALITY

Strengthening
the Tests of Academic
and Administrative
Effectiveness

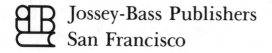 Jossey-Bass Publishers
San Francisco

For sales outside the United States contact Maxwell Macmillan International Publishing Group, 866 Third Avenue, New York, New York 10022

Printed on acid-free paper and manufactured in the United States of America

 The paper used in this book meets the State of California requirements for recycled paper (50 percent recycled waste, including 10 percent post-consumer waste), which are the strictest guidelines for recycled paper currently in use in the United States.

Library of Congress Cataloging-in-Publication Data

Bogue, E. Grady, date.
  The evidence for quality : strengthening the tests of academic and administrative effectiveness / E. Grady Bogue, Robert L. Saunders. — 1st ed.
      p.   cm.—(The Jossey-Bass higher and adult education series)
  Includes bibliographical references (p.) and index.
  ISBN 1-55542-406-6
  1. Educational accountability.   2. Education, Higher—Evaluation. I. Saunders, Robert L.   II. Title.   III. Series.
LB2806.22.B64   1992
379.1'54—dc 20   91-32020
                                                                       CIP

FIRST EDITION
HB Printing   10 9 8 7 6 5 4 3 2 1   *Code 9211*

*The Jossey-Bass
Higher and Adult Education Series*

Contents

Preface

Contemporary commentary within and outside the academy makes clear that the quality of American colleges and universities is coming under more intense scrutiny. Evidences are plentiful. Annual media rankings, new accreditation criteria, position statements of regional and national higher education associations, statements of governors, topics of national conferences, frequent book-length critiques of American higher education, public statements of faculty leaders and college presidents, and policy papers issued by centers for the study of higher education—all point toward an intensified concern for collegiate quality.

What are the origins of this more active quest for quality? Some initiative may be assigned to those within the academy who are doing what leadership in any organized enterprise should be doing— asking questions of purpose and performance. What are we trying to achieve? How good a job are we doing and how do we know? These are simple but penetrating questions, appropriate to any sector of our national life and certainly no less important for colleges and universities. Some portion of the concern for quality may be assigned to an intensified national interest in quality, driven by increased international economic competition. Another source of motivation is revenue reduction and cost-containment challenges—a probing of the conventional wisdom that quality and cost are always positively correlated. Finally, curiosity about quality may be associated with questionable qualitative performance at some colleges.

Whatever the origins of this renewed national interest in collegiate quality, the debate has opened for public and professional inspection a range of issues on the definition, the measurement, and the nurture of quality:

- Is quality in limited supply? By definition, can only a few institutions hope to achieve excellence? Are we to have pyramids of prestige based on size and selectivity, or will we expect and honor excellence of performance for each institutional mission?
- Should the educational mission of the American college focus entirely on the development of knowledge and skill? Is there a legitimate educational responsibility for moral and ethical matters?
- Is quality to be expressed in a single performance indicator or evidence, or does it take more than one data point to circumscribe the richness of both individual and organizational performance?
- How are the evidences on quality to be tried? What standard of performance will be deemed acceptable, and who will make the judgment?
- What is to be the primary decision motive for quality assurance efforts—improvement or accountability? To whom are colleges and universities first accountable?
- How can the definition and measurement of collegiate quality recognize and nurture diverse institutional missions and individual talents and simultaneously establish meaningful minimal performance standards?
- To what extent should information on quality be subject to public disclosure? Do commercial media reports on collegiate quality constitute a useful quality stimulus?
- What is the proper partnership role of campus and external actors on the quality stage? How can the principles of autonomy and accountability be constructively balanced?
- Is the current national interest in quality an ephemeral matter, destined to fade with time and to leave teaching and learning

relationships relatively undisturbed? Or will a strategic perspective on quality emerge, a perspective in which long-term commitments penetrate to the very heart of the campus and engage the active allegiance of faculty?

Purpose of the Book

The Evidence for Quality is designed to bring historical, technical, and philosophical perspective to these questions. We intend the book to be descriptive, furnishing a synthesis of contemporary practices and policies in collegiate quality assurance. We intend it to be evaluative, probing the strengths and limitations of each approach to quality assurance. We intend it to be assertive, emphasizing that quality assurance is a partnership journey of caring and daring, of perseverance and risk. And we intend it to be prescriptive, introducing an array of principles and practices that will serve as a foundation for constructing a strategic and effective quality assurance effort.

Certainly, we hope that the descriptive treatment of quality assurance practices will prove informative and that each chapter will promote enhanced understanding and appreciation of quality principles and practice. We expect, however, that the book will also stimulate curiosity and dissent, an outcome that would sustain our conviction that quality assurance should be a venture in decision and discovery, leading to renewal. Quality assurance exercises produce information that will affect decisions about both student and program performance, enabling us to both improve and account for performance. Quality assurance should also be an adventure in learning—a discovery exercise that challenges our understanding of purpose and performance and frames new questions.

We also accent the promise of quality assurance for strengthening a sense of community and producing an agenda of common caring. Too often questions of teaching and learning are addressed in professorial isolation and loneliness. Other questions of responsibility and reward, of reconciling tensions in teaching, research, and service are often analyzed and acknowledged but remain organizationally disengaged while individual faculty members struggle to negotiate the tensions in their careers.

The search for quality as discussed in this book should encourage faculty members to stand responsible both for their individual impact on campus life and students and for their collective impact on the community and culture that they help create. Neither in corporate nor in collegiate settings will quality emerge unless conversations breach departmental barriers and link all partners in common commitment. An effective quality assurance program will have faculty talking to one another across departments, colleges, and campuses much more than in the past.

Not all the outcomes of a college education, not all that is important to what happens in our classrooms and studios, not all the precious moments that link those who teach and those who learn, not all the value-added impacts of college can be or should be captured by some precise measurement. Where is the instrument powerful and sensitive enough to translate every beautiful moment into numbers?

We can, however, ascertain whether we are elevating the talent and vision of our students from the poverty of the commonplace to the upper reaches of their potential. And we can know whether we are cheating our students of their potential and promise. The first call on our accountability, therefore, is not to governing boards and agencies, not to legislators and other government officials, not to the media. The first call on our accountability is to our students. To know that some of our students have been exposed to low-quality climates requires no great philosophical agony in defining quality nor any technological feat in measuring quality but only the simple passions of caring and daring.

And on that point, we argue that quality assurance is not just an intellectual exercise. To be sure, it is an exercise that should call for our best thought and the engagement of our best minds. But it is an adventure that should tap our passion and our integrity as well. Failing to acquire and to apply information on quality is to confirm that we lack both caring and daring, a lamentable flaw of character in a community of curiosity.

How can we possibly give meaningful leadership to program and service improvements without data on quality? How can such timidity deserve the respect of our students? How can we teach our students the role of risk, courage, discipline, and perseverance in learning if we do not model these same values in learning about purpose and performance? Learning by doing, harnessing reflection and action—our search for quality offers an unparalleled instrument of learning, an opportunity to demonstrate the power and the character of a learning community.

Audience

The Evidence for Quality is designed for a range of readers interested in quality—in its definition, in its measurement, and, above all, in the way information about quality can be applied in decision making. Faculty and staff interested in developing and improving quality assurance programs will find the book useful. We also hope that friends in government and civic affairs who are interested in collegiate quality—governing board members, legislators, journalists, and other media representatives—will find the book of value in honing their knowledge of and sensitivity to questions of collegiate quality. Students of U.S. higher education—those interested in its past achievements and future promise—will find the book instructive, we believe.

Friendly critics are of mixed opinion about another possible audience for the book. We believe, however, that the book may also prove of interest to friends in corporate-sector enterprise who certainly have a serious engagement with questions of quality. We learn from them, and we believe there is room for two-way traffic here. Collegiate and corporate—we share common challenges in definition and decision, in evidence and standards, in timing and judgment. A lively and learning conversation is possible as our entire society searches for quality. Whatever may be the nature of the enterprise, asking questions of ends inevitably forces us to ask questions of beginnings.

Finally, we hope that international colleagues in higher education may find the book informative. The ways in which American higher education nurtures and assures quality will differ in part from those of other cultures and countries. Again, there is merit in bridges of learning that carry two-way traffic. We hope that international friends may find this book helpful—and candid in exposing our journey of discovery in ascertaining what seems to work well and what seems to warrant additional attention. And we anticipate with pleasure the opportunity of learning more about quality assurance from colleagues in other nations.

Overview of the Contents

Chapter One furnishes the background for the current intensified interest in collegiate quality and then offers a serious examination of current issues on how quality is defined and measured and how information on quality contributes to academic decision making. In Chapter One we also propose a definition of quality that takes into account both technical and ethical aspects. This definition allows us to link our presentation and evaluation of quality assurance approaches in the succeeding chapters.

Described in Chapters Two through Seven are current approaches to quality assurance: accreditation, college rankings and ratings, follow-up studies, professional licensure, academic program reviews, and college outcomes studies, respectively. These approaches are presented in the approximate chronological order of their emergence. For example, accreditation is clearly one of the oldest approaches to quality assurance; program reviews and college outcomes studies, on the other hand, have been a recent development. We present the strengths and limitations of each approach and show how each makes a contribution to academic decision making. Finally, we attempt to extract from each some fundamental principles, which we will use in fashioning a philosophy of quality assurance in Chapter Nine.

In Chapter Eight we describe the emerging role of state agencies in both quality assurance and quality enhancement. The relatively recent role of states in providing enhancement and incentive funding for quality—endowed chairs, economic development, enhancement of equipment and facilities—is impressive, whether viewed from a financial or a political perspective.

Chapter Nine emphasizes the renewal promise of our search for quality. The principal purpose of quality assurance is to improve academic decision making, and engagement with quality issues constitutes an unparalleled learning opportunity, a discovery venture. From previous chapters we draw a set of principles important in constructing a philosophy of quality for colleges and universities. For example, we believe that any instrument or system of quality assurance in American higher education must recognize varieties of excellence in both individual and institutional purpose and performance. We offer a streamlined quality assurance model designed to link these principles of good practice to the definition of quality offered in Chapter One. Finally, we reveal how the search for quality can revitalize higher education.

Chapter Ten is designed to be more prospective than retrospective, centering on the future rather than the past. We examine first the ethical, economic, and educational factors affecting the leadership climate in higher education today. We then urge the development of a strategic and unifying vision of quality—a vision in which a concern for quality penetrates to the heart of the college or university; a vision that engages the action allegiance of each one who gives meaning to the life of the institution; a vision that emphasizes the power of partnership; a vision that reveals the presence of competence, caring, and community.

Acknowledgments

We would like to express our appreciation to Richard Burns and other friends at the Educational Testing Service who encouraged the development of this book. We also salute the supportive contributions of Susan Jusselin, Mary Sue Love, Sammy Parker, Jackie Reed, and Dot Saunders, who assisted in the preparation of the manuscript and endured with patience and cheer the many changes and corrections. We wish to recognize the contributions of Gale Bridger, associate vice chancellor for academic affairs, Louisiana State University in Shreveport, who wrote and edited Chapter Four on follow-up studies. Thanks also to Louisiana State University and the University of Georgia for support. Finally, we express appreciation to Gale Erlandson, editor of the Higher and Adult Education Series at Jossey Bass, who, with a thoughtful blend of encouragement and challenge, helped improve style and substance. Whatever liabilities may remain we accept as our own.

We respectfully dedicate *The Evidence for Quality* to three men who over long years of service to American higher education have promoted through thought, word, and deed the causes of both quality and opportunity: Cameron Fincher, regents professor and director of the Institute of Higher Education at the University of Georgia; Fred Harcleroad, professor emeritus of higher education at the University of Arizona and former president of the American College Testing Program; and Allan Ostar, who recently retired as president of the American Association of State Colleges and Universities.

January 1992

E. Grady Bogue
Knoxville, Tennessee

Robert L. Saunders
Somerville, Alabama

The Authors

E. Grady Bogue is visiting professor in the Department of Educational Leadership at the University of Tennessee and is chancellor emeritus of Louisiana State University in Shreveport, where he served as chancellor for ten years. He received his B.S. degree (1957) in mathematics, his M.S. degree (1965) in education, and an Ed.D. degree (1968), all from Memphis State University. He served as interim chancellor of Louisiana State University Agricultural and Mechanical College in 1989. From 1975 to 1980, he was associate director for academic affairs with the Tennessee Higher Education Commission. Between 1964 and 1974, he held three different administrative appointments at Memphis State University, the last as assistant vice president for academic affairs.

Bogue has written four books, and his articles have appeared in such journals as the *Harvard Business Review, Educational Record*, the *Journal of Higher Education, Vital Speeches,* and *Phi Delta Kappan.* He has been a consultant on planning, evaluation, quality assurance, and leadership to colleges and universities, state-level planning agencies, and corporations. He was an American Council on Education (ACE) fellow in academic administration in 1974-75 and served as a visiting scholar with the Educational Testing Service in 1988–89. During his ACE fellowship year and the following five years with the Tennessee Higher Education Commission, he was director of the Performance Funding Project, which developed and implemented one of the first state-level performance incentive programs in American higher education.

Robert L. Saunders is dean emeritus of the College of Education and professor emeritus of educational administration and supervision at Memphis State University. Before his appointment there in 1970, he was associate dean of education at Auburn University, after several years as teacher and administrator in the Alabama public schools. He earned his B.S. (1947) and M.S. (1950) degrees in science education and his Ed.D. degree (1957) in educational administration, all at Auburn University.

Saunders served as president of the Alabama Education Association, the Southern Regional Council on Educational Administration, the Southern Council for Teacher Education, the Teacher Education Council of State Colleges and Universities, and the American Association of Colleges for Teacher Education and as executive secretary for the Southern States' Work Conference. For four years Saunders was vice chairman of the Tennessee Certification Commission, the policy and development body for the Tennessee Career Ladder Program; and for fifteen years he served as consultant to the Tennessee Superintendents' Study Council.

In addition to writing several monographs and articles in professional journals, Saunders coauthored *A Theory of Educational Leadership* (1966, with R. Phillips and H. Johnson) and *The Educational Manager: Artist and Practitioner* (1976, with E. G. Bogue). Saunders was a chapter contributor to *The Modern American College* (1981, A. W. Chickering, ed.) and to *A Practical Guide to Teacher Education Evaluation* (1989, J. B. Ayers and M. F. Berney, eds.).

THE EVIDENCE FOR QUALITY

ONE

Introduction: Defining Academic Quality

College quality: Is it measurable or mysterious? Is it to be found in reputation or results? Is it carried in the perceptions of our academic colleagues and our students, or does it exist independently of their opinion? Is it purchased at the expense of other principles important to American higher education—access, equity, autonomy, diversity—or does it enrich and support those principles? Is it directly related to cost or does it run independently of financial support levels? Is it found in media rankings or in the knowledge and skill of our graduates? Is it expressed in test scores or does it evade capture by existing performance measures?

Quality: Can you improve quality if you cannot define it? Can you measure it if you cannot define it? And if you cannot define it, does it really exist? This is where Robert Pirsig left us several years ago when he noted that "obviously some things are better than others . . . but what's the 'betterness'? . . . so round and round you go, spinning mental wheels and nowhere finding any place to get traction. What the hell is quality? What is it?" (Pirsig, 1974, p. 184).

Given the intensity and the complexity of the historic debate on the nature of quality, those who dare to write on the subject

1

might want to remember the fate of the fourth frog in Kahlil Gibran's parable on knowledge (1982). The story begins with four frogs on a log floating down a river. The debate concerns the question of whether the log or the river is actually moving. The first frog asserts that the log is different from other logs because it exhibits motion as though it were alive. The second frog takes issue, observing that the log is no different from other logs—it is the river that is moving. The third frog suggests that the movement is entirely within their own minds. "Each of you is right, and none of you is wrong," observes the fourth frog, suggesting that there are elements of truth in each point of view. Angered at the suggestion that each does not have access to the whole truth, the three frogs push the fourth into the river. That truth resides in ambiguity has furnished many a theme for writers and other artists, but it creates a disturbing tension for many.

In this book, we hope to reveal something of the ways in which American higher education has opened its search for quality. In this chapter, our aspiration is to engage some of the fundamental questions that must be confronted in that search—questions of definition, measurement, and decision application. We do not subscribe to the notion that every worthy and desirable outcome of American higher education will yield to measurement. But we do hold the conviction that quality can be defined, that quality can be measured, and that quality can be used to improve our impact on students and their growth as well as to enhance programs and services.

Would any college president or faculty member be willing to admit that he or she was producing a low-quality college graduate? Not likely. Would any president or faculty member be willing to admit that quality could not be improved at his or her college or university? Also not likely. But what does he or she have in mind when talking about quality? Whatever the definition (and we will venture a definition in this chapter), on one point a consensus appears to be emerging. If we are to judge by frequency and intensity of public commentary, colleges and universities should be more active in obtaining, using, and communicating data on quality.

The 1984 publication of the National Institute of Education entitled *Involvement in Learning* recommended that to enhance excellence in higher education, "institutions of higher education demonstrate improvements in student knowledge, capacities, skills, and attitudes between entrance and graduation" (p. 15). Later in the monograph, a further recommendation appears: "Faculty and academic deans should design and implement a systematic program to assess the knowledge, capacities, and skills developed by academic and co-curricular programs" (p. 55).

In the 1985 publication *Higher Education and the American Resurgence*, Frank Newman, the president of the Education Commission of the States (ECS), advanced the opinion that "higher education is entering a period of questioning of its purposes and quality" (p. xiii).

A major ECS paper, *Transforming the State Role in Undergraduate Education*, suggested that the "need to use assessment to improve teaching and learning is not reflected in current policies and practices" (Education Commission of the States, 1986, p. 17).

To Secure the Blessings of Liberty, a 1986 report of the American Association of State Colleges and Universities, recommended that "public colleges and universities should respond to these concerns by agreeing on and adopting a set of minimum academic skills and levels of proficiency that all students should attain, preferably by the end of the sophomore year" (p. 35).

In the June 1988 *Special Advisory for College and University Presidents*, the National Task Force on Higher Education and the Public Interest carried the recommendation that "higher educators must communicate to on- and off-campus constituencies: improvements that are being made in the quality of instruction; and what reliable assessment tools are in place" (Council for Advancement and Support of Education, p. 5).

One of the major goals expressed in the *1989-90 Annual Report* of the Southern Regional Education Board is that "by the year 2000 the quality and effectiveness of all colleges and universities will be regularly assessed, with particular emphasis on the performance of undergraduate students" (p. 11).

A report entitled *State Priorities in Higher Education: 1990* reported that accountability and effectiveness ranked in the top tier of issues related to higher education (Lenth, 1990).

A February 1991 issue of *Policy Perspectives*, published by the Pew Higher Education Research Program, University of Pennsylvania, suggested that revenue reductions and cost containment may cause institutions to develop more strategic visions of mission and that some national universities, the University of Michigan, for example, now admit that in some areas there may be an inverse relationship between cost and quality. *Policy Perspectives* notes that such observations are "hardly music to an industry accustomed to equating quality enhancement with increases in funding" (1991, pp. 1-2).

This is an impressive range and weight of commentary. No one would believe, however, that we are without dissenting voices on the subject of quality and measurement. In the July 5, 1990, issue of the *Chronicle of Higher Education,* Ernst Benjamin, in "The Movement to Assess Students' Learning Will Institutionalize Mediocrity in Colleges," argues: "Assessment promotes a misdiagnosis of the problem of undergraduate instruction. The deficiencies of undergraduate instruction are not due primarily to poor teaching and will not be remedied by improving the teaching of individual instructors. Rather, the problems of undergraduate instruction are systemic and are best summarized as inadequate 'involvement in learning'" (pp. B1-B2).

He also offers other cautions about possible unhappy links between assessment and funding, a narrowing of teaching interests and concerns to fit assessment needs, and intrusion of state agencies into curricular and teaching issues. These are helpful concerns, and we emphasize the constructive contributions of dissenting voices by recalling a line from Emerson's (1929) essay *"Compensation"*: "When a man is pushed, tormented, defeated, he has a chance to learn something; he has been put on his wits, on his manhood; he has gained facts; learns his ignorance; is cured of the insanity of conceit; has got moderation and real skill. The wise man throws himself on the side of his assailants. It is more his interest than it is theirs to find his weak point" (Emerson, 1929b, p. 164).

Dissent and criticism should not keep us, however, from our interest in the purpose and performance of our colleges and universities. Purpose and performance: What do we hope to accomplish and how good a job are we doing? These are premier leadership questions in any organized enterprise, corporate or collegiate. Such questions are perhaps more important to those holding the leadership of colleges and universities in trust, however, as we are expected to nurture leadership for every sector of our nation—economic, cultural, educational, social. In an essay entitled "First Glimpses of a New World," Robert Hutchins noted that "the most embarrassing question that can be raised in a university is what are we trying to do? . . . The administrator of an educational institution is to be forgiven if he evades this question and announces that education is what goes on in an educational institution" (1966, p. 178). Evasion of these leadership questions of purpose and performance—quality questions—is not a leadership option, however, for today's college educator, as this commentary suggests.

Without Care or Competence

Why do we need a definition of quality, a means of measuring quality, a program to improve quality? The accountability motive often will be cited—accountability to governing boards, to state agencies, to legislatures, to taxpayers, and so forth. But our first accountability allegiance rests elsewhere, as the following illustration will show.

A thirty-year-old woman enrolled in a graduate course has submitted a major paper. This paper is not just grammatically incorrect; it is incoherent! Her performance in the course has been marginal on every dimension, culminating in this disappointing and heartbreaking final paper. Any reasonable standard of acceptable performance for graduate study would not encourage a passing grade for this paper, much less for the course. It might be argued that each person contributing to the meaning of this student's bachelor's degree has committed an act of malpractice, cheating this woman of her potential and her dignity. She has adequate intelligence and talent for good work but has been denied the full use of that intelligence and talent by low and empty expectations. This is not a hypothetical illustration.

How could this happen? This woman is a graduate of an institution that is regionally accredited and of a program that is professionally accredited. Think of the simplicity of attitudes and actions it would have taken to discover whether this student could write a grammatically correct sentence, a coherent paragraph, a sensible essay. Think of the prescriptive and corrective action that could and should have been taken early in her collegiate career.

This example illustrates a mind left wasted, a mind left dispirited and disengaged. To know that this student has been exposed to a low-quality climate requires no great philosophical agony in defining quality nor any technological feat in measuring it. "We know when we are challenging talent and when we are not. We know when teaching is demeaning to bright and lively spirits. We know when classroom climates are never sparked by the exhilarating and exciting clash of minds and ideas. We know when we are treating our students with arrogance unworthy of those who hold the human spirit and mind in trust. And we know when programs are cheating students of their potential" (Bogue, 1985, p. 63).

At the risk of troubling some readers with an opening illustration of this tone, we believe that a modest display of passion is both legitimate and appropriate as we open our book-length conversation on quality. And although some might argue that our notions of quality should not be built on exceptional cases, we can counter with the proposition that the exceptions constitute powerful and pertinent evidence on collegiate quality. The concepts of "zero defects" and "do it right the first time" are as important to what takes place in our classrooms, studios, playing fields, and rehearsal halls as they are to what takes place in our manufacturing and service enterprises in the profit sector. Peters and Waterman made clear in their widely read work *In Search of Excellence* (1982) that passion and commitment are as important (perhaps more so) to quality as are rational models for quality assurance.

A precious work is the work that unfolds in our collegiate classrooms. Without care and competence, however, it is a work that can carry our students and our institutions into harm's way. Just one mind cheated of its potential, however, is adequate justification for reasonable efforts in quality definition and assurance. Just one such example accents the most basic reason for our quality search: the effective nurture of human talent, spirit, and potential.

One of the reasons that students like the one cited in the preceding example slip through our quality nets is that we are too often preoccupied in arguing about the philosophical and technical complexities inherent in quality definition and measurement. The arguments have an unfortunate tendency to immobilize our quality assurance efforts. Let us have a look at some of the conceptual challenges by exploring first the issue of definition.

The Definition of Quality

Certain conceptional assumptions are widely held by academics and laypersons concerning collegiate quality:

- Only high-cost colleges have quality.
- Only large and comprehensive colleges have quality.
- Only highly selective colleges have quality.
- Only nationally recognized colleges have quality.
- Only a few colleges have quality.
- Only colleges with impressive resources have quality.

These assumptions tend to produce what some call a pyramid of prestige at the apex of which the larger public and private colleges and universities, the "national" universities, reside. Making up the lower levels are the state and community colleges. Another unfortunate consequence of these assumptions is that some colleges have been raising their fees not so much because of financial needs as in response to the belief that students and their parents equate price with quality. See, for example, Ted Marchese's editorial appearing in the May/June 1990 issue of *Change* magazine (p. 4).

Some state college and university systems assert that the state can afford only one "flagship" university—usually the largest university in the state and most often the research university. (Should the term flagship be returned to the navy and left there?) Some states can (and obviously do) afford more than one research university, whereas others cannot. No matter what its Carnegie classification or size, no college or university can be completely comprehensive in any exhaustive sense—that is, have programs and services in every conceivable field of inquiry. Thus, the word "comprehensive" will always have a limited meaning, and every college and university—no matter what its mission, its size, or its Carnegie classification—will always have a limited mission.

These assumptions also suggest that quality is in limited supply. This assumption, indeed, constitutes the philosophic cornerstone for college rankings and ratings, and we have much more to say on this point in Chapter Three. Are quality and excellence in limited supply? They certainly are if you subscribe to a definition of quality based on assumptions of size, cost, and selectivity. However, a good argument can be made that one can find large, high-cost, and selective colleges of mediocre quality. And one would not have to search very long to find graduates of these institutions whose behaviors, skills, and values constitute occasional and unfortunate evidence of this mediocrity.

The philosophy of limited supply argues with the conviction that quality is not only attainable but essential to every campus. It also argues with the assertion that quality can and should be found within limited mission—because every campus will have a mission that is ultimately limited. And it argues with the belief that any campus without quality in its mission has no reason to exist!

Governors, legislators, board members, media, and civic friends—these are not the only members of the educational partnership who need to engage this question of definition. We watched recently as a newly designated doctorate-granting university ("doctorate" as defined in the Carnegie classification system) celebrated its new quality status and launched media campaigns to carry the celebration. The difference between a comprehensive university/college and a doctorate-granting university, as defined in the Carnegie classification system, is that a doctorate-granting university must "award annually 20 or more Ph.D. degrees in at least one discipline or 10 or more Ph.D. degrees in three or more disciplines" (Carnegie Foundation . . . , 1987, p. 7). Designed as a descriptive system of classification, the Carnegie designation was transformed into an evaluative label, suggesting a new and higher status for this institution.

Stripped to the raw essential of expression, the question for state systems is whether academics and laypersons will persist in viewing their system of higher education as one in which there is a quality pecking order—an order of prestige built on size, selectivity, and program diversity—or whether members of the partnership are willing to see quality potential in each campus mission, and whether they are willing to insist on quality in each mission.

The challenge of quality definition is certainly one of the first-order for American higher education. But is it a challenge unique to the collegiate sector of our national life? We think not. A book published by the American Management Association entitled *I Know When I See It: A Modern Fable About Quality* constitutes a venture into the definition of quality in the corporate and profit sector. The book concludes with this observation: "Customers aren't interested in our specs. They're interested in the answer to one simple question: Did the product do what I expected it to do? If the answer is yes, then it's a quality product. If the answer is no, then it isn't. At that point our specs and tolerance aren't wrong, they're just irrelevant" (Guaspari, 1985, p. 68).

Another authoritative writer on quality in the corporate sector is Philip Crosby. His definition of quality does involve a match to specifications. In *Quality Without Tears,* Crosby offers this simple definition: "Quality is conformance to requirements" (1984, p. 60). Crosby goes on to suggest that establishing requirements is essentially an exercise in addressing the question of what we want the product or service to do. More important, conformance to requirements can be used to define more clearly the expectations for those involved in production or service delivery. We note here that conformance to requirements can embrace some specification on customer acceptance and satisfaction. We are attracted to the simplicity and the power of this definition and will be returning to it shortly as we offer our definition of collegiate quality.

In his 1988 book *Managing Quality,* David Garvin traces four stages in the evolution of quality management in the corporate sector: inspection, statistical quality control, quality assurance, and strategic quality assurance. He identifies multiple dimensions of quality as follows:

- Performance, the "fitness for use" test: Does the product do what the consumer wants?
- Features, the "bells and whistles" that supplement product basic functions and add competitive edge.

- Reliability: How long till first failure or need for service?
- Conformance, the extent to which the product meets established specifications and manufacturer standards.
- Durability, closely related to reliability but addresses the question of length of product life.
- Serviceability, speed, cost, ease of repair.
- Esthetics, a highly subjective but measurable aspect of product sense appeal.
- Perceived quality: Is a Honda built in America perceived as a Japanese car? Of higher quality? (Garvin, 1988, pp. 49–68).

Garvin's book is helpful reading to anyone interested in quality definition, measurement, and improvement. He goes on to cite the differences in quality perspective and interests among design engineers, service technicians, and customers and then produces an informative analysis of the home air-conditioning industry between the best and worst performers. At the end of his book, Garvin says about a major goal of his analysis: "An equally important goal has been to test the conventional wisdom about quality, for a vast mythology surrounds the subject. It takes many forms: the belief that quality is undefinable and impossible to discuss objectively; that high quality is always associated with high costs; that automation is the key to Japan's superior quality; and that vice presidents of quality are required for superior results. None of these assumptions was supported by the results" (1988, p. 221). Sound familiar? There are good and parallel lessons for collegiate leadership in this book, which leads us to a series of questions to which we will return in a moment: questions of evidence and performance standard, questions of analysis and judgment, and questions of decision application and timing.

Here is an illustration to emphasize the relationship between mission and quality. Each of the authors owns and drives a different type of car. One lives on a farm and finds a small truck useful. The other has three children still at home and a dog and finds that a four-door van is not just satisfying but essential. Which of these vehicles has the higher quality? Perhaps the answer to that question can be found in this note taken from Abernathy, Clark, and Kantrow in *Industrial Renaissance:*

> Many domestic consumers regard a car with luxurious interior, stately dimension, and "boulevard" ride as being of high quality; others attach that label to a car with functional interior, aerodynamic styling, quick acceleration, and responsive handling. How to choose between them? In point of fact, there is no reasonable way to do so, for these cars were designed for quite different purposes and were intended to satisfy quite different sets of preferences. Evaluations of quality based on workmanship, reliability, and durability, however, would apply to both cars. It requires no leap of faith to believe that most consumers would view a car with obvious streaks in the paint job, windows that do not roll all the way up, doors that do not hang right, an engine that leaks oil, and an electrical system that fails after 500 miles as being of lower quality than a competitor's product without these failures. So much is common sense [Abernathy, Clark, and Kantrow, 1983, p. 64].

On this note, let us restate our conviction that each college and university has the potential for excellence within its own mission. With organizations and with individuals, however, the question of whether excellence is realized depends greatly on accessories of emotion—on investments of daring and discipline, caring and courage. These emotional elements that contribute to quality are also not in limited supply, but neither is their potential always realized in individuals or organizations. For concrete illustration of this point, see Peters and Austin's 1985 book *A Passion for Excellence*. What were those lines from Emerson's essay "Man the Reformer"? "Every great and commanding moment is the triumph of some enthusiasm. The victories of the Arabs who, after Mahomet, established a larger empire than that of Rome, is an example. They were miserably equipped, miserably fed. They conquered Asia, and Africa, and Spain on barley" (Emerson, 1929a, p. 75). An illuminating commentary on resources and results!

One final illustration from a service-sector enterprise concludes this venture in corporate-sector quality assurance. We commend Jan Carlzon's 1987 book *Moments of Truth,* a story about Scandinavian Airlines (SAS). As president of SAS, Carlzon discovered the relationship between customer satisfaction and airline operations: "But if you ask our customers about SAS, they won't tell you about our planes or our offices or the way we finance our capital investments. Instead, they talk about their experiences with the people of SAS" (1987, p. 2). Every interaction between an employee of SAS—whether pilot, baggage handler, or reservation agent—is a "moment of truth" in presenting the service face of SAS. Is this not also true of college and universities? Will our students remember the sophistication of our equipment, our per-student appropriation—or whether a faculty member or admissions clerk fashioned relationships marked by courtesy, competence, and caring?

Not content, however, to center attention totally on this interaction, Carlzon also talks about measuring results: "We thought we were doing very well on precision; our cargo people reported that only a small percentage of shipments did not arrive at their destination on time. But we decided to try a test anyway. We sent 100 packages to various addresses throughout Europe. The results were devastating. The small parcels were supposed to arrive the next day; however, the average was four days later. . . . Clearly we needed to start measuring our success in terms of our promises" (1987, pp. 107–108).

Is there a message in that finding for American higher education? We believe there is, and it will also play a part in our definition.

Let us come back to higher education and see what we can find on the definition of quality. Among the more thoughtful and helpful of those who have written on the issue of quality and excellence is Alexander Astin. We count *Achieving Educational Excellence* (1985a) and *Assessment for Excellence* (1991) as books that can be read with profit by educator and layperson. Astin contends that there are four conventional views of excellence in collegiate quality: excellence as reputation, excellence as resources, excellence as outcomes, and excellence as content. After examining the limitations of each of these views, Astin offers a "talent development" definition of excellence: "The most excellent institutions are, in this view, those that have the greatest impact—add the most value, as economists would say—on the student's knowledge and personal development and on the faculty member's scholarly and pedagogical ability and productivity" (Astin, 1985a, p. 61). There is an appealing simplicity to Astin's definition. It focuses on results. It asks the question, "What difference did we make in student knowledge, skill, and attitude?" His thought and his books merit review by collegiate educators, by board members, and by other civic friends, such as legislators.

A different definition is offered by Lewis Mayhew, Patrick Ford, and Dean Hubbard in *The Quest for Quality*. Mayhew and his colleagues argue for a more limited view on higher education mission, suggesting that some of the affective hopes that are assumed in Astin's definition are unlikely to be realized in colleges. They state that "colleges and universities, for example, can have little effect on the fundamental character traits such as honesty, optimism, or sense of humor" (1990, p. 24). They anticipate a more limited definition of quality with this preamble: "The emergence of an information-based, technologically driven economy requires citizens who are facile with the higher order cognitive skills of analysis, snythesis, and evaluation and who can express themselves clearly in verbal, written, or numerical form" (Mayhew, Ford, and Hubbard, 1990, p. 22). Their definition of quality, then, is as follows: "Quality undergraduate education consists of preparing learners through the use of words, numbers, and abstract concepts to understand, cope with, and positively influence the environment in which they find themselves" (Mayhew, Ford, and Hubbard, 1990, p. 29).

This vision of college purpose and quality definition may argue with the view that teaching is a moral enterprise. We are inclined to the perspective expressed by John Goodlad, Roger Soder, and Kenneth Sirotnik in *The Moral Dimensions of Teaching* (1990). In their view, teaching at every level is a normative venture. We agree. Our policies and practices in collegiate education convey moral posture and value; in the classroom and out, our behavior as faculty and administrators conveys a moral model.

Not even in science, known for its commitment to objectivity, are we without value principles that support inquiry, as Jacob Bronowski makes clear in *Science and Human Values* (1956). Thus, in the content of what we teach, we are anchored to a philosophy of values. Later in this book, in Chapter Seven on college outcomes, we will report how one state has publicly committed its system of higher education to a set of values.

This preliminary exchange on the definition of quality anticipates a principle that we hope to celebrate throughout this book: The definition and means of quality is a venture in learning and discovery.

The Measurement of Quality

A 1990 issue of *World* magazine features a lead article by George Fisher entitled "Measuring the Unmeasurable," the story of a major quality assurance effort at the Motorola Corporation. The article lead-in begins with the note that "everyone knows that quality is impossible to define. But that didn't stop Motorola" (p. 4). Though the program for Motorola is a multistep process, it also involves some relatively simple approaches to measurement. The article reports that chairman Bob Galvin encouraged the posing of these two questions at all levels of the organization and with its customers: "What do you like about Motorola and what don't you like?" (p. 4). At the collegiate level, we are inclined to expend considerable energy in debating the merits of measurement. If we just took the time to ask these same simple questions of our students and our civic supporters, we might be surprised how much we would learn.

Several questions associate with the measurement of quality. What evidence or indicators will we accept as appropriate operational expressions of quality? What evidence can we assemble, should we assemble, to reflect the performance and quality of institutions as diverse in their mission, their history, and their environment as Dallas County Community College, the Ohio State University, the University at Montevallo, and Rhodes College? Surely the evidence of quality at these colleges and universities will require more than one data point.

Once the evidences and indicators of performance are identified, the question of performance standard arises. What level of performance will be accepted or required as demonstrating an appropriate level of quality? Will we employ in these judgments a standard that is criterion based or norm based? Are we going to gauge program or personnel performance against a standard of predetermined acceptability or against the performance of other programs and personnel? Actually, we have three possible choices for performance standards:

- A criterion standard, in which performance is compared to a predetermined criterion level
- A normative or comparative standard, in which performance is judged against the performance of another program or person (or group of persons)
- A connoisseurship standard, in which performance is judged against the opinions and values of a panel of judges

One final question turns on who will make these judgments. For example, is it reasonable to assume that every college and university would like its students to communicate effectively in written form? One evidence for that quality goal could be an essay written by all students at some appropriate point in their college careers—at the end of the freshman year, the end of the sophomore year, or as a major paper in the senior year. Assume that an institution fashions a consensus on the form of such evidence. Who will evaluate or grade the essay: professors in the English department, professors from all departments, or civic friends and/or alumni? And what will constitute an acceptable performance level?

An array of quality indicators might be offered as evidence of collegiate quality: peer reviews as expressed in accreditation and program reviews, student and alumni opinion and satisfaction indices, reputational and ranking studies, student performance profiles on entrance and exit tests, professional licensure results, faculty research and publication productivity. One difficulty is that the variety of possible indicators constitutes an embarrassment of riches from which it is difficult to choose. In Chapter Nine, however, we offer a suggested profile of quality indicators that we think should constitute a fundamental information base on quality.

A second problem of quality assurance is that any one of these indicators—whether reputational and satisfaction studies or value-added and outcomes studies—can be and will be criticized for some philosophical or technical imperfection. Indeed, in the chapters to follow, one of our goals is to probe the strengths and the limitations of the major expressions of quality assurance now used by American higher education.

Because there are so many evidences of collegiate quality and because any single evidence may be criticized, there is often a proclivity to debate without action. We are immobilized by argument. We can, however, employ a useful principle—the principle of multiple evidences—to combat the tendency to do nothing. What might be the mood of an accounting department chairman and her dean as they contemplate the following performance profile?

- Of the last thirty accounting graduates, all but two passed all parts of the Certified Public Accountant (CPA) exam on first sitting. This rate is six times the state pass rate and twice the national pass rate.
- A recent alumni follow-up survey revealed that the graduates in this department accorded the department one of the highest satisfaction ratings of department graduates in the university and was the highest in the College of Business.
- The dean's office has received a dozen letters of commendation from firms hiring the graduates and only one letter offering a constructive criticism.
- The department's upper-division students have the highest scores in the university on the Educational Testing Service Academic Profile Test of general education skills, when compared to students from other departments and colleges, and all sophomore majors successfully passed the written essay part of the Academic Profile Test.
- A recent visitation team assembled by the state coordinating board reviewed the academic program in accounting and ranked the program as "outstanding" on a scale of four descriptors: low quality and should be terminated, marginal quality and should be improved, adequate quality, and outstanding quality.

Cogent arguments can be advanced about the limited power for any one of these performance/quality indicators taken in isolation. What is less debatable, however, is that these indicators offer a useful and happy performance profile for this program and its students. Refusing to judge the quality of student, program, or campus performance on the basis of a single indicator or evidence is, we believe, an important principle of quality assurance.

The measurement of quality, then, embraces a good bit of complication—selecting evidences and indicators of performance, making provision for both acquisition and analysis of data, setting an appropriate standard of performance, and identifying who will make the judgments of performance and how. Scientists will want an experiment and philosophers a logical argument. Lawyers will want an adversarial hearing, sociologists an opinion poll, and artists a panel of judges. Engineers will want a systems study and economists a cost-benefit or regression analysis. Appraising quality is an exercise in evaluation, an adventure in the pursuit of truth.

The Decision Application of Quality Information

Quality: What is it and how do we measure it? Why do we need information on quality? One could well argue that this discussion of decision utility should have been placed first in our discussion. From the perspective of campus partners involved in quality assurance, there should be little argument that the primary motive for any effort is that of improvement—of enhancing the instructional and learning climate of educational policy and practice.

A faculty-friendly approach: We want to emphasize early in our presentation the importance of designing a quality assurance system and adopting a quality assurance philosophy that will penetrate the heart of an institution—its classrooms and studios, its laboratories and faculty offices—and that will engage the active allegiance of its faculty and staff. A strategic approach is one characterized by long-term perspectives on the nature of quality; one built on the willing and active involvement of every member of the academic community; and one where the impact on instruction, research, and service is clear. We try to emphasize this perspective in each chapter, but we give the strategic perspective special treatment in Chapter Ten.

As for the accountability motive, we restate a point made earlier. Certainly, an aggressive quality assurance effort at the campus level enables a college or university to offer evidence of performance accountability to graduates, to boards, to legislatures, and to other civic friends. However, the first call on accountability belongs not to external groups but to our students.

Definition, decision, discovery: A decision-based quality assurance program is going to affirm the idea that the journey in definition and measurement of quality should also be a journey in learning and discovery. Action and decision inform thought, and vice versa. Knowledge and technology interact. Knowledge enables us to invent technology, and the technology in turn opens up additional avenues of inquiry. Knowledge advances by intent, accident, and serendipity. Elements of both reflection and action, of theory and raw empiricism, are involved in the search for truth. "Acting on the possible while awaiting perfection" we believe is a useful motto in developing programs of quality assurance. We need the initiator and the critic. And this brings us to a final matter on the decision application of quality assurance information—the question of public disclosure.

Many years ago, the Ohio Board of Regents published a monograph, *Management Improvement Program* (1973), in which the regents posed these planning and performance questions for campuses in Ohio: What is the distinctive mission of the institution, the reason it exists? What are the things the institution wants to do or to see happen? What will count as evidence for or against the claim that the goal or objective has been reached? How will an individual outside the institution be able to determine whether the institution is attaining its goals or objectives? This last question poses an intriguing test and suggests another useful, albeit debatable, performance principle, the principle of public disclosure.

Public disclosure of performance results is not a suggestion received with uniform comfort by faculty members and administrators, even though we are already exposed to such public displays as reputational rankings, about which we will say more in Chapter Three. Complaints about public disclosure are often prefaced with the recitation of real and imagined dangers:

- Educational goals are necessary for any assessment. However, by the time consensus is reached, goals may be trivial and unimportant.

- The methodology of assessment is not well developed. Existing instruments do not adequately reflect the variety of learning outcomes that should be nurtured.
- Not all variables contributing to quality are under institutional control, for example, funding levels, licensure standards, employment opportunities, and so on.
- Narrow definitions of quality and effectiveness will cause perversions in the educational process—the teaching-to-the-test syndrome.
- There is a tendency to believe that what can be measured is the only thing that is important.

Of course, colleges and nonprofit-sector organizations are not alone on this issue. American Airlines, for example, features itself as the "On-Time Machine," centering on on-time departures and arrivals, which is one of the performance variables monitored by the airline transportation industry. Delta Airlines prefers to use "Scheduled Flights Completed," a reliability performance indicator. Ford Motor Company features its corporate philosophy as one in which "Quality Is Job One." Chrysler touts its "Customer's Quality Bill of Rights." And General Motors sells cars on its safety record. Each company chooses a different quality indicator for public disclosure and accent.

We like what editor Ted Marchese had to say in the May/June 1990 issue in a *Change* magazine article entitled "Costs and Quality." He cited three characteristics of an effective quality effort: "External peer review of the undergraduate function; impacts on student learning as the first criterion for judging quality; and a process that results in public reports, with students and funders as intended audiences" (p. 4). Here is a call for public disclosure that we believe to be important and appropriate.

With this impressive array of interrogatories related to the issues of definition, measurement, and decision application of quality, it is easy to understand why there is mixed progress in quality assurance ventures among American colleges and universities. More impressive, however, are those faculties and institutions that take to heart that little motto we mentioned earlier: "Acting on the possible while awaiting perfection." These institutions and their forward-thinking faculties offer splendid models of action and discovery, and we will look at some of them in the chapters to follow.

Varieties of Excellence

Earlier in this chapter we promised to present a definition of quality, and we need to deliver on that promise. The philosophic and technical complexities cited in our discussion up to this point make clear that anyone who dares to offer a definition of quality for higher education agrees to become an academic target of high visibility. However, we believe that the debate and tension that inevitably surround any discussion of quality are part of the discovery process that should be associated with any college or university as a learning community. Our proposal is that educational quality be defined as follows: *Quality is conformance to mission specification and goal achievement—within publicly accepted standards of accountability and integrity.*

The first advantage of this definition is that it respects and affirms diversity of institutional missions and their historical and environmental settings. Consider, for example, the sweep of mission as one looks at the role of the Juilliard School of Music, the U.S. Naval Academy, the Emery Aeronautical Institute, Bemidji State University, Austin College, and the University of California, Berkeley. Add to this list the Gupton School of Mortuary Science and Maricopa Community College. Each of these institutions makes a contribution to the development of human talent in our nation, and a single-factor quality exercise hardly suffices to describe or define that quality.

A second advantage is that the definition requires an operational expression of mission and goals. Here is the "promise and deliver" challenge for colleges and universities. From those grand statements of intent that can be found in catalogues, the definition asks that institutions outline more clearly and specifically those knowledges, skills, and values they expect to be associated with their credentials and degrees. "What difference did we make?" is a question encouraged by this definition.

Also assumed is that the multiple stakeholders—faculty, governing board, state agencies, and so forth—are involved in the specification of mission and goals and in the assessment of institutional achievement and progress.

The third advantage of the definition is that it focuses debate on purpose—what the institution intends—so that arguments on quality—what it achieves—are not confounded over dissent that is actually related to purpose. Consensus building and partnership efforts are encouraged, we believe, by this definition. Asking questions of ends will drive the partners to ask questions of beginnings.

A fourth advantage of the definition is that it encourages public disclosure of institutional mission, goals, and performance results. The effect of public disclosure should be, as we previously noted, to open debate on purpose but to narrow debate on performance. Each of the questions associated with any quality assurance exercise—questions of decision, of evidence and indicators, of performance standards and modes of judgment, of who will judge and when—becomes a part of the public forum on quality. To that extent, then, the definition also promotes quality assurance as an exercise in learning and discovery.

A fifth advantage, at least in the authors' judgment, may elicit mixed reaction. The definition contains an ethical test. Contemporary media stories and book-length reports continue to highlight a brace of integrity issues in both corporate and collegiate sectors of our nation—ranging from deliberately diluted juice for babies, defense contract rip-offs, and check kiting by major accounting firms to acts of wrongdoing in the savings and loan industry. In the collegiate sector, we find padded enrollment figures traced to unenforced retention policies and fraudulent enrollments and prostitution of integrity in a host of other educational and administrative areas. Even though any one of these acts may be counted an exception to the general reality of integrity, can we claim, in either a corporate or collegiate setting, to produce quality while we are busy stealing from ourselves, our government, and our customers and clients? We think not. We plan to say more on the ethical environment in higher education in Chapter Ten.

One of the more obvious disadvantages of this definition is that colleges and universities could become quite proficient in achieving shallow and unworthy purposes, in serving missions of dubious distinction. Our conviction, however, is that the public-disclosure feature would offer protection against this potential liability, and likewise would offer some "consumer protection" to potential students.

In summary, this definition affirms the idea that there are varieties of excellence in both individual and institutional performance. Who can look at Harvard on the East Coast and Mills College on the West Coast, the University of Michigan in the North and the College of Charleston in the South and not realize the range of missions, each with the potential for quality. If we had to select one book most profitable for academic or layperson to read on the topic of quality and excellence, it would have to be John Gardner's *Excellence*, originally published in 1961 and issued again in 1984. Gardner offers a simple but illuminating illustration on what he calls "the full range of human excellence": "The Duke of Wellington, in a famous incident, revealed an enviable understanding of it. The government was considering the dispatch of an expedition to Burma to take Rangoon. The cabinet summoned Wellington and asked him who would be the ablest general to lead such an undertaking. He said, 'Send Lord Combermere.' The government officials protested: 'But we have always understood that your grace thought Lord Combermere a fool.' The Duke's response was vigorous and to the point. 'So he is a fool, and a damned fool, but he can take Rangoon'" (Gardner, 1984, p. 119).

A Journey of Caring and Daring

Reflecting that peculiar yet constructive lack of neatness that characterizes so much of our national life, Americans have fashioned a complex pattern of practices in our search for quality. Among those are the following:

- Accreditation: the test of goal achievement and improvement
- Rankings and ratings: the test of reputation
- Outcomes: the test of results
- Licensure: the test of professional standards
- Program reviews: the test of peer review
- Follow-up studies: the test of client satisfaction

In addition to these more conventional approaches to quality assurance, there are emerging models that bear the imprint of imagination and boldness. The partners involved in the definition, measurement, and application of quality are also becoming more numerous. To the historical and premier roles of faculties, we must add the interests of system and governing board staffs, coordinating agencies, regional compacts, legislative and executive officers. The state has become an active partner in both regulatory and incentive roles, and, of course, the federal government continues to be a player. In the chapters to follow, we will explore the strengths and limitations of each of these approaches to quality assurance and the roles of the partners in the process.

This book, therefore, is about the definition of quality, the measurement of quality, the decision application of quality information, and the renewing outcomes of quality assurance efforts. We intend it to be descriptive, furnishing an outline of contemporary practice and policy. We intend it to be evaluative, probing the advantages and the liabilities of each approach to quality assurance. We intend it to be explorative, searching for new approaches that might offer promise of improving our search and examining the issues of theory and practice that surround the search for quality.

In this first chapter, we have pointed to some of the convictions on which the book is constructed. The first of these is that our search for quality is a renewing and learning adventure in the best spirit of higher education. The second is that our willingness to risk, to try (to act on the possible while awaiting perfection) offers an opportunity to harness the power of reflection and action, which also respects an important principle of learning. Finally, we believe that the search for quality is a search for community.

Two recent publications accent the need for community. Several chapters in John Gardner's 1990 book *On Leadership* focus on shared values and standards. Gardner comments: "The disintegration of communities and the loss of a sense of community are clearly detrimental to the accomplishment of group purpose" (p. 113). What is the link between quality and community? We believe it to be simple and direct. Without community one will find neither caring nor courtesy, and without caring, there will be no quality, for there will be no standards.

A 1990 publication of the Carnegie Foundation for the Advancement of Teaching is entitled *Campus Life: In Search of Community.* What kind of community should higher education be? The lead-ins to the chapters of this special report speak directly to questions of quality:

- First, a college or university is an educationally purposeful community, a place where faculty and students share academic goals and work together to strengthen teaching and learning on the campus (p. 9).
- Second, a college or university is an open community, a place where freedom of expression is uncompromisingly protected and where civility is powerfully affirmed (p. 17).
- Third, a college or university is a just community, a place where the sacredness of each person is honored and where diversity is aggressively pursued (p. 25).
- Fourth, a college or university is a disciplined community, a place where individuals accept their obligations to the group and where well-defined governance procedures guide behavior for the common good (p. 47).
- Fifth, a college or university is a caring community, a place where the well-being of each member is sensitively supported and where service to others is encouraged (p. 47).
- Sixth, a college or university is a celebrative community, one in which the heritage of the institution is remembered and where rituals affirming both tradition and change are widely shared (p. 55).

These tests of community are also tests of quality. Purposeful, open, just, disciplined, caring, celebrative: These expressions of community and quality will yield to evidence on their presence or absence. Not only learning but also the climate for learning constitute a legitimate focus of inquiry in our search for quality.

The positive link between quality assurance and campus community is reinforced by Patricia Hutchings in her closing plenary address to the fifth annual American Association for Higher Education conference on assessment (1990). She shared several institutional illustrations in which faculty indicated that the potentially discomforting challenge of examining the outcomes of their programs often furnished the only time in which faculty in a department talked seriously with one another about learning—about what goes on, or should go on, in their classrooms and laboratories. Hutchings also emphasized that assessment promotes a performance view of learning that centers not just on what students know but what they can do with what they know. Here then is another perspective accenting quality assurance as an instrument of both discovery and community.

In an essay we cited earlier—"First Glimpses of a New World"—Robert Hutchins opened with this reflection: "I have been plagued all my life by two obsessions, the search for standards and the search for community" (1966, p. 177). The search for standards, for community, for quality—here is a magnificent obsession for those entrusted with the care of our colleges and universities. Failing to acquire and apply information on quality is to confirm that we lack both caring and daring. How can we possibly give meaningful leadership to program and service improvement without data on quality? How can we honor our responsibilities to the growth and nurture of our students without knowing what impact we have on their knowledge, their skills, their values? How can timidity in the search for quality command the respect of our students and our publics? How can we teach our students the role of courage, of discipline, of risk, of perseverance in learning and living unless we are willing to model these same qualities in learning about ourselves and our performance?

The dimensions of quality in American higher education are complex in origin and structure. To outline those dimensions more clearly, this book will first examine the major quality assurance systems already in place. Probably the best known quality assurance approach is that of accreditation, to which we will turn in Chapter Two. After a similar review of other contemporary practices—reputational studies, follow-up studies, professional licensure, program reviews, and college outcomes—the attention of the book will focus on policies and principles that show promise for improving the future impact of quality assurance in American higher education.

Part One

The Tests of Quality

TWO ᖇᘔ

Accreditation: The Test of Mission Fulfillment

To many, having a degree from an accredited college is tantamount to having a product with the collegiate "Good Housekeeping seal of approval." Indeed, accreditation is probably the most widely known and respected form of quality assurance among parents, government officials, and other civic friends of American higher education. Whether the general public has a high level of awareness of other approaches to be described in the following chapters may be a questionable matter. For example, only alumni are likely to know about institutional follow-up studies, and few laypersons will know of institutional efforts to improve quality through academic program reviews.

The involvement of peer educators in the identification and application of quality standards is unique to this country, an approach built on a long history. Collegiate educators from other nations are often fascinated with the decentralized approach because much of the quality responsibility in foreign countries resides in heavily centralized ministries. For example, in a visit to the Soviet Union a short time ago, one of the authors learned that all Ph.D. degrees from any university in any republic of the Soviet Union had to be approved in Moscow. That Soviet educators found the concept

29

of accreditation of great interest can thus be understood in context.

This chapter will reveal just how extensively accreditation is used as an instrument of quality assurance. A brief history of accreditation is followed by a classification of accrediting agencies by type and function. The chapter describes the improvement and accountability functions of accreditation and presents recent changes in philosophy, criteria and standards, and methodology—including the important shift in emphasis from process orientation to results or performance orientation. Descriptions of accrediting policy and procedure in four specialized fields are given: medicine, law, nursing, and teacher education. The chapter concludes with an analysis and evaluation of current problems and issues.

The Nature and Function of Accreditation

Though the two-year and community colleges are distinctly American, much of the American senior college and university system was patterned after features of European higher education. As noted, a major difference in American and European systems, and other systems as well, is the degree of government control. Many European and other countries have ministries of education that exercise direct control over universities. In some countries, for example, professorial appointments are made through a national system. In the United States, the jurisdiction over universities is primarily invested in state governments, which grant operational charters to both private and public institutions. The complex pattern of these institutions and the attendant complexity in campus governance patterns can be a source of confusion to some foreign educators. It probably would not be inaccurate to say that governance patterns can confuse Americans as well, including those who work within colleges and universities.

The federal government's role in American higher education has historically been somewhat distant and limited. Obvious historic exceptions have been the Land-Grant Act of 1862 and the GI Bill for financial support following World War II. In recent years, the federal government has continued to focus on support—scholarships, research, facilities, and so on—rather than quality assurance. The federal part in litigation surrounding the Fourteenth

Amendment is an example of recent activity that has had a sharp and direct impact on American higher education. Even so, higher education in the nation remains comparatively free of quality assurance control by the federal government.

The laissez-faire policy resulted in a wide variation among colleges and universities with respect to mission, organization, curriculum, and quality. Accreditation was invented as a way to "bring a semblance of order out of an increasing variation among institutions . . . a phenomenon peculiar to the United States" (Mayer, 1965, p. 11).

Accreditation can be defined as a status granted to an institution or a program within an institution that has been evaluated and found to meet or exceed stated criteria of educational quality (Young, Chambers, Kells, and Associates, 1983, p. 443). Another definition is "a process by which an institution of postsecondary education evaluates its educational activities, in whole or in part, and seeks an independent judgment to confirm that it is substantially achieving its objectives and is generally equal in quality to comparable institutions of postsecondary education" (Young, Chambers, Kells, and Associates, 1983, p. xi).

The word *accreditation* is often, and incorrectly, used interchangeably with *certification* and *licensure*. Whereas accreditation is a status ascribed to an institution or one of its parts, certification usually applies to an individual and connotes a process that determines that he or she has fulfilled requirements set forth in a particular line of work and may practice in that field of work.

Licensure is also a term applicable to an individual rather than an institution. Often related and sometimes linked to both accreditation and certification, licensure is the process by which an individual is granted the authority to practice in a particular field. It runs the gamut from vehicle operation to brain surgery, from barbering to flying jumbo jets. Chapter Five describes how in several professional programs the concepts of accreditation, certification, and licensure are interrelated, but each has a distinctive nature and purpose. In this chapter, however, we differentiate between them and focus on how and why accreditation serves as an indicator of quality.

Of the several beneficial purposes of accreditation, the two considered to be most fundamental are to ensure the quality and to assist in the improvement of the institution or program. Specifically, the accreditation of an institution or program says to the public in general and to institutional constituencies in particular that it has appropriate mission and purposes, resources necessary to achieve those purposes, and a history and record implying that it will continue to achieve its purposes (Young, Chambers, Kells, and Associates, 1983).

The needs of several constituencies are served when accreditation fulfills its purposes of quality assurance and institutional or program improvement. The general public is served by being assured that the institution or program has been evaluated internally and externally and conforms to general expectations in higher education. The public benefits when it can be assured that the accredited institution has ongoing and explicit activities deemed adequate to enable the institution to improve itself continuously and to make necessary modifications to accommodate changes in knowledge and practice in various fields of study. Accreditation decreases the need for intervention by regulatory agencies because accredited institutions are themselves required to provide for the maintenance of quality.

Accreditation benefits students in several ways: It assures them that an accredited institution has been found to be satisfactory and capable of meeting their needs; facilitates the transfer of credits among institutions; promotes admission to graduate degree programs; and serves as a prerequisite, in some cases, for entering professions.

Institutions also benefit from accreditation. There is first the stimulus for periodic self-evaluation and continuous improvement. Accreditation enables institutions to gain eligibility for themselves and their students in certain programs of government and private aid to higher education and helps institutions prevent parochialism by setting expectations that are national in scope. But the benefit most relevant to the theme of this chapter is the enhanced reputation of an accredited institution, primarily because of the generally high public regard for accreditation.

Admittedly, accreditation is based on the evaluation of institutional or program performance against a set of minimal standards. There may be, therefore, an understandable variance among accredited institutions—a perceived deficiency that we will treat at the end of this chapter. Here we only note that without accreditation the degree of variation would be much greater, and the public's ability to discern the differences between institutions of adequate quality and those of inadequate quality would be seriously damaged. Without accreditation the vagaries of reputational studies (see Chapter Three on college rankings and ratings) also would be greatly exacerbated.

A value of accreditation not fully appreciated by the general public can be found in the organized professions. Accreditation benefits professions in three major ways: (1) It provides for the participation of practitioners in setting the requirements for preparation to enter the profession; (2) it enables representatives of the respective professions to participate in evaluating the quality, appropriateness, and effectiveness of professional preparation programs and in weaving together theory and practice; and (3) it increases unity through collaborative activities of practitioners, representatives from the preparing arm, and students seeking entry into the profession. After all, quality assurance is important to the various professional bodies as well as to institutions, students, and the public. Professionals are often highly involved in recommending certain institutions to students and in communicating to students, parents, and the public their perceptions and judgments about institutional quality or the absence of it.

As noted earlier, accreditation is a voluntary, nongovernmental evaluation system devised, in part, to establish and maintain educational standards, a responsibility performed by central governmental authorities in many countries. Although accreditation remains a private and voluntary process, certain conditions and realities have moved it toward a quasi-governmental status. Actions by government funding organizations, foundations, employers, counselors, and professional associations have contributed much to this movement. In this regard, an institution electing not to become accredited does so at its own peril.

Most accreditation activity in the United States is conducted under the coordinating umbrella of the Council on Postsecondary Accreditation (COPA). A nongovernmental organization, COPA attempts to "foster and facilitate the role of accrediting agencies in promoting and insuring the quality and diversity of American post-secondary education" (Council on Postsecondary Accreditation, 1986, p. v). In its *Directory of Recognized Accrediting Bodies*, COPA lists six national institutional accrediting bodies, nine regional bodies (including three special accrediting bodies for vocational, technical, and career institutions), and forty specialized accrediting bodies (Council on Postsecondary Accreditation, 1989). Accrediting organizations functioning outside COPA (approximately seventy) "have been drawn into accreditation mainly because of its linkages to eligibility for federal funds and its credentialing" and are "well out of the mainstream of postsecondary education" (Young, Chambers, Kells, and Associates, 1983, p. 9). This chapter concerns itself only with COPA-recognized postsecondary institutions.

While we are speaking of COPA, we might note that the fabric of coordination around the agencies has grown slightly frayed. A March 27, 1991, article in the *Chronicle of Higher Education* reported on dissatisfaction with COPA's leadership, as perceived by heads of the regional accrediting agencies. They claim that COPA has furnished little leadership or direction on the major issues facing accrediting agencies, and they apparently have voiced the possibility of their withdrawal from the COPA umbrella. COPA is further cited for failure to curb the proliferation of specialized accrediting agencies and is accused of contributing to the balkanization of higher education, a splintering of purpose and resources attributed to the pleadings of special interest groups (Leatherman, 1991). We will return to some of these issues at the conclusion of this chapter.

Accreditation of institutions as total entities occurs through six national institutional accrediting bodies and nine regional accrediting associations. The national bodies are American Association of Bible Colleges, Association of Independent Colleges and Schools, National Home Study Council, Association of Theological Schools in the United States and Canada, National Association of Trade and Technical Schools, and the Association of Advanced Rabbinical and Talmudic Schools. The regional bodies include Middle States, New England, North Central, Northwest, Southern, and Western. Within these six regional bodies are three specialized bodies, as outlined previously, that accredit vocational-technical programs. An example of such a specialized body is the Commission on Occupational Educational Institutions (COEI) with the Southern Association.

In 1988, the nine regular regional associations included a total of 3,191 accredited institutions, 2,649 of which were accredited by the six regular regional associations and the remaining 542 by the three special bodies. The six national accrediting bodies listed 1,935 accredited institutions, 83 percent by just two of the bodies: the Association of Independent Colleges and Schools and the National Association of Trade and Technical Schools.

The forty COPA-recognized specialized accrediting bodies reflect broad coverage and considerable heterogeneity. The specializations range from the accrediting of programs in medical education to programs in music education, from interior design to librarianship, and from journalism to social work. Most of the specialized bodies are national in scope, and a few have multiple program subdivisions (for example, the Committee on Allied Health Education and Accreditation accredits programs in twenty-five subdivisions). As a general rule, the specialized accrediting bodies require institutional accreditation by the appropriate regional association as a precondition. Most of them are freestanding except for their affiliation with COPA.

Difficulties encountered by some institutions in meeting the conditions of this array of accrediting groups are numerous. As an example, one of the authors recently visited a major health sciences center as a part of the university's initial preparation for regional accreditation. That university averages one or more accreditation studies and visits every year; the investment of time, talent, and money to sustain this continuous pattern of visits is considerable. The chancellor of the university observed that folks in the university were about "self-studied out." Here is another issue of accreditation with which we will grapple at the conclusion of the chapter.

One can only imagine, however, the difficulties that would exist without the coordinating role of COPA, whose efforts at least bring some semblance of order to what otherwise would be a tangled web of requirements, expectations, and associational politics. Even with central coordination, however, institutions experience frustrations, as we have noted, in maintaining accreditation in their many areas of preparation.

The Evolution of Accreditation

As noted earlier, accreditation was initiated as a way to achieve reasonable standardization in higher education, thus serving a public need by helping to define institutional missions, to promote articulation among them, and to assist the general public in recognizing and appreciating quality. Voluntary accreditation guidelines and standards were seen as preferable to control and regulation by the central government. The need for some kind of accreditation arose first with problems associated with institutional definition, vast differences in institutional quality with no widely accepted basis for ascertaining quality, and difficulties encountered by students and institutions in the transfer of credit.

An early precursor, sometimes erroneously mentioned as the first accreditation, was legislation enacted in 1787 in New York that required the state board "to visit every college in the state once a year" (Selden, 1960, p. 30). Although this was an important development and a search for standards, the activity was not accreditation in the best sense of the concept.

Action by the American Medical Association (AMA) in 1904 also served as a precursor to accreditation, but the very first accrediting action was the American Osteopathic Association, which began reviewing and approving schools in 1901. In 1904, the AMA established a council on medical education that developed, a year later, a rating system for medical schools. Working rapidly, the council initiated "inspections" in 1906 and published its first list of classifications in 1907. Collaboration with the Carnegie Foundation in a study of medical education produced the famous Flexner Report in 1910. This report paved the way for the designation of the medical school at Johns Hopkins University as a prototype and also set the stage for closing many "inferior schools." Although not "accreditation" as it later came to be known, these actions had a lasting impact on medical education and established a pattern still revered today by other professions, although few have replicated it fully (Young, Chambers, Kells, and Associates, 1983).

Several aspects of Flexner's work merit a quick digression. First and notably, Flexner was not a physician. Indeed, he argued that those external to a field might, with the application of common sense and unfettered experience, be as effectively equipped to judge a field as those experts within: "The expert has his place, to be sure; but if I were asked to suggest the most promising way to study legal education, I should seek a layman, not a professor of law; or for the sound way to investigate teacher training, the last person I should think of employing would be a professor of education" (Flexner, 1960, p. 71). In addition, Flexner was not always inclined to courteous criticisms, euphemistic evaluations, and ambiguous advice in his reviews. His evaluation of one school concluded thus: "The school is a disgrace to the state whose laws permit its existence" (Flexner, 1910, p. 190). The matter of expertise external to a field we will consider again at the conclusion of this chapter.

The nation's first true accreditation of an institution of higher learning occurred in about 1910, by the North Central Association of Colleges and Secondary Schools, using standards developed in 1909. The association published its first list of accredited institutions in 1913 (Pfnister, 1959).

Citing ten significant events during the period of 1862 (and the passage of the Land-Grant Act) to 1914 (and the passage of the Smith-Lever Act and the founding of the Association of American Colleges), Young, Chambers, Kells, and Associates (1983) concluded that "accreditation was therefore born during a time of ferment and hope," sharing "the characteristics of the society that spawned it; idealistic, self-motivated, reform-minded, desiring improvement, believing in individual initiative and voluntary collective action, and distrustful of government (though seeing government as embodying the ultimate power to right wrongs)" (pp. 5-6).

Overcoming problems associated with definition, accreditation quickly moved to concerns and goals of a higher order—establishing, for example, membership requirements for the North Central Association and the Association of American Medical Colleges. A major development occurred in 1929 when the Higher Education Commission of the North Central Association appointed a committee on revision of standards. The work of this committee involved fifty-seven institutions and resulted in a seven-volume report. The report set forth a policy that was to have a lasting impact on regional and professional accreditation, namely, that institutions would be evaluated according to their own purposes, not by arbitrary standards. This action led to the self-study process, which remains embedded in virtually all accrediting efforts (Young, Chambers, Kells, and Associates, 1983).

To describe fully the development and evolution of accreditation since its outset would transcend the purpose of this chapter. Rather, a brief statement of major changes in accreditation during its eighty-year history will be given. Again, the exhaustive work by Kenneth E. Young and his associates (1983) is a major source document. According to this source, the major changes have been fourfold:

1. The universe of accreditation has changed as the concept of higher education has changed. It began as one of the degree-granting colleges and universities offering traditional academic programs and serving mainly full-time students immediately upon their graduation from high schools. Now it is more accurately described as postsecondary education comprising an ever-expanding variety of institutions, programs, and delivery systems involving a growing diversity of students of all ages with widely differing educational objectives.

2. The participants in accreditation have increased dramatically since World War II, when they consisted primarily of six regional associations and a few major professional associations. Today COPA recognizes six national accrediting bodies, nine regional bodies, and forty specialized bodies. Over 4,000 institutions (including duplicates) hold accredited status in one or more of these bodies and approximately 3,000 programs within institutions have approved status by one or more of the specialized bodies.

3. During the past seventy-five years, both the philosophy and practice have changed: from a quantitative approach to one relying more on qualitative factors; from regarding institutions as if they were all alike to recognizing and encouraging institutional individuality; from heavy dependency on external review to an emphasis on self-evaluation and self-regulation; and

from a focus of judging (accepting or rejecting) to a goal of encouraging and assisting institutions to improve continuously their educational quality.

4. Accreditation has changed through the years as society's expectations have changed. In retrospect, the initial expectations of accreditation seem rather mundane, for example, developing a consensus on the meaning of a high school, a college, or a professional school. Today, society places rather high expectations on accrediting bodies; in fact, accreditation helps to determine eligibility for certain funds, to define licensure requirements in several professions and occupations, and to help make decisions about the employment of graduates and the awarding of funds to institutions.

As in the beginning, however, the general public still has less than a full understanding of the importance and value of accreditation. The average citizen probably has an abiding faith that an "accredited institution" is more likely to be a quality institution than if it were not accredited, but he or she may understand few of the complexities and nuances involved in an institution's becoming and remaining accredited.

A recent and welcome change in accreditation is the focus on outcomes, especially on planned student outcomes. Concerted efforts have been made in recent years, particularly in the regional accrediting associations, to require institutions to set forth goals and objectives in a clear and measurable fashion, to describe procedures to be employed in seeking those goals and objectives, to identify indicators to be used in determining the degrees of attainment, and then to present evidence that the goals were, in fact, attained.

Indeed, Ralph A. Wolff, associate executive director of the Western Association of Schools and Colleges, suggests that the recent goal of emphases on assessment and outcomes is to create a "culture of evidence" (Wolff, 1990). We like that phrase. It suggests that institutional and programmatic conversations on quality should be linked to a simple yet powerful question: How do we know we have quality? Where is the evidence?

Policy groups and institutional officials support this change in approach and believe that in time it will greatly improve both the accreditation process and the public's understanding and appreciation of it. The new standards and procedures adopted in 1988 by the Southern Association of Colleges and Schools (SACS) are a good example of this change in accreditation (Thomas Carpenter, former president of Memphis State University, conversation with the author, 1989).

Another change in accrediting philosophy and procedure results from the recent emphasis on assessment. This change is of such significance that several of the regional accrediting bodies have revised their approaches to assessment and are placing greater emphasis on it, within the context of accountability. Wolff (1990) attributes the new emphasis to four challenges to accreditation during the past fifteen years.

1. The perceived failure of accreditation to respond effectively to nontraditional education, including programs operating away from the home campus
2. The absence of any reference to accreditation in a series of national reports on the baccalaureate and the reforms recommended therein
3. A call for increased accountability from state legislatures, the National Governors Association, and federal policymakers. The perception is that accreditation reports and decisions are not sufficiently grounded in the type of assessments necessary for state officials to make funding or other policy decisions
4. The establishment by the U.S. Department of Education of new criteria for the recognition of accrediting bodies' criteria that call for a focus on educational effectiveness

It is within this political context that several accrediting agencies have attempted to increase the visibility of their roles with institutions and to increase the emphasis on assessment.

The Southern Association of Colleges and Schools (SACS) initiated the movement in 1985–86 when it adopted a new criterion on institutional effectiveness as a part of its effort to link outcomes assessment to the process of accreditation. Noting that institutional quality is dependent not only on an institution's educational processes and resources but also on their successful use to achieve established goals, the Southern Association of Colleges and Schools (SACS) believes that all "institutions have an obligation to all constituents to evaluate effectiveness and to use the results in a goal-based, continuous planning and evaluation process" (Commission on Colleges, 1988, p. 13).

The action by SACS was followed rather quickly by the Western Association of Colleges and Schools, which revised several standards to accommodate the new emphasis on assessment and provided member institutions with implementing guidelines (Ewell, 1990).

More recently, the Commission on Institutions of Higher Education (North Central Association of Colleges and Schools) approved a statement of assessment and student academic achievement that made explicit the position that student achievement is a critical component in assessing overall institutional effectiveness. Also approved was new and more detailed language for two affected criteria (Farnsworth and Thrash, 1990).

Other regional associations are addressing assessment in a variety of ways. For example, the Commission on Institutions of Higher Education of the New England Association of Colleges and Schools is revising its criteria for accreditation with the expectation that the standard on evaluation and planning will explicitly require institutions to reassess periodically their plans as well as the effectiveness of their evaluation and planning activities (Sandra Elman, letter to the author, July 1990). The Commission on Higher Education of the Middle States Association of Colleges and Schools requires that in dealing with the standard on outcomes and institutional effectiveness, "institutions are required to make efforts to assess student achievement in general as well as in specialized areas of the curriculum, on an inclusive course-by-course basis, and when possible in comparison with student achievement elsewhere" (Commission on Higher Education, Middle States Association of Colleges and Schools, 1982, p. 18). The New England Association is in the process of revising its standards for accreditation, a process that will likely place greater emphasis on the role of assessment (Wolff, 1990).

Clearly, the regional accrediting bodies are responding to the challenge of better demonstrating institutional effectiveness, including student achievement.

The Accreditation Process

Does accreditation really promote and ensure quality? Perhaps our confidence in those goals will be enhanced by an examination of the process by which institutions become accredited, at the heart of which is the encouragement of efforts toward maximum educational effectiveness. Institutions are required to examine their goals, policies, procedures, and achievements; to consider the expert advice, suggestions, and recommendations of a visiting team; and to develop strategies for dealing with the visiting team's recommendations. Virtually every accrediting body requires institutions to maintain programs for continuous self-study and improvement in conjunction with the periodic review concept.

Although the various accrediting agencies have their own distinctive features and requirements, essentially the following procedures are employed in an institution's efforts to become accredited, either in whole or for separate programs (Council on Postsecondary Accreditation, 1986):

- Completion of an institutional or programmatic self-study, which includes the measurement of progress according to previously adopted objectives and consideration of the interests of the institution's constituencies; that is, students, faculty, administration, alumni, and the broader external community
- Review of the self-study by an accrediting commission and use of the study as the basis for evaluation by a site-visit team from the accrediting organization.
- Assessment of the institution or program by the site-visit team, which normally consists of professional educators, specialists, and members representing specific public interests.

A special comment on step 3, the site-visit team, is appropriate. This evaluation by an on-site team of peer educators constitutes a key element of the accreditation process. In some accreditation processes in fields outside of education, the accreditation of hospitals, for example, full-time paid professional evaluators make these visits and judgments. In colleges and universities, the evaluation team is ordinarily composed of peer faculty and administrators from institutions or programs of similar mission. Thus, the standard of acceptable performance on accreditation criteria resides in the values and judgments of these visiting teams. We should also remember that the original selection and definition of accreditation criteria are done in representative assemblies of institutional delegates. Thus, the concept of "peer judgments" marks the entire accreditation process and constitutes the philosophic foundation for this American approach to quality assurance.

- Review by the accrediting commission of the report of the site-visit team, the original self-study, and any response to it the institution may wish to make.
- Decision by the accrediting body regarding the accreditation status

Figure 2.1 furnishes a diagram of the accreditation process. Step 8 in that diagram does not fully describe the different decisions that can be made. Though these decision actions may differ by association, they vary from a completely positive action—original accreditation or reaffirmation—to a "notice" or "probationary" status requiring that the institution or program effect some improvement on particular standards or criteria within a specified time period. The ultimate negative action, of course, would be denial of accreditation or suspension of accredited status for a program or institution. As the figure indicates, an appeals process allows an institution to challenge negative actions.

Accreditation is normally granted for a specific term, usually from five to ten years, but accrediting bodies can review member institutions or programs at any time for cause or when a substantive change has been made, for example, proposed expansion to the graduate level.

It is apparent that the procedures and actions required to attain and maintain institutional and/or programmatic accreditation are exhaustive, time consuming, and expensive, both in actual dollars and in personnel time devoted to the process. The time and money are well spent, however, when educational effectiveness is enhanced by the process of accreditation and when institutional constituencies view accredited status as an assurance of quality.

Figure 2.1. Steps and Sequences in the Accreditation Process.

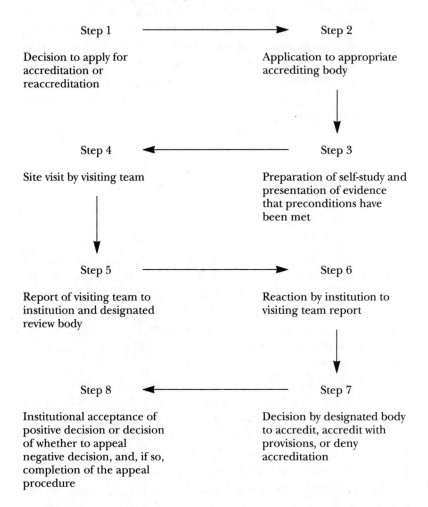

Step 1   Step 2

Decision to apply for   Application to appropriate
accreditation or   accrediting body
reaccreditation

Step 4   Step 3

Site visit by visiting team   Preparation of self-study and
                                                presentation of evidence
                                                that preconditions have
                                                been met

Step 5   Step 6

Report of visiting team to   Reaction by institution to
institution and designated   visiting team report
review body

Step 8   Step 7

Institutional acceptance of   Decision by designated body
positive decision or decision   to accredit, accredit with
of whether to appeal   provisions, or deny
negative decision, and, if so,   accreditation
completion of the appeal
procedure

In the following sections, a brief summary is given of the accreditation process in four fields: medicine, law, nursing, and teacher education. An understanding of the policies, procedures, and mechanisms used in accrediting programs in these areas of professional preparation (areas in which the public stake is very high) should further support the belief that accreditation is a valid guarantor of quality.

Accrediting Medical Education Programs

Informed opinion suggests, we believe, that the profession of medicine is probably the most advanced in today's society and occupies a position of high respect and prestige. Several factors have contributed to this admirable condition, one of which is the way medical education programs are accredited and the weight of accreditation in state policies vis-à-vis the license to practice. So important is accreditation in this field that, with only two or three exceptions, both certification and licensure require graduation from an accredited school (Jewett, 1985). Chapter Five deals more specifically with certification and licensure, which the authors contend are also valid quality assurances.

Programs in medical education leading to the M.D. degree in the United States and Canada seek accreditation through the Liaison Committee on Medical Education (LCME). Jointly sponsored, staffed, and financed by the Council on Medical Education of the American Medical Association (AMA) and American Association of Medical Colleges (AAMC), this body has served as the national accrediting agency for all programs in medical education since 1942. Before 1942, medical schools were required to be reviewed and approved separately by the AAMC and the AMA. Recognized by COPA, the Liaison Committee consists of eighteen members, two-thirds of whom are appointed by the two sponsoring organizations. The remaining six members are public members, students (nonvoting), a federal participant, and a representative of Canadian medical schools. Eligibility to sit on the Liaison Committee is clearly defined.

The accreditation process consists of six discrete steps, plus a seventh and a prior step for developing schools. Consistent with the generic process previously outlined, the procedure begins with an institutional self-study followed by an on-site team visit. The visiting team usually consists of four members, who are required to have broad experience in many facets of medical education, including university and hospital experience.

The team prepares a written report, step 4, setting forth the schools' strengths and weaknesses, suggestions for improvement, and recommendations to the LCME regarding accreditation, a power not always granted visiting teams in other accrediting agencies. The LCME makes the accreditation decision, which is then transmitted to the institution. Provisions exist for institutions to appeal decisions not to accredit.

All schools holding any type of accreditation are required to submit annual reports and any additional report deemed necessary by LCME. Schools granted ten-year approved status must submit a five-year interim report describing any significant changes. Eligibility for membership in the AAMC is an automatic by-product of accreditation by LCME (Council on Postsecondary Accreditation, 1986).

Accrediting Schools of Law

Two accrediting bodies exist in the field of legal education: (1) the Council on the Section of Legal Education and Admission to the Bar of the American Bar Association (ABA) and (2) the Association of American Law Schools (AALS). Although both have similar missions in regard to accreditation, the ABA Council grants accreditation to law schools in the United States, while the Association of American Law Schools accredits programs leading to the first professional degree in law (J.D. or LL.B.). Both accrediting bodies are recognized by COPA. The two bodies function separately and have no interdependent relationship; however, all AALS accredited programs are also accredited by the ABA Section of Legal Education and Admission to the Bar. Accreditation by the ABA Council is understandably a first order of business by law schools, because most states will not allow applicants to sit for the state bar examination unless they have graduated from a law school that has been approved by the ABA Council. This means, in effect, that the ABA Council on the Section of Legal Education and Admission to the Bar "acts as an agent for these various lawyer-licensing authorities and decides whether the school's graduates are eligible to sit for the bar exam" (Davis, 1987, p. 1).

No such linkage between accreditation and admission to the bar appears to exist relative to the Association of American Law Schools. Accreditation by this body appears to relate more to prestige and status. Not all schools of law approved by the ABA are also approved by the Association of American Law Schools. One hundred and seventy-five law schools hold approved status by the ABA, compared to 151 in the latter organization (Council on Post-secondary Accreditation, 1986).

As explained in more detail in Chapter Five, accreditation in legal education needs to be understood within the context of licensure and the authority to practice law. Unlike medicine, law does not issue a national license to practice in one or more of the country's fifty-three licensing jurisdictions; thus law is jurisdiction specific. Texas, for example, may require a different level of competence in the bar examination than another state. Moreover, this license does not permit the lawyer to appear in court; other licenses or permits are required to do so. In either event, however, graduation from an ABA-approved law school is a precondition in most states. This is a far cry from earlier years when it was common for a lawyer to earn his way through law school by practicing law (Rudd, 1985b).

As with medicine, accreditation plays an important role in the reputation and status of law schools. The strong linkage between program approval and licensure enhances that image, often causing the public to erroneously assume that such linkages exist in all professional preparation areas. With great control of the accreditation process in the hands of practitioners and their professional associations, institutions with accredited law schools sometimes fret about a shared control. They take considerable pride, however, in satisfying this important constituency and in believing that their programs are of high quality—that they have met the test of professional standards.

Accrediting Nursing Programs

The accreditation of nursing programs is the responsibility of the National League for Nursing (NLN). Established in 1952 through the merger of several national nursing organizations with the National League of Nursing Education, the NLN performs the accreditation role through four review boards, one each for baccalaureate and master's degree programs, associate degree programs, diploma programs, and practical nursing programs. Each board of review consists of ten members, nine peers from within the same discipline and one member from outside. A staff member from the NLN serves on each review board as a nonvoting member. Each board of review is vested with the power to determine the accreditation status of programs being evaluated. The NLN and its four review boards are recognized by COPA and are listed as a nationally recognized accrediting agency by the U.S. Department of Education.

As with most specialized accrediting bodies, including the two previously described (law and medicine), certain preconditions exist relative to other required accreditation. Nursing programs in institutions of higher learning, for example, must be accredited by the appropriate commission of a regional accrediting body. As a condition for eligibility to enter the accreditation process, hospitals with diploma nursing programs must be approved by the joint Commission on Accreditation of Hospitals. An additional eligibility requirement is approval without qualification by the state board of nursing. Again, there is strong linkage among the preparing arm of the profession, the broader profession, and the state mechanism. This linkage may pose problems for colleges and universities in regard to articulation, coordination, and the setting of standards; but it enables institutions of higher learning to demonstrate to these important constituencies their commitment to quality. Moreover, holding accredited status is demonstrable evidence that their programs have met the test of peer review and that graduates of the accredited programs hold "safe-to-practice" status within the world of nursing.

The accreditation process in nursing is very similar to the process used by other specialized accrediting bodies. Following the application and/or notification procedures, a self-study is prepared and submitted. An on-site evaluation team then visits, prepares its report, and submits it to the board of review, as well as to affiliates and the NLN. The board of review decides the accreditation status of the program. Provisions for comments by institutional officials and an appeal process are built into the accreditation process (Council on Postsecondary Accreditation, 1986).

Accrediting Programs in Teacher Education

Since 1954, authority for the national accreditation of programs in teacher education has resided in the National Council for the Accreditation of Teacher Education (NCATE). Prior to 1952, a system of quasi-accreditation existed, handled by the American Association of Colleges for Teacher Education (AACTE), currently a major stakeholder in NCATE. Founding members of NCATE were the National Education Association and the Council of Chief State School Officers.

Constituent members of NCATE include professional associations that represent various components of education (teachers, administrators, counselors), state and local policymakers, and professional specialty areas. More than twenty constituent organizations are involved, far more than in other specialized professional accrediting bodies.

NCATE is a member of COPA and is recognized by the U.S. Department of Education as a national accrediting agency. In July 1985, NCATE completed a major reorganization and restructuring process. Known as NCATE Redesign 1985, this process resulted in major changes in governance, the on-site visit process, and the type of accreditation granted (from program to unit). It is widely believed throughout the profession that the redesigned NCATE is a much stronger accreditation system, as evidenced by more demanding standards, broader representation of the total profession (for example, the recent affiliation with the American Federation of Teachers), creation of a National Board of Examiners (carefully selected and highly trained for on-site evaluation), and the establishment of an intricate system of eleven preconditions that must be met before the accreditation process proceeds further. For example, one of these preconditions requires the unit to present satisfactory evidence that it regularly evaluates its operation and the effectiveness of its graduates. Tangible outcomes that support this contention may be emerging. Of the first 130 educational units evaluated by the new standards, from Fall 1988 to Spring 1990, 28 percent were denied accreditation and another 13 percent were accredited with stipulations, a higher rate of rejection than in previous years (personal letter to Robert L. Saunders from Donna M. Gollnick, deputy executive director, NCATE, Nov. 29, 1990).

Once an institution has met the eleven preconditions, the accreditation process is very similar to the ones described earlier in law, medicine, and nursing. A self-study must be completed and a site visit follows. As noted above, the visiting team is composed of members of a board of examiners. The report of the visiting team is submitted to an audit committee of the Unit Accreditation Board, one of NCATE's four governance boards. The audit committee examines the team report and makes a recommendation to the Unit Accreditation Board, which, acting as a whole, considers and acts upon this recommendation. Accreditation decisions are of four levels: full accreditation, reaccreditation with stipulations, denial (which prohibits initial accreditation), and revocation (which terminates current accreditation) (National Council for the Accreditation of Teacher Education, 1987).

Despite improvements through the years and the rather dramatic changes in NCATE Redesign 1985, accreditation of teacher education at the national level is restricted by factors and circumstances beyond the control of the profession or the accrediting body. A serious restricting factor is the absence of a linkage between accreditation and certification/licensure. This means that, in the main, state certification is not dependent upon an applicant's having completed an NCATE-accredited teacher education program. The only exceptions are in Arkansas and North Carolina, and even in these states the requirement is not yet in full force (Viadero, 1989). The absence of this linkage serves as a disincentive, as evidenced by the fact that less than half (45 percent) of the nation's approximately 1,300 institutions with teacher education programs hold NCATE-accredited status.

A major obstacle to the effort in teacher education to develop a strong national accrediting system has been the reluctance of several major research institutions to seek accreditation by NCATE. Indeed, some of these universities holding NCATE accreditation frequently threaten to terminate the affiliation, the NCATE Redesign and its obvious improvement notwithstanding. As noted below in the section on problems and issues, one element of the dissatisfaction with national accreditation among research universities is the belief that many inferior institutions are able to attain accreditation by NCATE, a condition that, if true, seems to be changing. The founders of the Holmes Group (a significant and controversial consortium of approximately 100 research-oriented universities) were motivated in part by their dissatisfaction with NCATE and the possibility of seeking an alternative. That possibility did not materialize.

Before the Holmes Group initiative, the Association of Colleges and Schools of Education in State University and Land Grant Colleges and Affiliated Private Universities (ACSESULGC/APU) considered disaffiliation with NCATE and the establishment of an alternative accreditation system. Neither happened. ACSESULGC/APU decided to continue its support of NCATE; however, the association's dissatisfaction with NCATE was clear and most likely a major reason that NCATE Redesign 1985 was initiated.

Compounding the problem in accrediting teacher education programs is the large number of institutions with teacher education programs and the incredibly wide variance in state approval mechanisms. In some states, virtually any program can be approved, meaning that graduates of weak, non-NCATE-accredited programs can be certified and authorized to work side by side with graduates of NCATE-accredited programs—with no differences in rank, salary, or responsibilities (Saunders, 1987).

Other restricting factors are the size of the work force and the lack of public support. Trained professionals in education number more than 2.5 million, far more than in any other profession. It has yet to be demonstrated that the general public is willing to support teacher preparation to the extent that all certificated teachers are required to complete a preparation program that holds NCATE-accredited status.

Problems and Issues in Accreditation

The preceding discussion refers to various problems and issues associated with the accreditation of colleges and universities. In this concluding section, a more direct presentation is made of several problems and issues that are of concern to leaders in both accrediting organizations and institutions seeking reaccreditation or initial accreditation.

Young, Chambers, Kells, and Associates (1983, p. 380) caution that accreditation will not survive "just because it is a good idea." Future success, they suggest, will depend on how well individual institutions and organizations address problems carried over from the past and how well current and future leaders in the field enable the accreditation process to accommodate rapid and significant changes in education and society. Confidence in our ability to accommodate the changes is enhanced by the progress made in the past thirty years in responding to the seven issues identified in 1960 by Selden (1960, pp. 32-34) as critical to the future of accreditation:

1. Development of criteria that place less emphasis on minimum standards and more on continued institutional reevaluation, experimentation, and improvement
2. Making accreditation more stimulating for institutions of high quality
3. Accrediting increasing numbers of graduate schools without impairing independent research and individual scholarship
4. Meeting the need for quality assurance in specialized and professional programs without increasing the number of professional accrediting bodies
5. Simplifying the accreditation process without decreasing its effectiveness
6. Providing more information about the degree of quality of individual institutions attaining accreditation and what it means to be accredited
7. Meeting the government's increasing interest in accreditation without increasing its involvement and control

Few will argue that each of these issues has been satisfied completely, but many will contend that on balance the progress has been substantial, in fact, rather remarkable, considering the fact that accreditation is a voluntary matter.

Young, Chambers, Kells, and Associates (1983, pp. 382-386) have their own list of persisting issues that, as they put it, "still dog accreditation":

1. Control: government versus the private sector and, within the private sector, institutions versus external groups, particularly professional organizations
2. Voluntarism: the converting of accreditation by the federal government for its own purposes, and state agencies, acting at the

behest of professional groups, writing accreditation into licensing statuses

3. Sense of community: developing a sense of colleagueship among higher education professionals and staff members in accrediting organizations who often feel that they are not perceived as being in academe

4. Cooperation: preoccupation with the proliferation of accrediting bodies to the neglect of the need for better cooperation among bodies, president-based organizations (for example, American Council on Education), governing boards, and professional organizations that increasingly sponsor their own accrediting agencies

5. Focus on outcomes: Increasingly, professions defining their fields of practice in terms of proficiencies, and postsecondary education continuing to move toward defining their degrees in term of proficiencies, parallel and similar movements that may enable institutions and institutional accrediting bodies to develop a common focus, a condition that does not exist today

6. National coordination: an effective national mechanism needed to enable COPA to carry out its difficult role in surviving the pushes and pulls of its many and diverse constituent groups while at the same time building the necessary support from institutions

7. Public understanding: overcoming the perception that accrediting bodies function as "inspector generals," conducting "white glove inspection" not unlike governmental inspections, so that they become perceived instead as facilitators in the important tasks of goals clarification, self-evaluation, and peer review.

A very recent publication includes a chapter on the role of accreditation in the quest for quality. Mayhew, Ford, and Hubbard (1990, pp. 222–228) identify several issues associated with regional accrediting bodies.

1. Safeguarding the public interest, a stated goal of accreditation, cannot be met truly until a definition of comparability is established and accrediting associations clearly state that one insti-

tution barely meets minimum standards while another far sur-
passes them.

2. The claim that accreditation influences quality by withholding
    accredited status from institutions until they meet minimal
    standards has little basis because relatively few institutions have
    been so denied as long as their financial base appears reason-
    ably sound.

3. Whereas the shift from rigid standards to judging institutions
    according to purposes they have set for themselves has many
    benefits, this shift sometimes leaves institutions totally adrift
    when they are cited with obvious deficiencies. This problem is
    exacerbated by the lack of success by accrediting bodies in forc-
    ing institutions to cease questionable activities, as for example,
    in the case of many nontraditional off-campus programs.

4. The ability of accreditation, using historic instruments, to pro-
    vide obvious benefit to strong, high-quality, prestigious insti-
    tutions can be seriously questioned.

Despite the weaknesses and shortcomings cited by these authors, they conclude that "voluntary accreditation is still the best
mechanism for certifying undergraduate quality" (Mayhew, Ford,
and Hubbard, 1990, p. 231).

We believe that there are several additional accreditation concerns, problems, and issues, perhaps less sophisticated than those
cited above but no less troublesome to college and university leaders
as they endeavor to achieve and maintain accreditation of their institutions and programs. These concerns are presented as criticisms
of shortcomings of accreditation that, if unattended, might reduce
both the attractiveness and the effectiveness of accreditation—and
thus its value as a quality assurance.

One of these criticisms suggests that accreditation is little
more than "professional back-scratching." University faculty frequently hold greater loyalty to their particular discipline or profession than to their respective employing institutions. Serving on a
visiting team for an accreditation agency is sometimes used as an
opportunity to help a group of disciplinary colleagues achieve
higher salaries, lower teaching loads, and increased support services. "I'll help you now," the argument goes, "with the expecta-

tion that you or some other disciplinary colleague will return the favor when evaluating my institution." Some critics contend that this occurs all too often, even when discipline or professional kinship does not exist.

This criticism may be more imagined than real, and it is perhaps overdrawn. Members of visiting teams are not as free to sort out and act upon their own particular concerns (or ways to help a colleague) as this criticism implies. Rather, team members are expected to review information surrounding prescribed standards, to validate that information, and to clarify any points of conflict or inconsistency with what the self-study presented and what they see and hear during the site visit. Critics who subscribe to the fear of professional back-scratching often fail to appreciate both the nature and purpose of peer review in light of evidence produced and professional judgments rendered rather than opinions held. It is also possible that this criticism is based to a considerable degree on suspicion and hearsay. In any event, there is little evidence to support the criticism as a significant shortcoming of accreditation.

A second criticism charges that, despite considerable progress in the direction of results versus process, the progress is too little and too slow, pointing to standards that continue to stress numbers, procedures, and processes at the neglect of results—student achievement, goal attainment, and so forth. Regional accrediting bodies seem to have shown a stronger desire to focus on results than have national and specialized bodies. Performance of graduates, for example, seems to be more clearly associated with the concepts of certification and licensure, dealt with in Chapter Five, than with accreditation.

Closely aligned with this shortcoming of accreditation is the presumption or belief that the general public has neither a good understanding nor a deep appreciation of the importance of institutions' policies, processes, and practices. What the public wants, especially those that have a stake in a particular institution, is an answer to the ever-present and troublesome question: So what? What difference does accreditation mean to graduates, to their employers, to their communities?

It is probably true that the public has little appreciation of the advantages that accrue from accreditation, as noted earlier in this chapter. These advantages are more likely to be understood and appreciated by individuals and agencies whose work and responsibilities enable them to appreciate genuinely the importance of accreditation vis-à-vis self-renewal, the relationship between goal identification and goal attainment, and institutional and program assessment, to mention just three of the advantages. Efforts to answer the "so what" question by citing the several genuine advantages are not likely to convince skeptics, however, especially those who want one-liners.

A fourth frequently cited criticism of accreditation is that it is more a self-serving mechanism for professionals than a public benefit. Too much emphasis is placed on salaries, teaching loads, support services, and employee benefits, for example, and too little on indicators and determinants of quality. A part of the problem here is, again, the public's perception of quality and what makes it happen. Institutions must provide salaries, working conditions, and support services that enable them to attract and retain competent faculty. Not to do so would have deleterious effects on the quality of teaching and learning, and on research and service. Perhaps more effort should be made to help the public understand how student achievement is so closely intertwined with faculty competence, favorable working conditions, and adequate support services.

Another dimension of this criticism involves an accreditation strength that can be a liability. Throughout this chapter we have emphasized the constructive contribution of the peer review process. We may want to remember, however, the posture taken by Flexner concerning the merit of reviewers outside the field. It might be argued, as a point of criticism, that accreditation undertaken only by those who are practitioners within the field promotes a limited and predetermined perspective on what might constitute quality performance of a program or an institution. Those outside a field may not have been socialized to the "conventional wisdom" of an academic specialty or to higher education in general. Thus, they may be more inclined to ask those naive and obnoxious questions that could produce more effective evaluations. Having celebrated the merit of the peer review process, we run the risk of being accused of contradicting ourselves in acknowledging some validity to this criticism. This is not an either-or issue, however. We believe that inclusion of external members on both professional and regional accreditation teams has some merit. The inclusion of someone from a discipline outside the one being studied, in the case of professional accreditation, and the inclusion of a layperson outside education, in the case of regional accreditation, we believe is a practice worthy of salute—and a practice whose potential beneficial outcomes outweigh the risks.

This conviction does not come without an experience base that would suggest a contrary posture. Years ago, one of the authors received a regional accreditation team in which one of the visiting committee members was a lay member (owner and operator of a chain of retail business outlets). After only one day on campus, this lay member offered a number of snap judgments on several university staff personnel—including multiple recommendations for personnel termination. His confidence was undeterred by his ignorance of the complex history of both the institution and the affected staff, and his arrogance was a source of severe discomfort to the remainder of the visiting committee members. In the life of educational institutions, as in the life of many other organizational forms, the theory of a practice must be interpreted in the attitudes and behavior of individuals operating on the theory. The choice of the individual is as important as the theory on which his or her behavior may ride. On a point of theory, what we are saying is that the inclusion of external accreditation team members may constitute a useful counterpoint to this criticism.

A fifth criticism, referred to earlier in this chapter, is the rapidly escalating cost of accreditation, both direct and indirect. Fees paid to accrediting bodies and the costs of visiting teams are rising rapidly. Preparing for the visiting team, conducting the self-study, and maintaining liaison with the accrediting agency require substantial cash expenditures as well as many hidden costs, such as faculty and administrative time and energy. These problems are exacerbated by the proliferation of accrediting bodies, particularly in the specialized domain. They are troublesome to all institutions, but acutely so to those with weak or marginal financial resources, who are reluctant to voice this concern for fear that it would constitute prima facie evidence that the institution has insufficient resources to be accredited. Leaders in these institutions as well as those in institutions with better resources are increasingly tempted to risk the penalty of not seeking accreditation—especially in those programs where the penalty for nonaccreditation would not be great.

This criticism minimizes, if not ignores, the fact that many of the activities associated with the efforts to gain and maintain accreditation are essential to institutional effectiveness, even if accreditation were not involved. The recent emphasis on assessment, for example, should be an ongoing part of institutional life. The fact that it is required by accreditation agencies is not a good reason to label money and energy spent in these efforts as accreditation costs. In fact, few of the costs of accreditation are unique to accreditation but, rather, are expenditures good institutions make in the course of maintaining high quality.

A sixth criticism pertains again to public perception and understanding—and to the troublesome side effects of basing accreditation on the concept of minimal standards. It is not uncommon for institutions held in low prestige, both by their constituencies and fellow institutions, to achieve accreditation—sometimes national, regional, and specialized altogether. Often the achievement of accreditation leaves constituents and colleagues convinced that the achievement is indicative of weak standards of the accrediting body. Indeed, in some specialized fields of accreditation in which graduation from an accredited school is not a precondition for certification and/or licensure, high-prestige institutions often deliberately avoid accreditation. Their rationale is that more harm than good results from being accredited by an agency that will accredit institutions widely believed to be inferior. Stanford University, for example, cannot afford nonaccreditation of its law school, but it can—and intentionally does—afford nonaccreditation of its school of education.

Accreditation was never intended to bring all institutions into a single, monolithic band of like institutions, all of pristine quality. Rather, it was intended to set standards beneath which institutions could not fall without signaling to their constituencies and publics that serious questions exist about the appropriateness of their mission, the extent to which it is being achieved, and the likelihood that its purposes will continue to be achieved. Obviously, all institutions meeting minimum standards are not of the same quality. Some barely meet the standards; others greatly exceed them. Critics who expect all accredited institutions to be of equal and superior quality hold unrealistic expectations. These critics may be insensitive to the vagaries of reputational rankings, described in Chapter Three, and may be making their own assessments without specifying the criteria or information used. In any event, as noted earlier, the concept of minimum standards reduces the variation in institutional quality and assists the public in discerning the differences in institutions with adequate quality and those without.

A seventh criticism centers on the question of whether accreditation is meaningful to the larger, research-based, "national" universities. Some argue that accrediting associations would never deny such leading institutions accreditation. Why, therefore, should they be put through a process whose outcome is never much in question? What real benefit accrues to these institutions? At least one answer to this criticism rests in the original statement of two accreditation purposes: accountability and improvement. It could well be true that the "accountability" judgment might not be in serious question for these institutions (though arrogance on this point is not warranted). Surely, however, a learning community asserting that it could never benefit from the renewing scrutiny of its own faculty and staff and the external evaluation of peers would be a formidable and unhappy curiosity in American higher education.

An eighth criticism concerns the persisting problem of standards: their adequacy, their uniformity and comprehensiveness, their relevancy to quality, and their applicability to the exceedingly diverse nature of colleges and universities in this country. The matter of relevancy to quality and to student achievement was touched on earlier. It is difficult, however, to fashion standards that apply equally and evenly to all institutions that may justifiably seek accreditation. For example, standards that require faculty to be productive in research and publication are germane to graduate and research institutions, but their relevancy is questionable when applied to institutions that are primarily undergraduate and have no doctoral programs. The concept of mission achievement is deeply embedded in the accreditation process, yet standards often mitigate the concept by having a single set of standards that apply to all institutions irrespective of type, size, or mission.

This note on mission statements and mission achievement encourages our attention to yet another criticism of accreditation, which strikes at one of the foundations of the accrediting process. Readers may recall that accreditation was cited as "the test of mission achievement." One of the often cited strengths of accreditation is that it is designed to nurture diversity of campus missions, and, as we will note in other places in the book, notably in our final chapter, there are few national reports today that do not call for campuses to formulate more realistic and limited mission statements.

Two scholars at Mississippi State University, however, have conducted research that leads them to conclude that campuses may spend a lot of time fussing with their mission statements, but too few of these mission statements offer anything very distinctive about the campuses they are supposed to describe. In the Winter 1990-91 issue of *Planning for Higher Education,* Walter Newsom and C. Ray Hayes note that "the mission statement should be a declaration of the special purposes of an institution and whom it intends to serve. It is a revelation of the college's reason for being" (p. 28).

The authors surveyed 142 institutions in eleven southeastern states and received replies from 114. In reviewing and evaluating mission statements from these campuses, the authors found "that when we hid the institution's name, most of the colleges or universities could not be identified from their statements because they read alike, full of honorable verbiage signifying nothing. Not surprisingly, few colleges find much use for their mission statements. They are usually not guidelines for serious planning" (Newsom and Hayes, 1990-91, p. 29). If this is true, then our definition of quality, as offered in Chapter One, may be in some difficulty. How can any organization evaluate how good a job it is doing if it does not know or say what it is supposed to be doing? The solution, we believe, is not to abandon our definition of quality but to urge each campus to construct a mission statement that makes a more specific case for the distinctiveness of that campus. Newsom and Hayes outline a set of mission dimensions that includes target clienteles, intended outcomes and their priorities, region to be served, commitments for survival and growth, an outline of values and philosophical priorities, and matters of public image.

The standards and criteria of most regional and specialized accrediting agencies call for a well-developed and well-publicized mission statement, at both campus and program levels. Why, then, do we still find so many mission statements empty of meaning? Perhaps accrediting bodies need to be more specifically serious about one of the foundations of their own work. This would make a major contribution to the cause of quality.

A ninth issue centers on the question of whether a review every five or ten years constitutes sufficient pressure for a college or university to maintain and enhance its quality. Is there, in this long-term time frame, an incentive for an institution to float for years and then to engage in frenetic activity as the imminent arrival of the self-study period looms? Certainly, the activity of some campuses would suggest a "yes" to that question. Increasingly, however, the institutional effectiveness standards of accrediting associations require that institutions build their quality assurance efforts over a period of years. Campus faculty and staff awaiting the self-study stimulus for quality assurance action find themselves "behind the quality eight ball," inviting the hoisting of a red flag on their accreditation flagpole.

Finally, we take note of current controversies over the content of accreditation standards. As a first example, the Middle States Association of Colleges and Schools has apparently adopted a standard relating to the diversity of a campus and its success in attracting minority faculty and students. The adoption of this standard and its application in the accreditation review of Bernard Baruch College of the City University of New York has generated a lively controversy. The U.S. Department of Education is reviewing its recognition of the Middle States status with the federal government.

An article appearing in the December 5, 1990, issue of the *Chronicle of Higher Education* offered several criticisms of the Middle States policy posture. U.S. Department of Education review panelist Richard Kunkel, former executive director of NCATE, suggests that the Middle States position interferes with campus autonomy. However, officials of the Western States accrediting group, which also has a diversity requirement, suggested that the U.S. Office of Education was sending the wrong signal to colleges in holding up acceptance of the Middle States recognition (Jaschik, 1990).

Is diversity linked to quality, and are the policies and practices of a campus designed to promote diversity a legitimate point of inquiry for accrediting agencies whose purpose is to promote quality? A point that we will make throughout this book is that quality assurance is a venture in learning and discovery. Our journey in a quest for quality may be marked by moments of rest and renewal, but it is doubtful that it will have any final conceptual destination, which this point of controversy nicely illustrates.

A second example concerns the stance of regional accrediting associations with regard to the performance and integrity of intercollegiate athletic programs. In recent years, these associations have generally remained silent and aloof as stories of educational and financial abuse in athletic programs occupy front pages in local and national press. Is this silence justified by the absence of criteria or standards related to intercollegiate programs? Hardly so. For example, the *Criteria for Accreditation* of the Commission on Colleges of the Southern Association of Colleges and Schools contains this statement. "The intercollegiate athletics program must be operated in strict adherence to a stated philosophy and purpose in harmony with and supportive of the institutional purpose. The administration and faculty of the institution must have control of the athletic program and contribute to its ultimate direction with appropriate participation by students and oversight by the governing board. . . . All fiscal matters pertaining to the athletic program must be controlled by the administration and must be accounted for through the regular accounting and budgeting procedures of the institution. This principle pertains to all athletic expenditures and income from whatever source" (Commission on Colleges, 1991, pp. 36-37).

The teeth are there, what has been missing is the bite. In recognition of that challenge, the Commission on Colleges of the Southern Association of Colleges and Schools recently appointed a special committee to examine this issue. The committee will present to the December 1991 meeting of the Commission on Colleges a recommended set of new rules that link accreditation to the integrity of an institution's sports program. This activity at least reflects a leadership step on the part of a regional accrediting association to deal with a critical issue and reveals the commission's willingness to engage controversial issues, just as it did with its initiative on institutional effectiveness, to which we have already referred in this chapter. A front-page story in the May 19, 1991 issue of the *New York Times* (Weiss, 1991) promises a lively conversation in the December 1991 meeting, however. Although advocates of the proposed new rules feel that they will strengthen the role of accreditation in this area, others do not believe that they will have any significant effect. They do not believe that the Commission on Colleges would seriously jeopardize the accreditation of an institution having a strong academic program but an athletic program marked by either weakness or duplicity. Whether the teeth and the bite will come together remains to be seen.

A Concluding Perspective on Accreditation

Most of the ways colleges and universities have devised to assure their publics that quality programs exist are relatively new inventions. Accreditation, however, has been with us for most of this century. From its understandably meager beginning in 1910 when the process consisted of little more than evaluating a handful of institutions according to developed criteria, accreditation has evolved into a sophisticated process that, in addition to serving the quality assurance role, promotes the continuous improvement of member institutions and their movement toward a time when accreditation will become the true test of both effectiveness and quality.

That accreditation is a valued way to ensure quality can be seen by the impressive number of organizations and agencies that place credence in the concept. Students, their counselors, and their parents pay attention to accreditation when selecting a college or university. Institutions of higher learning have reciprocal articulation agreements based on respect for accreditation. Employers, philanthropic foundations, and governmental funding agencies increasingly require accreditation as a condition of eligibility for funding, grants, and employment. Additionally, the general public is more likely to perceive accreditation as a quality assurance than they are the more recently devised ways, such as program reviews and alumni surveys, which, in a general sense, go unnoticed.

Perhaps the greatest support for accreditation as a quality assurance is use by several professions. The fields of medicine and law serve as good examples of the importance attached to graduation from an accredited program, without which applicants for licensure and entry into the profession cannot even begin. Several other professions have virtually the same requirements, and still others desire such a condition.

During its eighty-year history, accreditation has undergone changes in philosophy and process that parallel and accommodate changes in society and in higher education. Examples of changes can be seen in the way specialized accreditation has kept pace with the specialization movement in American society, both among institutions and within them. A further example is the creation of special accrediting commissions in three regional accrediting associations designed to handle the accreditation needs of vocational and technical institutions and programs.

Currently, accreditation places great importance on goal formulation and attainment, a heavier emphasis on results obtained than on meeting externally prescribed standards and criteria. The concept of minimal standards still prevails, however.

Despite great improvement in accreditation, several issues and problems still surround the process. Noteworthy among the issues are the increasing costs of obtaining and maintaining accredited status; the proliferation of accrediting agencies and the inherent difficulty in articulating and coordinating with them; and the belief that professional fraternalism frequently invades the evaluation of institutions.

Accreditation has a long and rich history as a quality assurance instrument. Despite its imperfections, it remains the best known signal and perhaps the most effective instrument for nurturing and guaranteeing collegiate quality. As Kenneth Young and his associates remarked, "the genius of accreditation is that it began with the impossible task of defining educational quality and in just 25 years evolved, by trial and error, into a process that advances educational quality" (Young, Chambers, Kells, and Associates, 1983, p. 13).

THREE

College Rankings and Ratings: The Test of Reputation

In the Fall of 1983, *U.S. News and World Report* brought to newsstands over the nation a report and rating of "America's Best Colleges." This rating of American colleges and universities was repeated in 1985, 1987, 1988, 1989, and 1990. Although there have been a number of scholarly ratings published since 1911, the *U.S. News* journalistic exercises may have become the nation's most widely known quality reports. They have certainly become the most intensely debated approaches to quality assurance among college educators.

After describing a range of quality indicators, McGuire and others (1988) concluded that "given a universe of unsatisfactory output concepts, reputation—with all its flaws—is probably as good or better because it is broader and more representative of the range of important output components that are produced" (p. 356). In contrast, Robert Zemsky and William Massey offered this comment on the Fall 1989 *U.S. News and World Report* ratings: "The rankings of colleges and universities in *U.S. News* are as meaningless as the calculations spewed by Dustin Hoffman's character in 'Rain Man' . . . Admissions officers, presidents, trustees, and regents of institutions who use one year's *U.S. News* rankings to trumpet their status to prospective students, faculty, and donors wait nervously to see whether the next year's rankings will make liars of them" (Zemsky and Massey, 1990, p. 21). Later on in the chapter, we will have more to say on shifts in rankings and their meaning.

The entire process of rating and ranking is built on the philosophic premise discussed in our opening chapter, that quality is in limited supply. In other words, there can never be more than ten in the top ten or twenty-five in the top twenty-five, no matter what the actual performance level of a program or an institution or what impact the program or institution has on its students. Whether there is a definitive relationship between reputation and results is yet another issue to be engaged in this chapter.

Most organizations are concerned with both the perception and the reality of quality—that is, the public perception of and the hard data on product performance. One is not surprised then to see full-page advertisements in the *Wall Street Journal, USA Today,* or weekly magazines such as *Time* or *U.S. News and World Report* in which auto or airline industry executives pitch the quality theme. Indeed, in a 1988 *Time* magazine advertisement, Chrysler executive Lee Iacocca outlined a "quality bill of rights" to which customers of Chrysler are supposedly entitled (*Time,* 1988). Is there a lesson here for American higher education? It may not be enough for quality to show through in whatever indicator or evidence we may select to demonstrate quality. It may be equally important for us to attend to public perceptions of quality as well.

Do rating and ranking exercises make a meaningful contribution to quality assurance? We begin the engagement of that question by exploring first some of the more significant reports on both graduate and undergraduate rankings.

Rating Graduate Programs—The Origins of College Ranking

In his 1964 book *The Academic Man,* Logan Wilson said that ranking colleges has a history as early as 1911, when a list was published by the Bureau of Education, a rating of 344 institutions by the Association of American Universities. The leading institutions were, in order, Harvard, Chicago, Columbia, California, Yale,

Michigan, Cornell, Princeton, Johns Hopkins, Wisconsin, and Minnesota.

The study most often cited as the original study of graduate quality was reported by Raymond Hughes in 1925. As rationale for this early rating of graduate programs and schools, Hughes offered the opinion: "It has seemed that such a rating would be of distinct value to the college president or dean who is seeking men to fill vacancies on this staff. Such a rating also seems proper and desirable in printed form, so that any one interested can turn to it readily for a rough estimate of the work in a given field" (Hughes, 1925, p. 3).

The ratings began by securing from members of the Miami University (Ohio) faculty "a list of the universities which conceivably might be doing high grade work leading to a doctor's degree" (Hughes, 1925, p. 3). The Miami faculty also furnished a "list of from forty to sixty men who were teaching his subject in colleges and universities in this country, at least half of the names on the list to be those of professors in colleges rather than in universities" (Hughes, 1925, p. 3). Rating forms were returned, according to Hughes's report, from about half the respondents.

Hughes chaired a second study of graduate schools for the American Council on Education, and the results were reported in the April 1934 issue of the *Educational Record* ("Report of the Committee on Graduate Instruction," 1934). Whereas the 1925 study included a rating of about twenty fields, this one encompassed fifty different fields of study. Identification of the institutions offering graduate work was derived from a study of catalogues and reports of graduate deans. Learned societies in each of the fields were asked to supply a list of 100 scholars in that field, to whom the rating forms were circulated.

At the end of his introduction to the results, Hughes commented: "There was marked evidence of a lag in the estimate of departments. A department which has been strong, but which has lost good men and is really on the decline, has in several cases been rated too high. On the other hand, several departments that have recently developed much strength seem to be underrated. If this type of study could be repeated every few years, such errors would be corrected" (1934, p. 194). The time-lag liability of ratings and rankings is thus well identified. However, the next comprehensive ratings were not to occur within the time line suggested by Hughes.

In 1959 Hayward Keniston reported a ranking of graduate departments and institutions undertaken as part of an evaluation of the program at the University of Pennsylvania. Keniston describes the study approaches as follows: "A letter was addressed to the chairmen of departments in each of twenty-five leading universities of the country. The list was compiled on the basis of (1) membership in the Association of American Universities, (2) number of Ph.D.'s awarded in recent years, and (3) geographical distribution. The list did not include technical schools like Massachusetts Institute of Technology and the California Institute of Technology, nor state colleges, like Iowa State, Michigan State or Penn State, since the purpose was to compare institutions which offered the doctorate in a wide variety of fields" (Keniston, 1959, p. 115).

These rather important caveats notwithstanding, a review of the results will prove of interest. Appearing in the Keniston list of top twenty institutions are Harvard, California, Columbia, Yale, Michigan, Chicago, Princeton, Wisconsin, Cornell, Illinois, Pennsylvania, Minnesota, Stanford, University of California, Los Angeles (UCLA), Indiana, Johns Hopkins, Northwestern, Ohio State, New York University (NYU), and Washington. With the exception of UCLA, NYU, and Washington, all remaining institutions had appeared in Hughes's 1925 ranking. There has been, then, a considerable stability over the thirty-two-year history of the ratings. North Carolina and Iowa were not in the Keniston list, although they appeared in 1925. Can it be that the actual quality of these two universities declined during this thirty-two-year period? We will have more to say about this feature of collegiate rankings later in the chapter.

Two of the most frequently cited and best known of recent quality ratings of graduate departments and institutions are the 1966 study by Allan Cartter and the 1970 study by Roose and Anderson. Logan Wilson's foreword in Allan Cartter's report contains an arresting opening line: "Excellence, by definition, is a state only the few rather than the many can attain" (Cartter, 1964, p. vii). With this definition, Wilson supports the philosophic position of "limited supply" to which we earlier referred, which assumes a standard of performance that is comparative and relative rather than criterion based. The Cartter study is cited as the fourth such quality rating following Hughes's study of 1925, the American Council on Education study of 1934, and the Keniston study of 1957.

Cartter offers these introductory notes on the concept of quality. "Quality is an elusive attribute, not easily submitted to measurement. . . . In an operational sense, quality is someone's subjective assessment, for there is no way of objectively measuring what is in essence an attribute of value" (1964, p. 4). Arguing for the contributions of rankings and ratings, Cartter points to the limitations of diversity. "Diversity can be a costly luxury if it is accompanied by ignorance. Our present system works fairly well because most students, parents, and prospective employers know that a bachelor's degree from Harvard, Stanford, Swarthmore, or Reed is ordinarily a better indication of ability and accomplishment than a bachelor's degree from Melrose A & M or Siwash College" (Cartter, 1964, p. 3). As an editorial note, we find it interesting that Cartter had no difficulty naming the top institutions but fudged on his public disclosure of the supposedly lower-quality schools by resorting to pseudonyms and poorly disguised racial identification. Cartter then states this rationale for quality ratings: "Just as consumer knowledge and honest advertisement are requisite if a competitive economy is to work satisfactorily, so an improved knowledge of opportunities and of quality is desirable if a diverse educational system is to work effectively" (1964, p. 3).

To avoid criticisms of the earlier studies, Cartter used three panels of raters—department chairpersons, senior scholars, and junior scholars—in twenty-nine different fields of study.

In a replication of the Cartter study in 1970, Roose and Anderson published yet another rating of graduate programs. In a synopsis of the findings, they noted: "There is an increase in the rated quality of faculty of graduate programs, moving from 69.8 percent rated adequate plus or better in 1964 to 80 percent in 1969. Second, there is evidence of regional improvement. The south, for example, had only 59 percent of its faculties rated 'adequate plus' or better in 1964 but this percentage rose to 73 percent in 1969" (Roose and Anderson, 1970, p. 2).

In a section entitled "policy implications of the findings,"

Roose and Anderson warn of the limitations: "The superficiality of exclusive reliance on reputation as a measure of quality was well illustrated in a comment made to us by the former chief academic officer of a top rated institution about one of his distinguished faculty members: '_____' is highly regarded in his profession and has contributed importantly to the reputation of his department, but what has he done for students? In twelve years he has not turned out a single Ph.D." (1970, p. 24).

While we are reviewing the Cartter and Roose-Anderson reports, we note one of the more vigorous assaults on these two reports. In a monograph entitled *The Ranking Game: The Power of the Academic Elite* by W. Patrick Dolan (1976), we were drawn not so much to the body of the monograph as to the preface. William A. Arrowsmith begins this preface by labeling the reports as "quantified gossip" and "formidable professional sanctions against daring, diversity, and openness." Arrowsmith's prefatory remarks include the following judgment: "The Cartter Report and the Roose-Anderson reports are monstrosities, not simply because they are the patent product of reflex, bad faith and suboptimization, but because they are the regressive instruments of standardization which has no valid cultural or human purpose; which serves merely governmental, professional, administrative, or bureaucratic convenience. They simply have no educational purpose which is compatible with the needs of our culture or with the life of the mind" (Dolan, 1976, p. i).

Of this we may be certain. The person who dares to evaluate anything in higher education invites evaluation. We will never be without lively argument when it comes to the purpose and performance of American collegiate education.

In 1976, Mary Jo Clark, Rodney Hartnett, and Leonard Baird of Educational Testing Service (ETS) reported on an extensive study of quality indicators in three graduate fields. The opening pages of their report carry these warnings about the contributions of program ratings and give a rationale for multidimensional study of graduate quality: "Ratings of the reputation of a program among faculty members in the same field have a place in program evaluation; but they are not very helpful to those who may be seeking to improve their program, are highly related to program size and visibility, and only occasionally reflect recent changes (good or bad) in a program" (Clark, Hartnett, and Baird, 1976, p. 1.2). Their study involved an extensive review of the variety of evidences that should be examined to ascertain program quality: faculty, students, resources, and curricular characteristics.

As a final example of graduate study ranking, we explore a five-volume study that attempts to take advantage of the multidimensional approach advocated by the previous ETS study by Clark and others. The 1982 study edited by Jones, Lindzey, and Coggeshall, conducted under the aegis of the Conference Board of Associated Research Councils and published by the National Academy of Sciences, is by far the most ambitious of contemporary efforts— reviewing programs at 228 institutions (compared, for example, to 130 in the Roose-Anderson study). Within these 228 institutions, almost 2,700 programs in thirty-two disciplines were evaluated.

In their preface to Volume 1, the editors noted that at the time of the study American universities were producing over 20,000 research doctorates a year but "what might surprise us, however, is the imbalance between the putative national importance of research-doctoral programs and the amount of sustained evaluative attention they themselves receive" (Jones, Lindzey, and Coggeshall, 1982, p. v). They claim that collegiate educators are poorly informed about the quality of graduate programs and offer their study as a logical but improved continuance of the Roose-Anderson tradition.

This study employed sixteen measures for most of the fields reviewed: mathematical and physical sciences, humanities, biological sciences, engineering, and social and behavioral sciences. These sixteen variables were clustered in six groups: program size (three measures), characteristics of graduates (four measures), reputational survey results (four measures), university library size (one measure), research support (two measures), and publication records (two measures). Many of these measures are of dubious qualitative linkage. The number of faculty members in a program (program size measures) and the median number of years from first enrollment of a doctoral student to receipt of the doctorate (characteristics of graduate measures) may be of interest but hardly qualify as hard evidence on quality.

The qualitative heart of this study is embraced by the four

"reputational survey results," in which participating faculty were asked to evaluate these factors: the scholarly quality of program faculty on a scale from 0 to 5, the effectiveness of the program in educating research scholars, and the improvement in program quality in the last five years. Then the faculty evaluators were asked to indicate their familiarity with the programs they were evaluating. In Volume 1 on the evaluation of programs in mathematics and physical sciences, the comments of the editors are instructive: "It should be pointed out that the evaluators, on the average, were unfamiliar with almost one-third of the programs they were asked to consider" (Jones, Linzey, and Coggeshall, 1982, p. 24). Is this a condition designed to enhance confidence in the outcomes of the evaluation? We think not.

Under the measure of publication records, the editors report that a program was evaluated on the number of published articles attributed to it. The qualitative limits of this measure are reasonably obvious, but it ignores other major evidences of scholarship and also tends to bias the evaluation toward large departments.

In the May/June 1983 issue of *Change*, David Webster furnishes an informing review of the 1982 study. He is both complimentary and critical and describes the study as "the biggest, best, most expensive, most thoughtfully conceived, and carefully carried out academic quality rating ever done" (p. 14). Unlike what one might expect from a study of this nature, one searches in vain for systematic rankings of programs based on any one of the sixteen measures or combination of measures. Webster criticizes the authors for this approach: "By publishing endless columns of figures for institutions in each discipline it covers, without summarizing, combining, or averaging these figures, or ranking the institutions in any way, this most reluctant of all academic quality ratings is like the bible for some religious sects. Of which anyone is welcome to make any interpretation he or she wishes" (Webster, 1983, p. 16).

Webster then undertakes to remedy this difficulty by a numeric routine designed to portray shifts in institutional rankings from the earlier rankings (by Hughes, Keniston, and so on) to the Jones study. He publishes a table of results showing, among other movements, that Johns Hopkins had slipped twenty-three positions and MIT had gained fourteen positions from the 1925 Hughes study. Webster admits, however, that the results of this comparison cannot be considered very accurate for the simple reason that different groups of judges used different criteria with different groups of departments and different groups of universities.

Returning now to the original 1982 study, we find on page vi of the preface to Volume 1 that the three purposes of this massive study were to assist students in seeking the best match of graduate programs to their interests, to serve scholars in higher education, and to inform the judgment of those responsible for protecting quality. As an interesting and perhaps questionable commentary on these purposes, the copy of the study that we reviewed had never been checked out of the research university library in which we found it.

Webster cites this 1982 study as one of the more expensive ones undertaken, and we understand that as this book goes to press, a follow-up version is being entertained. Given the general liabilities of previous studies and the specific liabilities of this 1982 study, we wonder if funding agencies ever bother to obtain hard evidence on whether the three purposes above were well served and whether the study had any significant decision utility. It would be a simple matter, for example, to evaluate the achievement of the first purpose just cited by simply asking a random sample of students enrolled in research-doctoral programs whether they had ever heard of the study.

This study did not involve, by the way, major rankings of professional programs, other than engineering. Perhaps we should examine some of the work that has been done in such rankings. In 1973 Margulies and others ranked professional schools in such fields as medicine, law, and so forth. The authors sent questionnaires to deans in 1,180 schools offering degrees in seventeen different professional program fields. A comment on response rate in this study is instructive: "A look at the response rates shows that one explanation for the differences (in response rates) between types of schools is the prestige of the profession. The largest proportions of deans who did not respond are in those professions that research has shown to have the highest prestige. Inasmuch as the ratings of expert judges are of interest, even if they are statistically unreliable, we present the ratings of the eight types of professional schools with fewer than 20 respondents in the lower part of the table" (Margulies, 1973, p. 22).

The authors seem to suggest that we should be interested in ratings of these programs even though the representative participation of raters cannot be assured. It is no small curiosity that we are invited to find these results of interest even though they are statistically meaningless, and professionals in these high-prestige fields did not care enough to participate.

A second and more recent example is a *U.S. News and World Report* rating of graduate and professional programs. Not content with their venture into the rating of colleges and universities, *U.S. News and World Report* entered the field of graduate school rating in March 1990.This issue offered ratings in four graduate and professional fields: business, law, medicine, and engineering ("America's Best Graduate Schools," March 19, 1990). However, the issue is of interest for more than the ratings. An accompanying article is entitled "Why U.S. News Ranks Colleges" and opens with this lead: "The sad truth is that it is easier to learn about the relative merits of compact disc players than it is to compare and contrast America's professional schools. And some educators prefer to keep it that way" (p. 50).

Here is the closing comment of *U.S. News* editors: "The editors expect that like our study of undergraduate education, now going into its sixth edition, it will evolve, change and eventually merit the active cooperation of all the leaders of the graduate and professional school community. We trust they will come to understand that the 'light of public scrutiny' often can be as valuable a tool for improving higher education as it is for informing the reading public" (p. 50).

Discomforting though it may be to some collegiate educators, *U.S. News and World Report* makes a good point. We cannot continue to talk about quality without operational evidence of what we are talking about, and that is going to mean public disclosure. We are inclined to see the test of public disclosure—whether on ratings, outcomes assessments, results of peer reviews, or other evidence—to be a helpful trend. We encourage readers to review the rating results of graduate and professional schools in the four fields cited: business, law, medicine, and engineering. The larger national universities—Stanford, Harvard, Yale, and so forth—dominate the ratings.

In summary, what can we say about the reputational ratings and rankings of graduate programs and institutions having graduate programs? We certainly have to note an important consistency and stability in the results. One is hard pressed to find any list of top-rated institutions in which some of the national universities of the land cannot be found. The visibility and prestige of these universities, and the primary basis of these ratings, rest heavily upon the eminence of their faculties; and the eminence of the faculties resides heavily in their publication and research records. We are not surprised, then, that the top-rated universities and graduate programs are those whose faculties are publication productive and research oriented. Institutional size, history, and resources play important roles in this stability.

Reputational Ratings of Undergraduate Programs

Although the rating of graduate programs in the United States has a history reaching back to the early part of the twentieth century, the rating of undergraduate programs is of more recent origin. Of special interest is that a good portion of activity and initiative for such ratings has occurred not so much in scholarly studies, such as those previously discussed in this chapter, but in media and journalistic reviews.

A good lead example for the ratings of undergraduate programs is furnished by Lewis Solmon and Alexander Astin, who conducted a pilot study to rate undergraduate programs in seven fields in four states—California, Illinois, North Carolina, and New York. A more complete record of their study can be found in the September and October 1981 issues of *Change* magazine.

Respondents were all department members, approximately 15,000 in number. Rating criteria included these factors:

- Overall quality of undergraduate education
- Preparation of student for graduate school
- Preparation of student for employment
- Faculty commitment to undergraduate teaching

- Scholarly accomplishments of faculty
- Innovativeness of curriculum

Here is one interesting, and perhaps disturbing, result of the study. Princeton University appears in the top ten departments of business on each of the six criteria above—even though Princeton does not offer an undergraduate program in business. Solmon and Astin comment as follows: "The finding underscores the need to interpret the results of any reputational survey with care, since strong halo effects appear to be operating. In this report, we have not presented the results for business programs because of the confounding halo effects" (Solmon and Astin, 1981a, p. 27).

In the follow-up article entitled "Are Reputational Ratings Needed to Measure Quality?", Solmon and Astin conclude: "In short, while our analysis suggests that reputational ratings of undergraduate programs may indeed be unnecessary because they seem to be redundant with other known information about institutions, we must defer final judgment about the value of such ratings until additional ratings covering more fields and possibly more diverse quality criteria can be obtained, and until longitudinal value-added studies can be carried out to test the validity of such ratings" (1981b, p. 19). The last comment merits more thought because it offers a good lead-in to Chapter Seven on student outcomes assessment. Does attending a highly rated institution result in a demonstrated impact on student learning?

Other dimensions of the Solmon and Astin study also deserve attention. In their opening commentary, the authors point out that many raters chose not to respond for a variety of reasons: burdensome time commitments, lack of knowledge about departments to be rated, confusion over institutions included in the lists, and so on. The response rate is not cited in the article.

Another provocative finding of the Solmon and Astin study was that the position of an institution on the two lists of institutions provided to raters—a national list and a state list—did affect how raters responded. Indeed, the results were in opposite directions in two different fields. "California sociologists tended to rate the 'scholarly or professional accomplishments of faculty' in California institutions lower when those institutions were included in the national list rather than the California list. Chemistry faculty in New York tend to rate chemistry departments in their own state more favorably when they are included on the national list rather than a separate list, whereas sociology faculty in New York tend to rate their department more poorly when they are included in a single list along with the other national institutions" (1981b, p. 18).

What can we say about this study of ratings in undergraduate departments? The simplest answer may be that if one knows something about the admissions selectivity and size of a campus, then one can reasonably expect that institution to be viewed as a high-quality institution. Second, a variety of variables can affect the reliability and validity of these rankings—size of response, composition and arrangement of institutional lists, and so on. And finally, one cannot know from reputational rankings what direct educational benefit is conferred on a student; that is, whether the institution does, in fact, make a value-added difference. Our common sense is rewarded in this case. Many have experienced graduates of highly prestigious schools whose minds seem empty of meaning and hearts empty of caring. And many have seen graduates from the "Melrose A & M and Siwash College"—to borrow pseudonyms from Cartter—whose minds and hearts are making a difference.

As stated earlier, easily the most visible and widely known rating activities related to undergraduate programs in recent years are the surveys conducted by *U.S. News and World Report*. In 1983, 1,308 presidents were asked to name the nation's highest-quality undergraduate schools. Fifty percent responded. Commenting on the fact that only five of the seventy-six schools mentioned were public institutions, *U.S. News and World Report* writers observed: "Educators point to conditions found at many taxpayer supported institutions—among them larger class sizes, more graduate students serving as instructors for undergraduates and less selective admissions standards based on serving state residents than on attracting the nation's top students—as reasons for the predominance of private schools on the lists" ("Rating the Colleges," 1983).

Four years later, in the 1987 survey, 16 of 144 schools would be public, an increase from 6.5 percent to 11.1 percent of public institutions in the ratings. Can we suppose that quality conditions in public colleges changed that dramatically in four years?

Included in the 1985 survey were 1,318 institutions that offered liberal arts programs, with professional schools and military academies excluded. As in 1983 and 1987, the raters were college presidents, each of whom was asked to select the top five undergraduate schools from a list of colleges and universities similar to his or her campus in mission. Of the 1,318 presidents surveyed, 788 or 60 percent responded.

One of the best features of the *U.S. News and World Report* 1985 rating is the focus on diversity and innovation. For example, Evergreen State College in Washington was cited for its innovative curriculum in which students study special topical courses in small student-faculty settings. Evaluation of students at Evergreen takes the form of narrative entries rather than grades. Alverno College in Milwaukee, a smaller Catholic school for women, was cited for its development and evaluation of general education competencies in communication, analysis, problem solving, valuing, social integration, responsibility for global environment, responsible citizenship, and esthetic responsiveness. And Trinity University, a private liberal arts school in San Antonio, Texas, was cited for its aggressiveness in fund-raising and the attraction of top scholars with endowed chairs.

For the 1987 survey, 1,329 presidents were asked to rate colleges with missions similar to their own, as in the 1985 survey. Of the 1,329 polled, 650 responded—a 60 percent response ratio, as in 1985. Authors of the article indicate that "a small number of the presidents declined to participate in the survey and wrote to the magazine to say they felt that neither they nor their peers were in a position to judge the academic quality of institutions other than their own" (1987, p. 50). For 1987, the presidents were asked to rate the top ten institutions, rather than the top five as in the 1985 survey.

Once again, the writers of the story emphasize the curricular innovations that draw attention to the diversity of American higher education: the great books curriculum at St. Johns, global education emphasis at Earlham, value-added assessment at Northeast Missouri State University, freshman humanities seminars at Wofford College in South Carolina, one-course-at-a-time at Colorado College.

An informative addendum to the 1987 study is entitled "How the Rankings Changed: 'The Ups and Downs.'" It begins with this lead-in statement: "It doesn't take long for new college presidents to discover an essential truth about their vocation: Academic reputations are like campus trees, slow to grow, but once established slow to die" ("America's Best Colleges," 1987, p. 70).

However, a number of schools dropped out of the 1987 ratings, and the authors felt an explanation was in order. They explain that the disappearance of schools like Mills College in California, Wheaton in Massachusetts, Austin College in Texas, Old Dominion in Virginia, and Tennessee Tech came about because they were victims of their own success. These institutions and others had moved into more competitive Carnegie classifications.

Explaining why Harvey Mudd College, which ranked first among small comprehensive institutions in the 1985 survey, dropped completely out of the rankings, the writers said: "Harvey Mudd's slide into seeming academic oblivion is more apparent than real. Earlier this year, Carnegie reclassified Harvey Mudd, which emphasized engineering, chemistry, math and physics courses, as a specialized institution of engineering and technology. Because the *U.S. News and World Report* survey does not include a category for ranking specialized schools, Harvey Mudd did not even appear on this year's ballot. In brief after 1985, there was change in Harvey Mudd's category, not its quality" ("America's Best Colleges," p. 70). (This conclusion, both descriptive and evaluative, we should remember, is not the consensus of presidential raters but of the authors.)

In October 1988, *U.S. News and World Report* departed from the practices of its three previous surveys, revealing what was done and why: "This year, however, after extensive consultation with college presidents and other academic experts, *U.S. News and World Report* has made two major changes in its study. First, because academic deans and admissions officers often see education from rather different perspectives than do college presidents, they also have been included in the survey of more than 1,000 college officials. Second, because the expert opinions are just that, opinions, *U.S. News and World Report* has based its largest academic rankings on objective data as well as on the subjective judgments in the survey" ("America's Best Colleges," 1988, p. 50). The authors then indicated that these data included five measures of quality: admissions selectivity, faculty strength and instructional budget per student, resources for educational programs, graduation rates, and school reputational studies.

What happens to the reputational quality of a college or university when one changes both the rater and the criteria? Table 3.1 contains the rankings for national universities in 1987, 1988, 1989, and 1990 surveys. In 1988, four state institutions dropped out of the top twenty-five: the University of Wisconsin, the University of Illinois, the University of Texas, and the College of William and Mary. And how can we explain the wide swings in position for an institution such as the University of California, Berkeley, which in successive years occupied rank positions of five, twenty-four, thirteen, and thirteen among the national universities?

Does the real quality of these schools change that much in one year? Perhaps they would like to return to the more "global and subjective ratings" of college presidents rather than the more "objective ratings" rendered by deans and admissions officers. At the very least, four universities will now know the frustration of other schools that have not appeared in any of the *U.S. News and World Report* rankings, and perhaps they too may be scratching their heads about the meaning and value of reputational studies of quality.

The interest in collegiate ratings has spread beyond those reported in *U.S. News and World Report,* we should note. The March 1990 issue of *Southpoint* magazine carried a front-page picture of Duke business school dean Tom Keller in athletic sweats and baseball cap, leading a cheer for the business school at Duke. The cover caption is

> Hey! Hey!
> Whaddaya Say!
> MBA! MBA!

A paragraph early in this article is revealing: "Duke is on the cutting edge of a new breed of southern business schools slicing a wide swath through the old order. The schools promote themselves as brazenly as Donald Trump. They raid for faculty with the bravura

Table 3.1. Reputational Ranking of National Universities by
U.S. News and World Report.

1987	Rank 1988	1989	1990	School (State)
3	1	1	3	Yale University (Conn.)
4	2	2	4	Princeton University (N.J.)
21	3	4	5	California Institute of Technology
2	4	3	1	Harvard University (Mass.)
11	5	7	6	Massachusetts Institute of Technology
1	6	6	2	Stanford University (Calif.)
6	7	8	8	Dartmouth College (N.H.)
18	8	12	10	Columbia University (N.Y.)
14	9	10	16	Rice University (Tex.)
8	10	9	11	University of Chicago (Ill.)
16	11	14	15	Johns Hopkins University (Md.)
7	12	5	7	Duke University (N.C.)
10	13	15	12	Brown University (R.I.)
11	14	11	9	Cornell University (N.Y.)
19	15	20	13	University of Pennsylvania
17	16	19	23	Northwestern University (Ill.)
*	17	25	19	Georgetown University (D.C.)
*	18	23	*	University of Notre Dame (Ind.)
23	19	22	24	Washington University (Mo.)
15	20	21	18	University of Virginia
*	21	16	17	University of California, Los Angeles
25	22	*	*	Emory University (Ga.)
11	23	18	20	University of North Carolina, Chapel Hill
5	24	13	13	University of California, Berkeley
8	25	17	21	University of Michigan, Ann Arbor
23	*	*	*	University of Wisconsin
20	*	*	*	University of Illinois
25	*	*	*	University of Texas
22	*	*		College of William and Mary (Va.)
*	*	24	*	Vanderbilt University (Tenn.)
*	*	*	22	Carnegie Mellon (Pa.)
*	*	*	25	University of Rochester (N.Y.)

*Not ranked this year.
Source: "America's Best Colleges," U.S. News and World Report,
1987, pp. 49–87; 1988, pp. C3–C32; 1989, pp. 53–82; 1990, pp. 103–134.

of Carl Icahn. They are festooned with more corporate logos than
a stock car. They are more likely to be confused with a Grand Hyatt
than an ivory tower. With a combination of blue smoke and mir-
rors, substance and drive, they are shaking up the rankings of the
nation's top business schools" (Helyar, 1990, p. 38).

As a parenthetical note, among the top twenty-five business schools cited in the previously mentioned 1990 *U.S. News and World Report* ranking, there were four in the south: Duke led the way at ninth, followed by the University of Virginia (eleventh), University of North Carolina (seventeenth), and the University of Texas (twenty-fourth).

Whatever else might be said about the search for status reflected in the *Southpoint* article, the least is that there are elements of hype and passion that are new to collegiate forums. The recurring presence of articles in *U.S. News and World Report* and other magazines such as *Southpoint* illustrates a move beyond dispassionate and objective studies, with the good and the bad that come with the departure.

In the August 16, 1989, issue of the *Chronicle of Higher Education,* James W. Schmotter, associate dean of Cornell University's Johnson Graduate School of Management, reported on the behavior of faculty and staff in Cornell's Johnson Graduate Schools. Apparently, they engaged in a frenetic bit of behavior when the school did not make the top-twenty list of the 1987 *U.S. News and World Report.* However, in November 1988 Cornell's Graduate School of Management was ranked fifth in a *Business Week* ranking. Dean Schmotter reported the change in behavior as follows: "Suddenly all was sweetness, light, and self-congratulations at the school. Everywhere reprints of the *Business Week* article appeared; student and staff morale increased dramatically. Alumni congratulations (and contributions) poured in, and applications for fall 1989 enrollments skyrocketed, rising more than 50 percent" (p. A40).

Schmotter concludes that college faculties and administrators have themselves to blame for these consequences in swing of result and mood. He suggests that ratings fill an information vacuum because higher education "itself has not been able to develop a means of evaluating and certifying quality that is either relevant or intelligible to those who invest in it through their tuition payments or gifts" (p. A40). He recommends that "developing clearer institutional goals and employing more honesty and accuracy in presenting them to the public are good ways to begin to reclaim the ground we in higher education have ceded to our colleagues in journalism" (p. A40). We believe this advice is consonant with our position on public disclosure and our definition of quality as conformance to mission specification and goal achievement.

This exploration of media rankings would not be complete without reference to the annual *Money Guide* publication of "America's Best College Buys." The entire issue of the Fall 1990 *Money Guide* is devoted to "exclusive rankings of the top 200 schools for your money." Here is another ranking, this time of "America's Ten Best College Buys," followed by a more extensive listing of the top 100 public and top 100 private college "College Value Rankings," with this lead: "If assessing academic quality is tough, trying to calculate a school's value—its quality relative to price—is an even more difficult task. Here's how we did it: We used statistical analysis to determine how much each school might be expected to cost, based on 17 measures of academic performance, and then we compared that figure to actual cost" (Gilbert, 1990, p. 72).

According to *Money Guide*, the top ten best college values in the Fall of 1990 were Cooper Union for the Advancement of Science and Art, California Institute of Technology, Rice University, the New College of the University of South Florida, State University of New York, Geneseo, State University of New York, Binghamton, Trenton State College, State University of New York, Albany, the University of Virginia, and the University of Florida.

To this point, we have made no mention of a cluster of rating reports that can be found in most collegiate libraries: *The Gourman Reports* (1983), which offer a rating of both undergraduate and graduate programs to two decimal places. In the 1983 rating of undergraduate programs in Louisiana, for example, the top three schools were Tulane, with a rating of 4.53; Louisiana State University and Agricultural and Mechanical College, with a rating of 4.35; and Louisiana State University in Shreveport with a rating of 3.38. Centenary College, which has appeared in the *U.S. News and World Report* lists of best liberal arts colleges for more than one year, was ranked thirteenth in the state with a rating of 3.06. What do these ratings mean? Not much.

The Gourman Reports are filled with puffed-up rhetoric about their own importance, and there are grammatical inaccuracies throughout. Nowhere in these reports are we told precisely what data were gathered, by whom they were obtained, by what means, or on what date. Nor are we told who rendered the judgments that led to the ratings expressed to the hundredths of a decimal point. Yet *The Gourman Reports* have been used by economists and other scholars studying the relationships between college quality and a host of other variables, such as alumni earnings, student choice, and so on.

In a devastating critique of *The Gourman Reports,* David Webster concluded that "Jack Gourman is not a reasonable arbiter of educational quality. Students, librarians, book reviewers, and scholars need to reexamine his reports and pronouncements on college and university performance. And more importantly, we need to look again at our willingness to accept such rankings from an individual who simply has the power of the printed page behind him" (Webster, 1984, p. 55). Our fondness for numbers and our search for "number one" can lead even academics down unhappy paths.

What role do these rankings play in American higher education? We will visit that question again at the conclusion of this chapter. In terms of one of the principal purposes of quality assurance—improvement—the *Money Guide, U.S. News and World Report,* and *The Gourman Reports* ranks are relatively empty. They may prove of some value to those who have the financial capacity to afford these top-ranked colleges and to those who can move from where they are to where these schools are. For those who live within service and financial range of these schools, the rankings may be of some understandable pleasure. For the schools appearing in the rankings, there is the pleasure of national recognition, perhaps accompanied by enhanced enrollment attraction, though we want to say more of that in a moment.

Returning to the discussion on quality definition of Chapter One, it may help to remember the complexity of variables associated with the definition and measurement of quality. To the customer who cannot afford a high-priced luxury automobile, its quality is irrelevant. To the student of modest means living in rural Tennessee or Texas, America's best college buy may be Columbia State Community College or Kilgore Junior College. (It is of some interest that this entire sector of American higher education—community colleges—is omitted in both the *Money Guide* and the *U.S. News and World Report* rankings!)

Americans love numerical shorthand, as noted by Robert Hutchins: "He (the American) is not at home with anything he cannot count, because he is not sure of any other measure. He cannot estimate or appraise quality. This leaves him with quantity" (Hutchins, 1966, p. 178). The competitive edge in our national personality leads us to label rather than understand, to prefer averages rather than depth. There is something highly satisfying about the weekly polls that describe who is on top in collegiate football and basketball. Stories on recruiting violations, ethical misconduct of both coaches and alumni, or misuse of drugs by players will not stay our pleasure in finding out who is in the top ten or twenty.

Quality Ratings and Quality Reality

Here, then, is a brief glimpse of the history of ratings and rankings as an instrument of quality assurance. Do these ratings make a substantive contribution to quality assurance? What are the limitations? Let us begin our summary by posing a few questions suggested by a review of the studies previously cited.

Who is an effective judge of program and institutional quality? A variety of raters has been employed by these studies. It certainly seems important to know who is doing the rating and whether the rater has reasonable knowledge and authority on which to base his "informed opinion." The earlier graduate rankings used department chairpersons as raters, but Allan Cartter criticized this approach, suggesting that chairpersons were not always the most distinguished scholars in their fields. Later the studies used deans and faculty in departments and programs being rated. The *U.S. News and World Report* ratings of undergraduate programs first used presidents as raters. To what extent might the judgments of these presidents be as much influenced by their knowledge of other presidents as their knowledge of the institutions in question? In few if any of the studies do we find graduates as raters, with the exception of the study by Clark, Hartnett, and Baird (1976).

What criteria are used by the raters to judge quality? Earlier studies obviously touched on the criteria of faculty accomplishments and library holdings. Later studies, such as those in the *U.S. News and World Report*, asked for more global assessments. The study of undergraduate quality by Astin perhaps utilized the most extensive list of criteria. Astin's findings, however, lead to the next question.

To what extent do reputational ratings contribute information not already available from other sources? A number of these studies suggest that if one already has knowledge about program size, selectivity, library holdings, and number of graduates, one can predict program and institutional standing in the ratings.

Is there a relation between perceived prestige, as reflected in ratings, and perceived influence? In a study sponsored by and reported in *Change* magazine, Richard Johnson stated: "There are at least three senses in which the term 'leading' can be used: (1) Prestige—the degree to which an institution is looked up to or admired; (2) innovation—the frequency with which an institution is first in generating new ideas or programs and (3) influence—the degree to which other institutions follow the leading institutions' example. Here then is a paradox: All institutions tended to agree on a set of leading institutions which influences other colleges and universities. But when reporting on the influence on their own institutions, they also agreed that these national influential institutions do not influence them" (Johnson, 1978, p. 50).

How extensive is the "halo" effect? We recall the finding in Astin's study of undergraduate programs in which Princeton University was identified as a leading institution in undergraduate business, even though it did not have an undergraduate program in business. Do strong departments and programs tend to bathe weaker programs in a positive light? The evidence suggests that this is so.

Is the philosophy of limited supply of excellence justified? The use of ratings as an instrument of quality identification assumes, as we have shown, that excellence is indeed in limited supply. As additional schools develop high performance records on any criterion of quality—student growth and performance, faculty research and publication, library holdings, or curricular innovation—there can still be only five in the top five or ten in the top ten.

What about the stability of ratings? There appear to be mixed results on this question. One cannot argue with the apparent stability of the national universities' profile in the ratings of graduate programs. However, there are movements in and out of those ratings, suggesting that quality is a fleeting condition, and our common sense suggests otherwise. In the first *U.S. News and World Report* ratings of undergraduate institutions, only 6.5 percent of the institutions were public. Just four years later that percentage had almost doubled to 11.1 percent. Had the quality of public institutions changed that much over four years?

In this chapter, we have pointed to other equally puzzling illustrations of instability. For example, we noted the position swing in the *U.S. News and World Report* ratings for the University of California, Berkeley—from fifth place in 1987 to twenty-fourth place in 1988 and then back up to thirteenth place in 1989 and 1990. Surely the quality of this national university cannot be that mercurial in actuality. And what can we say about the complete absence of the Cornell Graduate School of Management in the 1987 *U.S. News and World Report* rankings and its fifth place in the *Business Week* rankings just one year later, as outlined in the earlier citation by James Schmotter?

What effect does the structure of rating studies have on the response? We have evidence that the way in which questions are posed and studies structured can have an effect on the results. Harvey Mudd College was ranked first in the 1985 *U.S. News and World Report* study but, because of a classification fluke, did not even appear in the 1987 study. Astin found that raters responded differently in their ratings depending on whether an institution appeared on a national list or a state list.

What can we say about rate of response and confidence in ratings? We have seen that ratings are offered as a justifiable expression of quality because they constitute an aggregation of informed opinion. Yet most of the studies report response rates of 50 to 60 percent. Although these response ratios are respectable for questionnaire research, there is little discussion on the margin of error in conclusions occasioned by these response ratios.

Do ratings make meaningful contributions to program and quality improvement? In their informative monograph *A Question of Quality: The Higher Education Ratings Game*, Lawrence and Green (1980) point out that the "results of such studies contribute little to a program's self knowledge or its efforts toward improvement" (p. 10). Global ratings simply do not offer the specific information necessary for improvement, although program improvement is cited by most educators and evaluators as the principal reason for any venture in educational evaluation. Thus ratings must be counted as making a relatively empty contribution to this important goal.

Do ratings tend to encourage labeling? In their widely read book, *The Academic Marketplace,* Caplow and McGee used the terms "major league, minor league, and academic Siberia" as florid terms often used to describe various sectors of American higher education (1958, p. 14). The mixed use of metaphors from baseball and political geography describes an assumed pyramid of prestige topped by the national universities, which, as we have seen, everyone is willing to identify. There are no ratings, however, of the five or ten worst institutions or programs, and no one is willing to venture their names. They remain covered by Cartter's barely disguised terms "Melrose A & M and Siwash College."

To what extent do ratings encourage a limitation of esteem as well as mission? Reputational studies have succeeded in identifying the diversity existing in American higher education. Read again, for example, the rich descriptions of undergraduate programs found in the *U.S. News and World Report* studies. Whether these studies promote a diversity of esteem and respect for the variety of missions in American higher education is not clear.

One of the finest books ever written on the subject of excellence is Gardner's *Excellence,* first published in 1961 and revised in 1984. In perhaps the most often quoted line from that book, Gardner advocated a diversity of esteem and high expectations in these words: "The society which scorns excellence in plumbing, because plumbing is a humble activity, and tolerates shoddiness in philosophy because it is an exalted activity will have neither good plumbing nor good philosophy. Neither its pipes nor its theories will hold water" (p. 102).

Do ratings make a significant contribution to consumer choice decision? This argument has been advanced by more than one source cited in this chapter. The essence is that a college education is a product (similar to a compact disk or an automobile), that potential students and their parents need to know something about the quality of that product, and that ratings furnish this discriminating evidence. One has to ask, however, whether potential students have been noting the wild swings in the rankings for the University of California, Berkeley, over the past three years, the disappearance of the University of Texas from the rankings between 1987 and 1988, and the in-and-out placement for the Cornell Graduate Schools of Management as carried in two different journalistic publications.

On this topic of consumer choice, we repeat an observation made earlier in this chapter. When almost 40 percent of those attending undergraduate schools in this nation attend two-year colleges, and those two-year colleges are not included in media rankings, a legitimate question can be asked about the value of the rankings to the majority of college students in this nation. We wonder whether the variable most closely correlated with these rankings is the sales volume of the issue; if you are in the business of selling magazines, that is of legitimate and keen interest.

Thus, we have some questions concerning the decision value of ratings to potential students. Here, however, is a good topic for a useful thesis or dissertation. To plot the history of enrollments, gifts, and other benefits that supposedly follow discriminating student choice based on ratings might help bring speculation on this topic to heel. What would the facts tell us about these relationships?

To what extent do ratings recognize the occasional "maverick" character of American higher education? One of the conventional quantitative signals of academic quality is the number or percentage of the faculty with a doctoral degree. Although few would argue with the general validity of that indicator, is there room in our reflections and ratings for the power of exceptions? David Webster carries the point in this comment: "One frequently used 'objective' measure of rankings of institutions and individual departments was by the percentage of their faculty, or senior faculty, who possessed Ph.D.'s. Around 1970, one well-known department would have been ranked quite low in such a quality ranking—fully three of its senior professors had no Ph.D. One had a law degree, one had only an M.Ed., and the third had only a B.A. yet these three members of Harvard's social relations department—David Riesman, Christopher Jencks, and Erik Erikson—might possibly have been better scholars and teachers than some professors who did possess earned doctorates" (Webster, 1981, p. 22).

The Test and Testimony of Reputation

College ratings and rankings constitute a test of reputation. What have we learned about reputation and how it is formed? The first and most obvious point is that the formation takes time. We might not be surprised, then, that older institutions are better known and represented in many studies of reputation. Indeed, an institution that has been serving this nation for a hundred years or more has earned its way.

Second, size can combine with time to produce a larger number of graduates. When these graduates occupy positions of responsibility, one is also not surprised to find his or her alma maters well represented in reputational studies. And as the production levels of other American universities grow, we will not be surprised to note some expanding diversity in the institutions appearing in those ratings.

Third, national reputations associate more with publication than with teaching, more with article and book citations than with the knowledge and pleasure of one's graduates. We are not surprised that institutions attracting frequently published research scholars are favored, certainly in graduate reputational studies.

Finally, reputations can be built on some sense of distinction in curriculum or climate. We should also not be surprised that institutions are more easily recognized for quality if they have such a distinction: great books at St. Johns, expository grades at Evergreen, work emphasis at Berea, general education competencies at Alverno.

Not appearing in reputational studies is a large range of institutions that are perhaps younger, smaller, less selective, a little more routine in climate and curriculum, but not necessarily of low quality. Those institutions and programs occupying the top positions in reputational studies have no justification to hold in disdain or arrogance those not appearing there. The halls of history are filled with the sounds of bare feet going up the stairs and golden slippers coming down. Graduates of Harvard, Chicago, Yale, Columbia, and Stanford will be working for graduates of Melrose A & M or Siwash College. And researchers from more prestigious schools may be scooped by an obscure scholar working in one of the "academic Siberia" laboratories. All of this gives life to the power of diversity in American higher education.

There is, by the same token, no justification for those not appearing in reputational studies to hold jealousy or prejudice against their colleague institutions for these accomplishments and recognitions. Not only achievement but daring and perseverance are represented in these ratings. With institutions as with individuals, there is little to gain in throwing oneself against the record or reputation of another. To be inspired by the lessons of risk, imagination, achievement, and perseverance demonstrated by those programs and institutions that have earned their way to prominence is a healthy response. To understand that recognition is to be earned by time and distinction is also a healthy response.

With these reflections in mind, we can begin to understand some of the constructive contributions made to quality in American higher education by ratings and rankings, the lifting effect of reputational studies.

Keeping the Concern for Quality Visible and Active

Certainly reputational studies serve this rather fundamental and simple purpose. Robert Hutchins once said something to the effect that a first-class university is essentially an ongoing and lively argument. Conversations on the nature of quality open the possibility of new action and understanding.

Reflecting the Power of Innovation

A careful review of the ratings studies, particularly those of undergraduate programs and institutions, illustrates the variety of curricular and program innovations recognized in those studies. These experiments, some small and others large, can furnish both information and inspiration for other campuses. This is a worthy out-

come, and reputational studies deserve a salute for that purpose
alone.

Demonstrating the Power of Perseverance

A review of reputational studies helps develop a greater appreciation for the long and distinguished history of some of our national
institutions. In a nation that thrives on everything "instant"—from
coffee to personal gratification—important lessons are to be learned
in the power of perseverance. Northeast Missouri State University
has been recognized in the reputational studies and in other places
for its daring approach to value-added instruction. What many
folks do not recognize, however, is that Northeast has been developing this program since the early 1970s. The university earned this
recognition over a long period of time.

Creating a Competitive Edge

We know both the advantages and dangers of competition in our
society. An overemphasis on competition delivers a "dog-eat-dog"
mentality in which overly ambitious personalities and institutions
climb over the backs of colleagues to fulfill their selfish desires. On
the other hand, the absence of the competitive edge can cause both
personalities and organizations to lapse into a stupor of mediocrity
or explode into arrogance.

  These summary reflections on the strengths and weaknesses
of reputational studies may leave some readers yearning for a set of
one-armed authors, so that equivocation is not encouraged by the
phrase "on the other hand." So let us state our conviction clearly:
We are not inclined to see reputational studies as a very useful
quality assurance tool.

  Although scholarly exercises and media studies of ratings can
serve to keep the quality argument in ferment and encourage the
"culture of evidence" about which we spoke in Chapter Two, there
continue to be equivocal linkages between quality reputation and
quality reality. We find no significant evidence that reputational
studies furnish a very meaningful tool for enhancing student
choice. Nor do we find that reputational studies make a demonstra-

ble contribution to the most fundamental goal of evaluation and quality assurance—improvement. Finally, we find no obvious value of ratings to the other major quality assurance goal—establishing accountability with major higher education stakeholders.

Reputational studies concentrate on asking questions of those who are responsible for the design and delivery of higher education, but there is a more important respondent. Few Americans who purchase either products or services in our nation today escape a follow-up telephone call or questionnaire to ascertain customer and client satisfaction. As we shall see in Chapter Four, higher education is not a newcomer to the use of client satisfaction indices as an instrument of quality assurance. We pay attention to our clients and customers: our students.

FOUR ⬥

Follow-up Studies:
The Test
of Client
Satisfaction

Years ago the Packard automobile company advertised its cars with
the simple line: "Ask the Man Who Owns One." Whether that was
an adequate quality test for Packard may be debatable, because the
company is no longer in business. However, the simple expedient
of seeking feedback from customers and clients—our students, in
the case of colleges and universities—remains a key element in any
effective program of quality assurance.

Contact with faculty in classrooms and studios, contact with
registrars and financial officers, contact with campus security officers and secretaries: Each day thousands of impressions are developed as our students attend classes, check their degree progress with
the dean's secretary, order a transcript, pay a traffic ticket, or check
out equipment in the gym. A large university produces a million
such contacts a week, each one conveying the spirit of the university
to its students.

Although each of the quality assurance instruments explored
in Chapter Two and Chapter Three, accreditation reviews and reputational studies, makes contributions to a comprehensive program
of quality assurance, in none of them do we find a primary focus
on the perceptions and satisfactions of the student. To emphasize

the importance of hearing from our students, it is not necessary either to diminish the premier role in quality assurance held by faculty from our own campuses and by peer colleagues from other campuses or to demean the contributions of media friends and other interested partners with board or state agencies.

After all, our students are the only ones who can furnish a view of what our colleges or universities look like from the receiver's perspective. What do our students think about our programs and services? How can their thoughts be used in improving educational and administrative services? These are simple questions, yet often ignored in the press of daily business. This point was highlighted in one of the early national efforts to obtain follow-up data. In their Carnegie Commission report *Recent Alumni and Higher Education,* Spaeth and Greeley (1970) offered a comprehensive national perspective on alumni assessments of their alma maters. In the foreword to the Spaeth and Greeley book, Clark Kerr supplied this view of student and alumni feedback: "Often neglected, too—at least until the next fund drive—is news of the whereabouts and progress of recent alumni. This is unfortunate since they, of all persons, are especially qualified to contribute insight into the ways in which college failed or served them and perhaps how it may best serve the future" (Spaeth and Greeley, 1970, p. v).

This note reminds us of good advice in the same spirit issued by Robert Townsend in his book *Up the Organization* (1970). In a short passage entitled "Call Yourself Up," Townsend, former chairman and chief executive officer of Avis Rent-A-Car Company, suggests: "When you're off on a business trip or a vacation, pretend you're a customer. Telephone some part of your organization and ask for help. You'll run into some real horror shows. Don't blow up and ask for name, rank, and serial number—you're trying to correct, not punish. If it happens on a call to the Dubuque office, just suggest to the manager (through channels, dummy) that he make a few test calls himself. . . . Then try calling yourself up and see what indignities you've built into your own defenses" (Townsend, 1970, p. 31). Townsend not only calls us to view our organizations through the eyes of our customers and clients but affirms the improvement motive for quality assurance, a motive that we emphasize throughout these chapters.

A college president of a state university received an irate letter from a recent graduate complaining of treatment by the university registrar's office. Here is the essence of the complaint. It seems that the graduate had sent a five-dollar check to the registrar's office along with a transcript request. His letter and check were summarily returned with a form letter in which the following impersonal line had been checked: "Transcripts Are Three Dollars." Apparently an uncaring clerk had failed to see the wisdom of sending the transcript along with a two-dollar refund. Not only did the university president get a copy of the sizzling verbal missile, but information copies were distributed to the governor of the state, to area legislators, and to local newspaper editors. A little irritation goes a long way.

Within moments of receiving the letter, the president called the graduate with a personal apology and had the transcript personally delivered to the graduate, who lived just an hour away from the campus. Opportunities to see ourselves as our students and graduates see us are found not just in questionnaires and surveys but in the daily operational moments of our institutions. Accreditation reviews, assessment of student knowledge and skill, rankings, and ratings contribute useful elements to a comprehensive quality assurance program. They are powerfully complemented, however, by the simple expedient of asking our students what we are doing well and how we can improve the remainder.

The purpose of this chapter is to explore the nature of student follow-up studies at the national, state, and campus levels; to outline some of the instruments and approaches available for follow-up studies; to demonstrate how these studies can have constructive decision impact; and to explore some of the issues of both purpose and process in the conduct of follow-up studies.

Perspectives of Time and Method

A few months ago a friend bought a new automobile after having driven a four-wheeled treasure for eleven years. The former car had performed superbly for 150,000 miles with routine maintenance. Its body style had been compatible with newer models for over a decade. The manufacturer never asked those who owned the vehicle if they were satisfied. By contrast, less than a month after the new car was acquired, its manufacturer (a different corporation) sent a questionnaire to determine owner satisfaction. The new owner's first response was to complete the survey with highly positive feelings; after all, the car was new and performing well. However, the company's quality assurance process would be better served by asking these questions later; for this owner's standards are long term— after three years, five years, not one month.

Our graduates' standards are long term, too. Immediate gratification is nice: a job, a degree to hang on the wall. Promotions, advanced degrees, greater earning power, an improved quality of life happen over time, but we also need to measure our quality, in part at least, by students' standards within *their* time frame.

Long-term follow up of graduates of our institutions is but one kind of measure of client satisfaction. In actuality, all assessment is a kind of follow-up. Examples are readily discerned. The final examination in a course is a follow-up measure of the instructional quality in that particular class. The number of students who continue in good standing may be an indicator of satisfaction with previous instruction. Retention rates of students from entry to graduation may be a measure of student satisfaction. Success rates of developmental students in freshman English and mathematics courses are follow-up measures of developmental education quality. Tests for licensure or professional school admission are comprehensive follow-up indications of undergraduate learning.

Quantitative measures that provide such data are easy enough to obtain. By searching our sources of information, we can obtain evidence to evaluate performance and goal achievement. How many developmental/remedial students satisfactorily complete their freshman year? How many first-time freshmen complete their freshman year? How many first-time freshmen complete their first semester in good academic standing? How many freshmen persist to graduation? How many baccalaureate graduates go on to graduate school? How many accounting majors pass the Certified Public Accountants (CPA) examination, or teacher education majors the National Teachers Examination (NTE), or nursing school graduates their licensure examination, or law school graduates the bar examinations? How many graduates get jobs? How much money do they make? In fact, constantly improving computer data bases and increasingly user-friendly access to those data may lull institutions into the mistaken notion that here is all the information they need to establish proof of quality and of adequate performance.

There is no doubt that such quantitative information is valuable, but some question exists about whether numbers alone can testify to client satisfaction. Let us consider, then, what it is that we want to know: What should a higher education institution expect of its products (its graduates and the recipients of its services, including research)? What should its graduates (its clients) and other constituencies expect of a higher education institution?

The interactive nature of these expectations is nicely illustrated in two national follow-up studies. In the opening comments of this chapter, we cited the Spaeth and Greeley study *Recent Alumni and Higher Education*. The authors report that their study was "based on a sample of 40,000 graduates of 135 accredited or large colleges and universities. Data were collected in 1961, 1962, 1963, 1964, and 1968" (1970, p. 3). For what purposes? Spaeth and Greeley report that they were interested in alumni views on the goals and performance of their own colleges, alumni interests in literature and the arts, alumni political and social attitudes, alumni financial contribution profiles, and alumni views on the role of college in career planning and attainment.

The relationship studies possible among these questions and alumni classification variables such as age, race, sex, and field of study are endless. For example, Spaeth and Greeley developed three goal indices—personality development, career training, and intellectual accomplishment—which they then correlated with selected variables of college quality and control and with selected graduate variables such as sex and age.

Readers interested in understanding the rich potential in mining such studies for meaning are encouraged to review the original book-length report. We found one of the author's evaluative and concluding comments to be of particular interest: "If we were asked to make a single recommendation on the basis of the data presented in the present study, it would be not that education hie itself into the inner city, nor that it create more work study programs, nor that it establish marathon encounter groups on campus—though all these activities may be virtuous and praiseworthy—but rather that it concern itself more with the analysis and development of values, which is something rather different from 'changing values.' The college's perceived contribution to value formation seems to be the strongest predictor of alumni satisfaction seven years after graduation" (Spaeth and Greeley, 1970, pp. 179–180). Where does this finding place us on the question of institutional and student expectations? It might suggest that reading Victor Frankl's *Man's Search for Meaning* (1959) could be as important as reading basic texts in psychology or physics.

One other simple reflection can be noted here, one to which we will return in other chapters. If there is dissonance on the goals of higher education, we should not be surprised to see satisfaction indices vary with one's perspective on goals. The student who comes to college looking for personality development as a goal of primary interest, as opposed to the other two goal indices developed by Spaeth and Greeley—career/professional goals and intellectual/general education goals—will look back on his or her college experience with that goal in mind. Moreover, student perspectives on the importance of these goals change not only during the college experience but also during the years after graduates exit our doors. The very act, however, of getting a handle on these changing perceptions is one of the benefits of follow-up studies, benefits clearly evident in the extensive data from the Spaeth and Greeley study.

A personal and poignant commentary carried in the Spaeth and Greeley book clearly illustrates the importance of student goal perspectives and also illustrates the merit of open-ended options in follow-up studies. A businessman responding to the study offered these reflections on college experience: "College is supposed to teach a person how to think and how to live. A person must learn the meaning of life, and unless a person learns this he will be unhappy forever, and will probably make others unhappy. My college tried to mold my intellect, which I have since realized is not man's most important faculty. Man's spirit, his soul, is totally neglected by college, just as it is neglected by our materialistic world, and as a character in 'Karamazov' says, 'without God anything is possible' " (Spaeth and Greeley, 1970, p. 61).

This graduate gave an unhappy and dissatisfied evaluation of his college education. It is clear that his evaluation was based on a keen view of college purpose. If the college from which he graduated is disappointed, it may take pleasure in at least two achievements. This graduate obviously developed continuing curiosity about life, and he has been exposed to at least one good book by Dostoevski. Finally, we have to note that some learnings—especially those about the meaning of life—are less likely to emerge during the years of college life than after our graduates have experienced the pain and pleasure of grappling with life problems where the answers cannot always be found in the back of a book.

A second nationally renowned study is the work begun by Alexander Astin in the early 1960s and continuing to this day. In his book *Four Critical Years,* Astin (1977) outlines the cooperative institutional research program (CIRP), in which many institutions over the country have participated. Annual reports of this study appear in the *Chronicle of Higher Education* and profile shifts in student aspirations and values, while students are in college and after they graduate.

Astin's chapter on "Satisfaction with the College Environment" contains a host of correlate findings. Two that might be easy to predict, but not always easy to take advantage of, are the fact that close faculty-student interaction promotes student satisfaction, as does involvement with the life of the institution. Astin has invested a large portion of his talent and career in this extensive longitudinal study of student perceptions, and his work is exemplary of thoughtful questions and well-conceived methodology driven by a scholarly perseverance over the years.

This work, by the way, illustrates yet another advantage of follow-up studies. By showing our students and our graduates that we are interested in their perceptions and evaluations, we model a performance curiosity and willingness to risk that we hope to nurture in their lives as well.

The value of student follow-up results in addressing issues of accountability—that is, the shared expectations of institutions and their graduates—has also been demonstrated by the work of Stevenson, Walleri, and Japely (1985) at Mt. Hood Community College. Their efforts were directed toward determining student satisfaction with educational services "especially after they have some time in which to reflect" (p. 81). Other important insights into the way various people perceive the institution's purpose, programs, and performance are provided by surveys designed to measure the attitudes of an institution's various constituents. "These attitudinal surveys take many forms, address a range of publics, and generate a wealth of information to be ploughed back into the planning/ evaluative process" (Bridger, 1989, p. 48).

We turn now to a review of survey instruments appropriate to the follow-up process, the kinds of information that may be acquired by survey, and the best use of the information generated.

Formal Follow-up Processes

Ewell's *Information on Student Outcomes* (1983a) included a listing of student development and satisfaction indicators that are measurable either by use of test results and the usual demographic and scholastic records maintained by institutions or by student self-reported attitudinal responses. In this report, Ewell has examined six data-gathering instruments, comparing his outcomes dimensions with them to identify which of the instruments measures directly or indirectly the various outcomes. Ewell's process is one that might well inform our own review. Among the instruments he uses for comparison are the Student Outcomes Information Services (SOIS) and the American College Testing Program/Evaluation Survey Services (ACT/ESS). Not included in Ewell's listing is the family of survey instruments offered by Educational Testing Service (ETS)—including Institutional Goals Inventory (IGI), Institutional Functioning Inventory (IFI), Student Reaction to College (SRC), and Program Self-Assessment Service (PSAS). A description of those instruments useful in follow-up studies follows.

American College Testing Program

The American College Testing Program Evaluation/Survey Service (ACT/ESS) now offers twelve survey instruments for use by college and universities. Each is an optical-scan instrument containing two or four pages of questions designed to permit a general evaluation of an institution's programs and services. Institutions have the option of designing twenty to thirty additional questions for inclusion in each survey. The American College Testing Program also offers a catalogue of additional items, from which institutions may select in lieu of writing their own questions. In addition, each instrument provides space for the participant to write comments or suggestions. Since 1979, over a million ACT/ESS instruments have been administered at more than 750 institutions. This extensive use of these materials has made possible normative data for comparative studies as well as an opportunity for longitudinal studies within institutions. Among the surveys available from American College Testing Program, those of particular benefit for our purposes are reviewed below.

The Alumni Survey. The Alumni Survey is useful in ascertaining the impact of the institution on its graduates, particularly, as in the Mt. Hood experience, after graduates have had some time away from the institution. Four-page surveys are available for two-year and four-year institutions and provide information in the following sections: background information—tailored to the two-year or four-year graduate; continuing education—providing extensive information on formal education since graduation or departure; educational and college experiences—gauging the graduate's perception of the value and impact of his or her education in areas such as quality of life, skills development, and independent living; employment history—providing valuable information for alumni and placement offices, as well as for various academic programs planners; and additional questions, mailing addresses, and comments and suggestions—providing additional information that may be useful locally.

The Student Opinion Survey. With two-year and four-year forms, the Student Opinion Survey is used to examine the perception held by enrolled, continuing students of their college services and environment. The two-year form also includes items to explore the student's reasons for selecting the college and his or her overall impression of the school. Included are background information; use of and level of satisfaction with various campus services and programs; level of satisfaction with the college environment in areas such as academics, admissions, rules and regulations, facilities, registration, and general; and additional questions, comments, and suggestions.

The Survey of Academic Advising. The Survey of Academic Advising is used to obtain information regarding student impressions of academic advising services. The four-page form includes background information, advising information—including frequency of adviser-and-advisee contacts and the period of time the student has been assigned to the current adviser; academic advising needs—in which the student identifies topics discussed with the adviser and expresses his or her level of satisfaction with the adviser's assistance; and additional questions, comments, and suggestions.

The Survey of Current Activities and Plans. Designed for applicants to the institution who chose *not* to enroll, the Survey of Current Activities and Plans requests background information; impressions of the college; educational plans and activities; employment plans; and additional questions, comments, and suggestions.

The Withdrawing/Nonreturning Student Survey. The Withdrawing/Nonreturning Student Survey is produced in both a two-page and four-page format. In both, the student who chooses to leave college before completing a degree is asked to provide background information and to indicate reasons for leaving. These reasons are grouped in the following categories: personal (health, moving, marriage, social), academic (suspension, instructional quality, not challenged), institutional (scheduling problems, inadequate advising, programs or facilities), financial (availability of work or financial aid), and employment (conflict between work and school). Both forms also provide space for comments and suggestions. The long form, in addition, asks the student to rate his or her satisfaction with various institutional services and characteristics.

ACT offers a variety of flexible services, and institutions may elect to purchase one or more of the survey instruments or to contract for a full range of mailing, scoring, and reporting services.

Student Outcomes Information Services

The Student Outcomes Information Service (SOIS), co-sponsored by the College Board and the National Center for Higher Education Management Systems (NCHEMS), is similar to ACT/ESS. The questionnaires focus on six different points during and after college: entering student, continuing student, program completer and graduating student, former student, recent alumnus, and three-to-five-year follow-up.

Offered in formats for both two-year and four-year institutions, the questionnaires provide background demographics and survey educational experiences, plans, and goals. They also identify the need for, use of, and satisfaction with institutional services and give perceptions and impressions of the institution as held by the various survey populations.

Perhaps the most significant differences between the SOIS and ACT families of surveys is the coordinated, research-oriented approach of the SOIS, which is supported by a carefully written handbook, *Student Outcomes Questionnaires: An Implementation Handbook*, by Peter T. Ewell (1983b). This takes the novice practitioner through the process step by step and carefully points out techniques and essential steps to help guarantee successful, usable survey results. As with ACT, data processing and questionnaire analyses are available, as well as annual summaries of information from participant institutions.

Educational Testing Service

The Educational Testing Service (ETS) College and University Programs offer a different array of survey instruments focusing primarily on program planning and evaluation. Several elements of ETS offerings are pertinent to our topic and are described below.

The Program Self-Assessment Service (PSAS). The PSAS consists of a set of questionnaires that addresses areas such as curriculum, program purposes, departmental procedures, faculty activity, student accomplishment, and the general environment for work and learning. The PSAS assumes that the perceptions and assessments of those most directly involved with any department or program can contribute to an improved quality and functioning of the area surveyed. Thus, the service offers three assessment questionnaires: for faculty, for students who major in the department or program, and for recent graduates of the program. Responses provide a profile of the targeted program or department and can assist in the program review process by identifying areas of strength and those that need attention.

The Graduate Program Self-Assessment Service (GPSAS). The GPSAS is the parent of the previously described PSAS. GPSAS is co-sponsored by the Graduate Record Examination Board and the Council of Graduate Schools in the United States. Instruments have been developed for both master's and doctoral-level programs and address the parallel constituent groups identified in the PSAS discussion, that is, students enrolled in the program, faculty, and recent graduates. Survey questions provide information on sixteen areas of program characteristics, including environment for learning, scholarly excellence, teaching quality, faculty concern for students, curriculum, departmental procedures, resources (such as library and laboratories), faculty work environment, student accomplishments, and others.

The Student Reactions to College (SRC). The SRC survey is used to solicit opinions from enrolled students about their college experiences, including instruction, counseling, out-of-class activities, administrative affairs, and so forth. The 150-item questionnaire is grouped into nineteen areas of interest and provides information about the needs and concerns of students. There are separate forms for community colleges (SRC-2) and for four-year colleges and universities (SRC-4).

The Institutional Functioning Inventory (IFI). The IFI is helpful to faculty, students, and administrators who wish to assess administrative policies, teaching practices, and academic and extracurricular programs. The questionnaire consists of 132 items; students respond only to items 1 through 72. The IFI grew out of a study of institutional vitality supported by the Kettering Foundation; comparative data are available for public universities, four-year state colleges, private liberal arts colleges, community colleges, and private junior colleges.

The Student Instructional Report (SIR). The SIR, a brief, objective questionnaire, helps instructors gain information about students' reactions to their courses and instruction, offering students the opportunity to comment anonymously. It covers six factors: course organization and planning, faculty-student interaction, communication, course difficulty and work load, textbooks and readings, and tests and/or examinations.

The SIR is not intended to replace regular student-faculty communication. It does, however, provide an additional means by which instructors may examine their teaching performance. Extensive comparative data are available through Educational Testing Service based on SIR administration in the United States and Canada. The questionnaire can be obtained in Spanish and in a Canadian version in both French and English.

All of the Educational Testing Service instruments offer space for optional local items, and, as with the American College Testing and College Board/NCHEMS, the services of basic data processing and reporting are available. Special services and professional assistance may be negotiated as well.

Some selective combination of this wealth of instruments for measuring values, attitudes, and programmatic strengths and weaknesses can yield insightful data for the institution's efforts to ensure quality. The key word is "selective," for too much, too often, to the same people can be counterproductive and yield inaccurate or severely biased data. A careful selection of instruments includes those that will examine the various dimensions and standards established as important to the particular institution and its clients.

Inventories of Good Practice in Undergraduate Education

The Johnson Foundation has published two documents designed to help institutions discern whether their undergraduate policies and practices match seven principles for good practice in undergraduate education. The two surveys include an institutional inventory and a faculty inventory. Built on the work of higher education scholars Arthur W. Chickering, Zerda F. Gamson, and Louis M. Barsi, seven good practices are advocated:

1. Good practice encourages student-faculty contact.
2. Good practice encourages cooperation among students.
3. Good practice encourages active learning.
4. Good practice gives prompt feedback.
5. Good practice emphasizes time on task.
6. Good practice communicates high expectations.
7. Good practice respects diverse talents and ways of learning (Johnson Foundation, 1989, p. 11).

Utilization of these introspective surveys on any campus will certainly demonstrate the "discovery" potential of a quest for quality. Having faculty complete the inventory is certain to generate a lively conversation on teaching responsibility and practice, and having students share their perspectives concerning the presence or absence of these good practices on our campuses should also furnish adequate stimulus to lead off a faculty development workshop.

UCLA Center for the Study of Evaluation

One other instrument that may prove useful for institutions interested in obtaining student feedback is the *College Student Experiences Questionnaire (CSEQ)* authored by C. Robert Pace (1990) at the Center for the Study of Evaluation at the University of California, Los Angeles.

The brochure describing the CSEQ states that "the CSEQ is an instrument which measures the quality of effort students put into using the facilities and opportunities provided for their learning and development in college" (Pace, 1990). Fourteen scales contain a series of behavioral statements that furnish "quality of effort" measures for each of fourteen activities. For example, under the activity "course learning," behavioral activities range from "took notes in class" to "did additional readings on topics that were introduced and discussed in class." Similar behavioral scales are included for the other activities.

The CSEQ also furnishes an opportunity for students to offer "opinions about college" via two questions that constitute a form of satisfaction index. Finally, students can give their ideas on "the college environment" and "estimates of gains" in five goal clusters: goals related to personal development and social competence; goals related to science and technology; goals related to general education, literature, and the arts; goals related to intellectual skills; and goals related to vocation.

We have reviewed a number of commercially available instruments, many with analytical support and normative reference group data, features that make them particularly useful where personnel and support services are in short supply on campus. Providing the opportunity to include locally developed optional questions, these instruments may be tailored to the local environment.

Other Survey Options

Obviously, where special needs cannot be met through instruments such as those described above, two other options exist: contracted survey services or campus-developed surveys.

Contracted Services. Most management consultant services and marketing consultants are capable of developing and conducting surveys to determine perceptions about an institution's reputation, purposes, and programs. A number of agencies now market themselves primarily to the higher education community. There are several advantages in contracting for survey services. One is that the contract is usually for a turnkey process (that is, it includes tailoring the survey to the specific needs of the client, gathering and processing the data, and presenting and interpreting the results to the appropriate groups). Another advantage is that those surveyed may regard the contractual process more favorably because it is individualized and carries the identity of the contracting institution. Providing on-site consultants who may lend added credibility to the process and the findings through discussion with others is a third advantage.

We cite three disadvantages of contracted services. First, an institution can expect the contract cost to be significantly higher than that for already developed instruments. Second, the resultant data will not have the benefits of comparability to normative or summary data from other institutions of the same level or type. And third, the time required for the full development of such services may be counterproductive.

These disadvantages can be negated, however, when the institution's needs are determined to be met best by a specially designed survey. Frequently, for example, institutions are interested in gleaning community perceptions of institutional performance, through telephone sampling or similar marketing techniques. Such services contracted by local sampling and marketing agencies can be quite successful and not unduly expensive. This approach should, in fact, be selected if (1) available commercial instruments do not meet the institution's identified need, (2) the expertise or labor force is not available in-house, or (3) the contracted arrangement can provide the data required in a cost-effective and timely manner (Bridger, 1989).

Campus-Developed Surveys. Locally developed survey instruments take time and expertise. However, many campuses will have individuals in their social science or education departments or in their offices of institutional research who have knowledge of the methodology necessary to develop these surveys. And, of course, their services are likely to be cheaper. H. R. Kells, in *Self-Study Processes,* reminds us that "a poorly designed instrument, used at the wrong moment with an unreceptive audience, will yield little or no useful information and it may damage the sense of community and morale at the institution involved" (1980, p. 69). On the other hand, recognizing and using local expertise to produce a well-developed survey and to provide prompt analysis and dissemination of results may be the most effective way to gain a sense of ownership for the entire assessment/evaluation process. For those who determine that locally developed surveys will serve them best, a look at the content of commercial surveys reviewed earlier in this section may give the developer a head start on the general areas to include.

Earlier in this chapter we pointed out other sources of

follow-up information, using assessment tools and quantitative data generated primarily for other purposes. Thus, surveys are recommended to serve purposes that cannot be met by other existing data sources. There are obvious limitations and potential biases in survey data. Oversurveying a population is one way to guarantee biases and unreliability of responses. For example, surveying students at entry, as continuing students, and at exit would result in their responding to very similar questions in a one-to-two-year time span between surveys. Disregarding the "irritant factor" (the resentment at being asked repeatedly to respond), the purpose of this kind of follow up is by nature longitudinal. Our most efficient measures of enrolled student growth and outcomes are within the classroom, through performance assessment, and by observation of various student interactions. In fact, if we must limit our activity, there is no more valuable measure of our institutions' successes over time than the views held by alumni (Marcus, Leone, and Goldberg, 1983). If an institution must make a choice of commercial instruments, the alumni survey is probably the one to select.

An interesting quasi-commercial/locally developed alumni survey development approach was taken by the Tennessee Higher Education Commission (1987), when a group of survey specialists developed a survey and distributed it to all 1986 baccalaureate and associate graduates from Tennessee public institutions. This approach obviously had the advantage for the commission of enabling comparisons among state institutions concerning alumni perceptions of institutional quality and program strengths and weaknesses.

Among other surveys developed locally, a simple employer check sheet, also aimed at assessing long-term performance attainment, is a useful tool. A suggested format for such a check sheet has been developed at Louisiana State University in Shreveport (LSUS) to parallel items on other instruments allowing for cross-tabulation and statistical analysis. See Exhibit 4.1 following.

Coordination of survey activity should be encouraged. The surveying institution should prevent the possibility of a graduate's receiving a request from the placement office, from the alumni office, from his or her academic department, and from institutional research all within a three- to five-year time period. These offices can send one survey at three- to five-year intervals and gain valuable

**Exhibit 4.1. Five-Year Employer Survey,
Louisiana State University in Shreveport.**

Please help us evaluate our effectiveness by promptly responding to this short questionnaire. Your responses will be used for statistical tabulation only and will not identify your firm or employees.

1. Among the employees in your agency, please estimate the number of new (less than 5 years since graduation) college graduates (bachelor degree or higher). _____

2. How many of these now college graduate employees graduated from LSUS? _____

3. Are most of the other new college graduates from
   ( ) private colleges and universities,
   ( ) Louisiana public colleges and universities,
   ( ) out-of-state public colleges and universities?

4. If you know of LSUS graduates among your employees, how does their performance compare with other colleges' graduates with respect to

5. For the needs of your business/agency, how do your LSUS graduates perform with respect to

Better	About The Same	Worse	Unable to Judge			Superior	Fair	Inadequate	Unable To Observe
0	0	0	0	1.	Writing effectively	0	0	0	0
0	0	0	0	2.	Speaking effectively	0	0	0	0
0	0	0	0	3.	Understanding written information	0	0	0	0
0	0	0	0	4.	Working independently	0	0	0	0
0	0	0	0	5.	Learning on his/her own	0	0	0	0
0	0	0	0	6.	Understanding graphic information	0	0	0	0
0	0	0	0	7.	Using the library	0	0	0	0
0	0	0	0	8.	Following directions	0	0	0	0
0	0	0	0	9.	Caring for his/her own physical and mental health	0	0	0	0
0	0	0	0	10.	Working cooperatively in a group	0	0	0	0
0	0	0	0	11.	Organizing time effectively	0	0	0	0
0	0	0	0	12.	Recognizing rights, responsibilities, and privileges as a citizen	0	0	0	0
0	0	0	0	13.	Planning and carrying out projects	0	0	0	0
0	0	0	0	14.	Understanding and applying mathematics in daily activities	0	0	0	0

Exhibit 4.1. Five-Year Employer Survey,
Louisiana State University in Shreveport, Cont'd.

Better	About The Same	Worse	Unable to Judge			Superior	Fair	Inadequate	Unable To Observe
0	0	0	0	15.	Understanding different philosophies and cultures	0	0	0	0
0	0	0	0	16.	Persisting at difficult tasks	0	0	0	0
0	0	0	0	17.	Defining and solving problems	0	0	0	0
0	0	0	0	18.	Understanding the interaction of man and the environment	0	0	0	0
0	0	0	0	19.	Leading/guiding others	0	0	0	0
0	0	0	0	20.	Recognizing assumptions, and making logical inferences, and reaching correct conclusions	0	0	0	0
0	0	0	0	21.	Understanding and appreciating the arts	0	0	0	0
0	0	0	0	22.	Understanding and applying scientific principles and methods	0	0	0 0	

information, which of course does not preclude other kinds of communication to maintain close touch with alumni. The more in touch we are, the better will be the response rate when alumni are surveyed.

The Decision Focus. Let us examine the experience of one campus in using the ACT alumni survey as but one example of the kind of information available, the limitations on its interpretation, and the applications to the planning and evaluation process. Louisiana State University in Shreveport (LSUS) graduated its first baccalaureate students in 1975. Ten years later, each graduate of its first five classes was surveyed using the ACT services for all mailing and contact. A response rate of about 42 percent yielded a sample of students from each class and all program areas.

The resulting data compilation provided information on job history, satisfaction with the degree, continuing education, and salary levels. A secondary benefit has been the updating of alumni files with current employers and addresses. In addition, the survey asked alumni to rate the contribution of the institution to a number of needs—such as the development of writing skills, personal financial management, personal health maintenance, independent work habits, and use of the library. These ratings were compared to user norms to provide a picture of the rating of the university's programs and services by its alumni. This survey procedure has since been conducted two additional times.

LSUS is a commuter campus serving both students in the eighteen to twenty age range and a somewhat older and more mature student population. Many of the students attending the university are already managing independent households. The low rating given to the goal of personal finance can be better understood in this context. While the university faculty has, at least until now, not regarded skill in managing personal finances as a high-priority goal for the general education component of the curriculum, it is entirely possible that their perspective might warrant reassessment. In the spirit of our previous discussion on the relationship between student perceptions of goal and performance, this finding does present the university faculty with an interesting question of educational goal and curriculum content. Should the practical business of equipping our students with some exposure to personal financial planning become a general education goal of the university?

Other, more pressing concerns were low ratings of satisfaction with degree choice by students who completed general studies degrees and the question of personal health maintenance. Alumni rate the university low in this area. Although national trends have focused on health concerns, a nonresident environment and a nontraditional population here complicate the effort. The point is that items from the survey have been analyzed and discussed in appropriate groups and have contributed to the total pool of information for campus decision making.

The survey used at LSUS offered the opportunity for alumni to write additional comments. These anecdotal comments recognize individual instructors or courses the graduate remembers, make an explanatory statement about a response item in the survey, state feelings about the university (positive or negative), and offer suggestions for new programs or revisions to old ones. All comments are routed to the appropriate individual or office and provide yet another, more personal, dimension to the follow-up studies.

Interviews

The discussion thus far has centered on the application of paper-and-pencil instruments for obtaining data—with a particular focus on questionnaires. Perhaps the simplest and oldest means of acquiring feedback, however, is that of the interview. Although we do not intend this book as a handbook on evaluation and research methods, a word about the use of interviews as a tool for acquiring feedback from students and constituents is appropriate at this point.

Although the immediate advantages of questionnaire follow-up include the merit of surveying larger populations at lower cost, the disadvantage is that communication meaning conveyed in more personal settings is lost and the opportunity to pursue unanticipated threads of thought is unavailable. Interviews can be structured, and thus parallel the application of questionnaires, or unstructured. Interviews can be used to take advantage of "critical incident" types of data. An institution might choose to evaluate its registration services by sampling students who completed the registration process and asking them to describe the most effective and satisfying dimension of the registration process and then asking them to contrast the first response by describing the most dissatisfying and most in-need-of-improvement aspect.

Panel interviews in focus-group settings can take advantage of the response freedom and flexibility afforded in interview settings, the economics of having access to the ideas of several respondents at the same time, and the ideological multiplier effect when the ideas of one respondent stimulate thought in another. However, disadvantages also exist. There is always the danger of one or more respondents dominating the session, as well as of "groupthink," as members of the group yield their reflective independence to a group mood or momentum. In addition, there are limits in the potential to explore the background of the respondents.

Nevertheless, focus-group settings can be an effective tool for acquiring evaluative feedback from our students and other constituent groups. For example, an institution interested in evaluating and renewing its general education requirements may want to conduct group interviews with different constituent groups, such as alumni, currently enrolled sophomores or seniors, and perhaps a sample of community representatives. One of the advantages of focus-group interviews is that they can also test new concepts. A college thinking of implementing a new general education requirement may choose a focus group to test the merit of the proposal, for example. A research university graduate department desiring to evaluate its doctoral program may elect to conduct group interviews with clusters of recent graduates.

Readers interested in more detailed background on the structure and conduct of interviews can look at a chapter on this topic appearing in Guba and Lincoln's 1981 book *Effective Evaluation*. Two other sources entirely dedicated to interviews are Downs, Smeyak, and Martin, *Professional Interviewing* (1980), and Donaghy's *The Interview: Skills and Application* (1984).

Informal Follow-up Approaches

Most of us who have been involved for many years in colleges and universities have experienced the special pleasure of hearing from students who long since left our classrooms. Their informal anecdotes, like those in the alumni survey, provide another follow-up dimension. The anecdotes, by their nature, tend to be positive, and they often provide insight into the best that our institutions have to offer.

- A former student was working as a clerk in a local supermarket some ten years after she had sat in a professor's English classroom. As she checked the professor's groceries, she began reciting Chaucer's Prologue to *The Canterbury Tales*.
- Another student who had been in a writing class was working as a mechanic. He told of the short stories he often wrote in the evenings "for the fun of it."
- An independent businessman successfully completing his first year of operation gave credit to a support service of an institution's business school—a small business development center

that had provided the businessman with assistance in setting up his business following guidelines of good management practice.
- An M.Ed. program graduate had recently been appointed to a principalship when she wrote to thank several of her professors for the knowledge gained in their courses that had prepared her for her new role.

But, of course, we do occasionally hear complaints.

- A student who had graduated from an honors program at a large research university was having difficulty in her legal research and writing course as a first-year law student. She blamed her honors program. That program (not surprisingly) had bypassed the usual freshman composition courses where college students often hone the basic skills of writing and term-paper techniques.
- A first-year teacher who was struggling to maintain order in her inner-city classroom discounted her "ideal" student-teaching experience in a magnet school that had selective admission criteria.

When a new chancellor first came to the city, he noted that everywhere he went, ordinary citizens told him of some experience with his university: a downtown businessman who had taken a computer class to learn a new skill, the wife of a wealthy oilman who returned to college and earned a degree after many years (and then gave back to the school as she had gained), an employer who indicated he always hired graduates from that university first, and individuals who praised first one and then another member of the faculty. Such feedback leaves us with a pleasant glow about our institutions and also serves as a legitimate method of follow-up if the feedback is routed to the appropriate office—recorded, compiled, and used to effect continuation or change in programs or procedures. "While relatively less valid and reliable than objective data, subjective data do usefully portray the state of that world of people, human values, preferences, aspirations, and interpersonal dynamics that the . . . decision-maker ignores at his own peril" (Jones, 1982, p. 20).

This accent on informal and quiet approaches to the acquisition of perception and performance data prompts the recollection of beautiful dialogue from Elspeth Huxley's *The Flame Trees of Thika*. In the closing pages, Lettice remarks that "the best way to find things out is not to ask questions at all. If you fire off a question, it is like firing off a gun; bang it goes, and everything takes flight and runs for shelter. But if you sit quite still and pretend not to be looking, all the little facts will come and peck round your feet, situations will venture forth from thickets and intentions will creep out and sun themselves on a stone; and if you are very patient, you will see and understand a great deal more than a man with a gun" (Huxley, 1959, p. 272).

What a marvelous thought and what a wonderful complement to the more formal approaches described in this chapter. With questionnaire and interview guide in hand, we may indeed be poised to learn something about institutional and program performance from those who know that performance most directly and intimately. Perhaps, however, our questionnaire and interview studies may so disturb the organization that we will have the social equivalence of the Heisenberg uncertainty principle in physics. When the optical scanner is turned off and the institutional research office is closed, when we are not on collegiate safari hunting for client responses, and when we are in quieter and more relaxed repose, perhaps even in those moments we can learn about our colleges and universities if we are receptive.

Follow-up: In Units of One

In these concluding thoughts on the merit of follow-up studies is a timely place to remember the theme of Jan Carlzon's book *Moments of Truth* (1987), previously referenced in Chapter One. Customers and clients, Carlzon reminds us, will remember less the sophistication of our equipment, the health of our financial ratios, and the attractiveness of our annual reports than the quality of personal contact with members of our organization.

Think of the thousands of contacts between a college or university and its students: in our classrooms and laboratories, in our registrar and placement offices, in our cafeterias and residence halls, in our bookstores and our deans' offices. Each of these contacts is a "moment of truth." We have only to search our own memories to establish the validity of Carlzon's observation. Which is carved most deeply into our memory—our feelings about the equipment we used or our gratitude for those faculty and staff members who challenged our aspirations and our talent through the quality of their caring?

The qualitative impact of colleges and universities is delivered in units of one, and our students are the only ones who can see the university from the client perspective. Formal and informal approaches to follow-up studies are a quality assurance instrument of mutual benefit. Listening to our students, to our graduates, and to our community is a learning exercise that sets a good model for each of these three constituents. And the feedback we obtain from these follow-up studies can make us stretch to our intellectual and emotional heights, encouraging a college and university to continue education about itself, a discovery exercise with constructive potential.

FIVE

Licensure: The Test of Professional Standards

Licensure is a form of quality assurance that may go relatively unnoticed as a means for colleges and universities to evaluate program quality. In many professions the only route to practice is by completing a college or university preparation program. When students are assisted in this rite of passage and find that their preparation program has enabled them to attain licensure easily, they may assign their success to the "quality" of their preparation program.

Thus, institutions whose accounting, nursing, law, engineering, teacher education, and medical graduates consistently score well on licensure and certification examinations may tout these performance scores as evidence of program quality. There are some obvious dangers here, however. In one state, for example, the supply of lawyers in the state led to a severe tightening of standards on the state bar examination. Thus, law schools that may have found their bar examination performance satisfactory in one year might discover that the same level of performance would prove unsatisfactory in a following year. What can be said, then, about the quality of professional preparation programs under conditions of shifting standards?

This chapter defines and describes licensure as an instrument of quality assurance and treats the advantages and liabilities to

119

which we alluded in our opening remarks. The chapter also relates licensure to accreditation because, as we noted in Chapter Two, the two are interwoven in several fields—with the result that neither licensure nor accreditation can be employed separately as an indicator of quality. The licensure process for four professional fields is described: law, medicine, nursing, and teacher education. The accrediting process for these same four fields was outlined in Chapter Two. A concluding discussion engages some of the problems and issues associated with licensure.

The Concept and Value of Licensure

Webster's *Ninth New Collegiate Dictionary* tells us that a license is "a permission granted by competent authority to engage in a business or occupation or in an activity otherwise unlawful." Licensure is, according to the same source, the "granting of licenses especially to practice a profession." The term "licensing" is used increasingly to describe the process or procedure by which one becomes licensed and is often used interchangeably with licensure. The word "credentialing" is also often used interchangeably with licensing, but such use strains the standard definition of licensing.

Discussion about licensure is further complicated by the use of "certification" as a synonym, such as in the granting of a certificate to teach. The word "certificate" is legitimate, however; Webster's *Ninth New Collegiate Dictionary* defines it as "a document certifying that one has fulfilled the requirements of and may practice in a field." Remember, however, that both "license" and "certificate" have accepted meanings not within the context or the purpose of this chapter. All certificates do not carry the right to practice. In the case of the proposed national certificate being developed by the National Board for Professional Teaching Standards, as a current example, it is not anticipated (for the foreseeable future) that the certificate will have a licensure function. Indeed, recipients will have already been licensed (or certificated) by their respective states, typically through a department of education acting on behalf of a state board of education (National Board for Professional Teaching Standards, 1989). A license to operate a motor vehicle or to fish or hunt, for example, is a use of the word that is not pertinent to our treatment of licensure.

Young's definition of licensure is helpful: "Licensure is a process by which an agency of government grants permission (1) to persons meeting predetermined qualifications to engage in a given occupation and/or use a particular title and (2) to institutions to perform a specified function" (pp. 457–458). But his definition of certification as "a process by which a non-governmental organization grants recognition to a person who has met certain predetermined qualifications specified by that organization . . ." (p. 457) fails to take into account that state governments (specifically state boards of education) grant certificates to teachers (Young, Chambers, Kells, and Associates, 1983).

In any event, in this chapter we use "license" to describe the authority one is granted to practice a profession, and "licensure" describes the process or procedure one goes through to attain the authority. "Certification" will have two meanings: (1) a process by which one is granted the right to practice, just as in licensure and (2) a process by which a person has met prescribed requirements to hold a position or title or to engage in a specified practice after licensure has been attained.

Licensure has several purposes that serve the public interest. Chief among them is reasonable assurance that a licensee has fulfilled requirements set forth by experts in a particular field, usually functioning in behalf of the state, that are considered essential for safe entry into that field. The process, therefore, is designed to prevent incompetents and charlatans from practicing.

A second useful purpose of licensure is the identification and publication of the knowledge and skills deemed by expert practitioners and teachers to be necessary for good performance. This enables schools and colleges to prepare students for the profession more effectively and efficiently. Admission requirements, instructional programs, and exit requirements can be established and maintained with greater confidence and effectiveness than would be the case if licensure were not involved.

A third benefit is the opportunity provided licensed professionals to use their own training and experience in devising requirements for initial licensure, and to revise and upgrade the curriculum as the profession grows in knowledge and maturity and as new discoveries and inventions place new responsibilities on the professional. The knowledge base underlying licensure in medicine, for example, is very different today from what it was at the turn of the century or, for that matter, just a decade ago.

Assisting in regulating, policing, and promoting professions is a fourth way that licensure serves the public interest. In addition to controlling entry, licensure is almost always accompanied by stated conditions that will result in revocation of the license and, thus, the right to practice. Several professions require additional study beyond initial preparation and licensure, as well as other ways of maintaining proficiency. Maintaining a license requires approval by both internal and external publics. A doctor's associates, for example, may submit charges that, if proven, can result in license revocation. Similarly, malpractice complaints and suits may produce sufficient evidence to cause the appropriate body or agency to move for the accused's license to be revoked.

Several professions are not sufficiently well developed in terms of "accepted best practice" to permit the litigation of malpractice complaints. But several are: Medicine and law are considered to be so well developed that even the lay public (jurors in malpractice suits) is permitted to render judgments—albeit after expert opinion has been given.

A fifth benefit to society, and the one most germane to this chapter, is the use of licensure as a form of quality assurance. This benefit has at least two dimensions. First, prescribed licensure requirements virtually require colleges and universities to keep their respective curricula closely attuned to the requisite knowledge and competencies. Preparation programs can exceed but not fall below licensure prescriptions. To do otherwise would be institutional suicide, for no institution can long survive without a reasonably high proportion of its graduates meeting professional licensure requirements and, thus, becoming licensed to practice. The public rightfully expects institutions they support to ensure that students aspiring to practice in a profession are able to do so; and the public has the right to believe, with reasonable confidence, that satisfactory completion of an institution's approved program will result in the authority to practice.

With this background, we believe the reader will gain deeper insight from the following descriptions of how the concept of licensing works in four professional fields: law, medicine, nursing, and teacher education. In the case of teacher education, a somewhat fuller treatment is made of licensure for three reasons. First, teaching is the largest of all professions and one in which the public has a great stake. Second, the reform of education is a high national priority, and teacher preparation and licensure are at the core of many reform efforts. Third, unlike the other three fields described, licensure for teachers is in a state of flux with several new directions and concepts emerging.

Licensure in the Field of Law

Unlike medicine, law does not issue a national license to its practitioners. Rather, lawyers are licensed to practice in one or more of the fifty-three jurisdictions throughout the country. States may, and do, require different levels of competence in their bar examinations. Licensure that results from passing a particular state's bar examination does not carry with it the right to appear in court, which requires additional licenses or "permits." Moreover, in the United States there are two judicial systems, state and federal; a separate permit is required before a lawyer can appear in either of the systems. The United States Court of Appeals and the Supreme Court also require separate permits. Thus licensure in law is jurisdiction and system specific (Rudd, 1985).

A license to practice law usually requires the holder to have graduated from an accredited law school and to have passed a state bar examination, as noted in Chapter Two. This linkage between accreditation and licensure, in our opinion, strengthens both the accreditation principle and the legal profession. A negative consequence is that the linkage effectively removes accreditation from its voluntary status—a condition some accreditation leaders view as detrimental to accreditation, also noted in Chapter Two.

The Multi-State Bar Examination, developed by the National Conference of Bar Examiners, is used in virtually all states and often takes up the first day of the state bar examination. The second day is usually given to tests developed by the respective state board. States have the right to establish their own cutoff scores, resulting in variability among the states (Augstyn, 1985).

Responsibility for admission and exit requirements and for the training curriculum is shared between the profession at large and the preparing institution. As the unevenness of legal training received under the "reading law" tradition attracted increasing criticism, responsibility for supervising the academic education of would-be lawyers gradually became the jurisdiction of colleges and universities, most of which established law schools for that purpose. The "bench and bar" were unwilling to relinquish total jurisdiction, however, and ultimately devised the system that allows the practicing bar to retain considerable control over the education of persons who aspire to join them in the practice of law (Davis, 1987). Again, this circumstance is a double-edged sword: Institutions often chafe at not having full control of their curricula, admission, retention, and exit requirements; but considerable benefits accrue when their graduates achieve approval from the profession in the form of passing the bar and being permitted to practice.

Licensure of Medical Doctors

Unlike licensure for lawyers, licensure for doctors is national in scope and function. The ability to move from one state to another and to be licensed in those states without having to be reexamined was a strongly felt motivation of medical leaders when the National Board of Examiners was established in 1915. The policy of reciprocity has remained to this day.

The examination and the other requirements imposed by the national board for its certificate have become the path to licensure for about 80 percent of the medical school graduates in the country. The examination is recognized by all of the country's fifty-three licensing authorities except three: Texas, Louisiana, and the Virgin Islands (Jewett, 1985).

An alternative licensure route open to graduates of medical schools is the examination developed by the Federation of State Medical Boards. A substantial number of medical schools use the examination (commonly called FLEX) as an internal evaluation of students, but students electing the FLEX licensure option are not eligible to take the examination until after graduation. Most students find that taking the national board examination (the National Board of Medical Examiners) is the more functional route to licensure because it can be taken during the course of their medical education. Part One of the exam is given at the end of the first two years of medical school, Part Two during the last year, and Part Three after six months of residency. All three parts must be completed satisfactorily within seven years. Passing scores are set at the national level with little concern for "manpower" needs (Jewett, 1985).

Although national board certification (licensure) rests heavily on the examination, there are two additional requirements. First, the candidate must graduate from a medical school approved and accredited by the Liaison Committee on Medical Education, a body jointly sponsored, staffed, and financed by the Council on Medical Education of the American Medical Association and the Association of Medical Colleges. Second, one year of postgraduate training in residency accredited by the Accreditation Council on Medical Education, or a Canadian equivalent, must be completed (Jewett, 1985).

Both the national board examination and FLEX assess the medical school graduate's capability for practicing without supervision. Part Three of the national board examination and FLEX 2 determine whether an individual is able to practice without supervision; FLEX 1 determines whether an individual can practice under supervision.

In response to increasing numbers of United States citizens and aliens who are educated in foreign medical schools but desire to practice in the United States, the National Board of Medical Examiners developed the Foreign Medical Graduate Examination. Non-U.S. citizens must satisfy this examination in order to be admitted to a residency program in the United States. The test was developed as the equivalency of Parts One and Two of the National Board Examination.

The licensure mechanism for medical doctors is long standing, intricately designed, and powerful. The control of licensure by the profession and the close linkage between accreditation and licensure is unequaled by other professions; the states have effectively delegated their licensing powers to the several medical boards vis-à-vis accreditation and licensure. Medical schools whose graduates attain licensure, as most of them do (although there is some attrition between Parts One and Two on the national board exam) (Jewett, 1985), have little problem convincing their constituencies that their programs are of high quality, especially since quality is both defined and measured by the medical profession itself.

Licensure of Nurses

In nursing, licensure and certification are not used synonymously. In this field, a license is required to practice. Certification is not a precondition for practice and is, in fact, usually granted only after several years of practice. Certification is given in several levels and types—such as nurse generalist, nurse practitioner, and clinical specialist.

Licensure in nursing is the responsibility of the National Council of State Boards of Nursing (NCSBN), a national standards board comprising executives of the respective state boards. This council recommends standards for licensure and sets standards for the national licensure examination, although licensure itself is awarded by the state agencies (Fabrey and Rupp, 1985).

As with doctors and lawyers, testing plays an important role in the licensure of nurses. A national examination for licensure is required by each state; the results then are used by each state board. The examination is prepared by NCSBN, which also sets cutoff scores. There is no separate or additional licensure examination beyond the national examination.

As is not often true in the licensure of doctors and lawyers, applicants for a nursing license must have completed an accredited preparation program. Accreditation procedures were described in Chapter Two.

As noted above, nursing utilizes the concept of certification as an extension of licensure, not unlike the way in which doctors can become certified in certain specialty areas in addition to their generic license. The structure for certification is more decentralized and fragmented; in addition to the American Nursing Association, approximately twenty nursing organizations certify nurses in one or more specialty areas. No national standards board exists for certification examinations. Thus, in nursing, certification is used not as a license but, rather, as a professional recognition tool and as a factor in hiring and promotion decisions, often enhancing job mobility (Fabrey and Rupp, 1985).

Licensure of Teachers

In education, the distinctions between certification and licensure are blurred. Concerning the authority to practice, the terms were virtually synonymous until recently, but distinctions are developing; certificates as extensions of licenses are beginning to appear on the scene. The National Board of Professional Teacher Standards, mentioned earlier, is developing a national certificate that also will be for persons already licensed.

Historically, most states have used the term "certificate" to mean license, or, at least, persons have been authorized to teach on the basis of a state-awarded certificate. Use of the term "license" has increased in recent years, however, both formally and informally. Tennessee, for example, systematically changed its certification procedures and requirements in 1988 as a result of the career ladder program. In the process, the word "license" was used where the word "certificate" was used formerly; a certification system was created for teachers electing the career ladder certificate option and meeting its requirements (Tennessee, 1987). In this section, we use both terms interchangeably except when noted, since both mean the process by which a person is granted the authority to teach or otherwise serve an educational role in schools K–12 for which a certificate or license is required.

No national licensure mechanism exists for teachers; consequently, there is no national standards board for licensure. National accreditation exists through the National Council for the Accreditation of Teacher Education (NCATE), but accreditation of a program by NCATE is not a prerequisite and does not lead to national licensure for graduates of an accredited program. Moreover, slightly less than one-half of the country's schools, colleges, or departments of education have NCATE approval. Only two states, Arkansas and North Carolina, require graduation from an NCATE-accredited program as a precondition for state certification and in neither state is the requirement in full force. Thus, licensure in teacher education is altogether a function of the states. Indeed, in earlier years several large systems, Chicago, for example, trained and certified their own teachers. That practice continued until quite recently but is now extinct (Leviton, 1976).

The typical state mechanism for handling teacher licensure is for control to be vested in the state board of education; the state department of education is assigned responsibility for implementing policies, rules, and regulations previously developed or approved by the board. Certification advisory committees have become commonplace as a means for teacher educators, school leaders, and school practitioners to have a voice in recommending policies, rules, and regulations, as well as curriculum content.

Practitioner input has increased in recent years by the establishment in several states of professional practice boards, mechanisms advocated strongly by the National Education Association (NEA) for over two decades. Jordan (1988) notes that although state-level boards or commissions on standards and practices are found in virtually all states and have existed since the 1920s in New Jersey, forty-one such bodies were created after 1960 and thirty within the past two decades. Jordan points out that whereas these bodies have several important functions, only the state standards boards in California, Minnesota, and Oregon are fully autonomous. Since Jordan's study, Georgia created a fourth fully autonomous standards board in the spring of 1991. With state-level balances of power vis-à-vis teacher licensure (and other aspects of standards and practices) being challenged by the national teacher organizations and various public and political forces supporting school reform, the door may be opening for education to "become more involved in setting licensing standards" (Jordan, 1988, p. 34).

A plan for establishing and monitoring standards for the governance of the teaching profession was adopted by the NEA board of directors in February 1987. The plan extends the concept of state professional standards boards to a national configuration and presses for significantly greater autonomy in licensure and various other governance matters. Implementation would move teaching closer to the status held by medical, legal, and nursing education. Additionally, it would go far toward establishing the kind of "interlocking interrelationships between program approval, program accreditation, and licensure" that strong professions have already attained (Saunders, 1987).

Most states do have program approval mechanisms, but they are subject to the vagaries of political protectionism. Members of state boards of education are usually elected by popular vote or are political appointees. Consequently, they often find it difficult to resist strong pressures from area and state politicians to keep open a teacher training program found by a state visiting team to be inadequate. Put candidly, few if any states have been able to maintain program approval requirements stronger than the weakest teacher education program could meet if it had a reasonably strong political support system.

A significant aspect of the NCATE Redesign 1985 (see Chapter Two) is linkage with state approval systems. If it is successfully implemented, those states that satisfy NCATE standards for state approval policies, procedures, and requirements will be recognized by that national accrediting organization and will become a part of a coordinated system of approval and accreditation.

The education reform movement of the 1980s edged states a little closer to a national testing system for teachers—a licensure device currently used in medicine, law, and nursing. Rampant criticism of teachers and of schools of education provoked several legislatures to mandate testing programs for teachers. Compared to only ten states in 1980, currently about forty-four of the fifty states require some kind of standardized, norm-referenced test as a condition of certification; the National Teacher Examination is the most commonly used (Sandefur, 1988). Cutoff scores vary greatly among states, however; and unlike the situation alluded to earlier in medicine, cutoff scores and personnel needs do seem to be positively correlated. In fact, twenty-seven states have developed alternative teacher certification programs, established in part as a way to widen the applicant pool and thus increase the number of entry-level teachers. Less than half of the twenty-seven alternative programs mandate a standardized, norm-referenced test as a requirement (Council of Chief State School Officers, 1989).

A promising movement in the certificate/licensure arena in teacher education is the work of the National Board of Professional Teaching Standards, alluded to earlier. The efforts of this board, sponsored and initially funded by the Carnegie Corporation, could unintentionally be the forerunner of a national standards board that influences and possibly controls licensure. We say this could be unintentional because the board is currently focusing on the voluntary certification of experienced teachers in accordance with "high and rigorous standards . . . calibrated to an advanced level of teaching proficiency, contrasting again with minimal, entry level state licensing standards" (p. 3). However, this organization's plan to develop "high and rigorous standards for what teachers should know and be able to do" and to establish "an assessment system to determine when candidates meet these standards" (National Board for Professional Teaching Standards, 1989, p. 3) looks very similar to the work of national standards boards in legal and medical education early in this century.

Support for this eventuality can be inferred from comments made by Jordan (1988, p. 33) on the emergence of voluntary national certification: "Even though voluntary national certification standards may appear to be nonthreatening, how long can credible and well-publicized 'voluntary' standards remain voluntary?" Although Jordan was pondering the impact on state and local school boards, the possibility also exists relative to national standards being developed along the lines found in medicine and nursing.

The growing belief among state legislators and other policymakers that teachers should be licensed only after passing a standardized, norm-referenced test, as mentioned above, is yet another movement that could propel teaching and teacher education toward a more tightly controlled and more prescriptive licensure and program approval system. Several states that require teacher candidates to pass a standardized examination (in pedagogy, teaching field content, and basic skills) have legislated ways to hold schools of education accountable for their students' failure rates. The typical arrangement is to put schools of education on notice when less than 70 to 75 percent of their graduates in a given year attain a designated cutoff score. Failure to correct the condition in a specified number of years, usually three or four, results in disapproval of a school's program by the state and thus in their graduates' ineligibility for state licensure. The movement has been vigorously opposed by many teacher educators, among others, who cite the movement as being unfair, racially motivated, and without precedent in other fields of professional licensure.

It is not our intention to argue the merits or demerits of the movement but, rather, to cite it as yet another "straw in the wind" that seems to be blowing toward a more rigorous and demanding system of preparation, accreditation, and licensure. The reader may know that when the medical profession used the famous Flexner report and subsequent grants from Carnegie and Rockefeller to upgrade medical education, three openly avowed intentions were the use of the medical school at Johns Hopkins as a prototype, the replication of that model throughout the country, and the elimination of inadequate schools of medicine.

Summarizing the situation in teacher licensure, the authority to license practitioners remains largely in the hands of state authorities. There has been increasing input from the teaching profession but only modest relegation of authority to professional bodies. Indeed, during the reform decade of the 1980s state agencies tended to increase their authority, elevating standards and requirements for licensure in accordance with their own conceptions of needed corrective action. Many of the state initiatives have been met with strong opposition from the profession, an anomalous circumstance when one remembers that the stronger professions themselves elevated standards for both preparation and licensure. Once the standards were visibly and credibly high, states were willing to relegate much of their licensing authority to the respective professions. Both teacher educators and the broader profession might profit from an objective reading of the professionalization of legal education, medical education, nursing education—and others—vis-à-vis the development of standards for both accreditation and licensure.

There are, however, several reasons for guarded optimism: NEA's effort to develop a professional governance system, along with the sponsorship of state professional standards boards; NCATE's redesign for national accreditation, which includes a piece on improving state approval systems; and the increasing use of knowledge-based standardized tests as a condition of certification and licensure.

Problems and Issues

As with accreditation, and as noted in Chapter Two, licensure is not without its problems or its critics. Even the several ways licensure was described as serving the public interest are not without dispute. Cited below are several of the criticisms frequently voiced, along with some of the problems and issues being addressed.

1. Licensure is self-serving. This liability was also mentioned as a liability of accreditation in Chapter Two, and the rationale is similar: Professional groups use the process of licensure to promote their own interests. In the case of medicine, for example, there is widespread belief that licensure is used purely and simply to control the number of persons entering the profession, that this is done to maintain a shortage of doctors, and that both the number of patients and the fees charged are intended functions of that controlled entry.

Other charges of self-service have been made, such as the one that teacher certification is essentially a monopolistic control mechanism by schools of education that prevents many qualified persons (such as graduates of arts and sciences colleges) from being professionally licensed. The degree to which colleges and universities influence, if not dictate, the requirements of licensure in several fields and the requirement of having to complete an institutional program as a precondition of licensure are often cited as additional evidence that it is self-serving.

In making this criticism, critics put the professions in a difficult position. The public is protected when licensure requirements have an expert professional opinion base, and when respected and successful practitioners have a strong voice in helping assure that both preparation programs and licensure requirements are closely attuned to competencies and skills needed for effective performance. Yet professionals exercising these judgments are sometimes suspect, viewed as pursuing selfish interests rather than protecting the public. See, for example, "Arrogance and Altruism in the Professions" (Bogue, 1981). Without the contributions from the organized professionals, however, licensure would be much more precarious and less likely to achieve its purpose.

2. Licensure is not a proven way to exclude incompetents

from practicing. Friedman (1962) contended almost three decades ago that there is no persuasive evidence that licensure does in fact sort out the competent from the incompetent. Similar allegations of more recent origins are seen from time to time.

Frequently, the evidence cited to support this criticism lacks credibility; like beauty, competence often is in the eye of the beholder. Some are quick to judge doctors, lawyers, nurses, and teachers as incompetent and unworthy of the license bestowed upon them. Sometimes our bases for the accusations are valid and provable; more often they are not. Although every profession has some prescribed way for revoking licenses, it is still rather rare for a professional license to be revoked.

Malpractice suits, especially those in medicine, attract a great deal of attention, especially when the size of the award is great. The publicity and notoriety surrounding these cases tend to mislead the general public into believing that malpractice suits are commonplace, but, despite their increase in recent years, only a very small percentage of patient-professional relationships reach litigation, and the situation is similar in other professions.

3. Licensure excludes many competent and deserving persons. This criticism is related to the accusation of being self-serving but includes also the belief that licensure requirements are not always wise and just. As noted above, many persons believe that the pedagogical requirement built into teacher licensure is unnecessary, even harmful, in the sense that it precludes the entry into teaching by arts and science graduates who have an adequate preparation. For a contrasting view on the knowledge base of teaching, see Bogue's comments on "A Need to Know" (Bogue, 1991). Bar examinations and those in the several subfields of medicine and health care are not immune from this type of criticism, despite their having been developed by knowledgeable and highly experienced professionals.

The accusation that licensure requirements are not always job related is a relatively new dimension of this criticism and one with a strong social implication. This criticism asserts that (1) blacks and other minorities are disadvantaged in their efforts to pass licensure examinations because of unequal education backgrounds and differences in their cultural backgrounds and (2) portions of the examination that pose difficulty for these groups are not job related, that is, not essential for effective performance. Considerable litigation has taken place in this arena, the watershed case being Griggs v. Duke Power Company in 1971 (Rebell, 1976), which directed that examination and other entry-level requirements must be job related.

4.   Licensure mitigates the voluntary nature of accreditation. In several professions, strong linkage exists between accreditation and licensure, as noted in Chapter Two. We cited some advantages of the linkage and suggested that it is a necessary condition for a strong, mature profession. Teaching, for example, was described as not fully developed as a profession, in part because of the absence of a linkage between national accreditation and state licensure (certification).

But that is one edge of the proverbial double-edged sword. The other edge is that from the perspective of institutions, accreditation loses its voluntary nature when certain of their graduates cannot be licensed without having first completed an accredited preparation program. Simply put, institutions cannot afford not to have their professional programs accredited and, consequently, must sometimes abide by terms and conditions imposed by others that they would not agree to otherwise (Young, Chambers, Kells, and Associates, 1983). In this country, accreditation was conceived as voluntary and some of its leaders contend that its great benefits will cease if it does not remain so. There is mixed opinion on whether accreditation's voluntary status is threatened by the federal government's requirement that accreditation be a condition of eligibility for federal funds.

5.   There are disturbing and counterproductive contradictions between licensure and the actions of policymakers. Sykes (1989, p. 32) contends that the "three functions of licensure systems—creating supply, constructing categories of competence, and inventing conceptions of quality—are difficult to reconcile." Using teaching to make his point, Sykes notes that several actions by policymakers in the various states appear "simultaneously to tighten and loosen the connection between qualifications and assignments in teaching, and to raise and lower entry standards" (1989, p. 32). Among the actions cited by Sykes are (1) administration of both entry tests and performance evaluation during the initial year of teaching, (2) enactment of alternative certification programs that

usually relax professional education and other requirements, (3) issuance of substandard certificates permitting unqualified individuals to teach, and (4) assignment of teachers to classes outside areas of competence (to affect the number of available practitioners).

Licensure: Serving Public and Academic Interests

Licensure systems have become rather commonplace in American society, with a large number of occupations regulated and/or controlled by state agencies, and there are no signs of reduction. Indeed, the concept of licensure as a means of protecting the general public seems to be more firmly entrenched than ever, a continuing stream of criticism and dissatisfaction notwithstanding. Institutions of higher learning are inextricably involved in licensure, whether they like it or not and whether or not their best interests are always served.

This chapter has been concerned with the licensure of professionals, the method by which persons aspiring to practice in a certain field of endeavor become authorized to do so. Professional licensure was treated first in a general way and then with more specificity in law, medicine, nursing, and teaching. Professional licensure was shown to serve the public interest in several ways, such as the assurance that a licensee has fulfilled requirements believed by experts to be essential for effective performance in a particular field. Two other benefits cited were the preventing of incompetents and charlatans from practicing and the setting forth of program and curricular guidelines for institutions to follow in their preparation programs. A benefit of licensure especially pertinent to the theme of this book is the opportunity provided colleges and universities to use licensure as a quality assurance. Maintaining preparation programs that are closely attuned to what credible experts say is necessary for effective performance and successfully preparing aspirants for the prescribed entry requirements constitute a justifiable basis for institutions' claiming that they have programs of high quality.

Licensure practices were examined in some detail in law, medicine, nursing, and teaching and in the first three fields depicted as standing, well developed, rigorous, and credible. We discussed licensure in teaching as being less well developed, standing primarily as an uncoordinated series of state mechanisms and, consequently, highly susceptible to state and local political policymaking— even political machinations. The chapter concluded with a brief description of five problems and issues in licensure, citing assertions by critics and supporters concerning problems that must be solved in order for proponents to make good on their claim that it is a viable and valuable societal instrument.

SIX

Academic
Program Reviews:
The Test
of Goal Achievement

$\mathbf{A}$s with many of the other approaches described in these chapters, the evolution of academic program review as an instrument for quality assurance is primarily a movement of the last quarter century. However, Fred Harcleroad (1980, p. 1) suggests that "academic program evaluation in the United States of America began on September 23, 1642," the day that Massachusetts Bay Company governor John Winthrop went to preside over nine seniors graduating from Harvard College.

The historic roots of evaluation may go back to that early day in Harvard's history, but both the literature and the activity in this field clearly point to the emergence of academic program reviews as a quality assurance development of the past twenty-five to thirty years. For example, a survey of almost 900 institutions by Barak (1982) showed that more than three-fourths, 76 percent, of the institutions' current policies and procedures were initiated since 1970. This more recent emergence of program reviews as an instrument of quality assurance is affirmed by Conrad and Wilson (1985), who note that "it was not until the 1970's that forces largely outside the academy were to make program review (internal as well as external) a central feature of academic program planning in the majority of institutions and states" (p. 4).

Our goal in this chapter is to outline the distinctive features of academic program review as an instrument of quality assurance, to identify some of the educational and political factors that led to its emergence, to reveal the variety of actors involved—institutional, state agency, and so forth—and to examine some of the strengths and limitations of this approach to quality assurance.

Academic Program Review—A Definition

What exactly is meant by "academic program review" and how do the features of this approach to quality assurance differ from other approaches described in this book?

Essentially, an academic program review is a comprehensive evaluation of a curriculum leading to a degree. This review will ordinarily involve the acquisition of historic, current, and projective data on program purpose, resources used and needed, and an evaluation of performance. The evaluation of performance may involve elements of previously described quality assurance approaches—peer judgments and student outcome measurements, for example.

Academic program reviews may be initiated and conducted within a college or university, within a system of institutions, by a state-level governing or coordinating agency, or by some element of state government, such as a legislative audit agency. The reasons for such reviews may be financial, educational, political, or ethical:

> *Financial:* to ascertain whether there is a need for additional support, whether resources can support existing programs, whether current resources are being applied with effectiveness and efficiency
>
> *Educational:* to ascertain whether a program should be implemented, revised, improved, or terminated; to determine quality of program performance
>
> *Political:* to ascertain whether a program is being operated within state guidelines or whether students are being protected from programs of questionable value and quality

Ethical: to ascertain whether the program is being operated according to ethical standards set forth by the institution and/or the governing body, whether the purposes of the program are commensurate with the purposes of the institution as a whole, or whether the operations of the institution or a particular program are characterized by good management practices, efficiency, and integrity.

This may be a useful time to spend a moment on the meaning of terms, because *program review, program evaluation,* and *program audit* can be found in similar contexts. In a 1979 monograph, *Developing a Process Model for Institutional and State-Level Review and Evaluation of Academic Programs,* the Ohio Board of Regents offered these distinctions: The word *review* signaled a state agency role, the word *evaluation* an institutional or faculty initiative, and the word *audit* a legislative or executive initiative. Although the association of these three terms with the actors cited may have some validity, all center on the evaluation of program performance and potential and raise these questions:

1. Is the program achieving those goals for which it was designed, and are the goals still relevant to the mission of the unit or institutions in which the program is located?
2. Are the resources required to operate the program being applied in the most effective and efficient way possible?
3. Are there ways in which the impact and the efficiency of the program can be enhanced or improved?

Our previous outline of decision purposes, however, suggests other reasons for program review. Reviews can be conducted, for example, to determine whether a new program should be started, whether an existing program should be terminated, or whether institutional operations are in conformity with stated guidelines and regulations—programmatic, financial, and ethical. These purposes clearly speak to evaluation intents that go beyond the conventional purposes of program improvement. Moreover, they suggest possible evaluation roles beyond faculty and campus. Thus, one of the distinctive features of academic program reviews is the potential involvement of organizations and agencies external to the campus.

An earlier book-length treatment on *The Profession and Practice of Program Evaluation* (Anderson and Ball, 1980) offers several reasons for program review that embrace those we have cited but also contain other purposes, among them (1) to contribute to decisions about program installation; (2) to contribute to decisions about program continuation, expansion, or "certification"; (3) to contribute to decisions about program modification; (4) to obtain evidence to rally support for a program; (5) to obtain evidence to rally opposition to a program; and (6) to contribute to the understanding of basic psychological, social, and other processes (pp. 14–42). We draw the reader's attention to the last three decision purposes, as they suggest both political and educational rationales.

An illustration here will indicate how and why agencies external to the campus may become involved in campus evaluation. In the late 1970s, one of the authors was serving with the Tennessee Higher Education Commission (THEC), a coordinating agency for higher education in the state, with responsibilities in master planning, new program review and approval, budget review and recommendations, facility review and recommendations, and review of existing programs (but with no power to terminate academic programs). A routine legislative audit conducted on a state college campus revealed that it had failed to implement its retention policy for two years. As a result, the auditors found that approximately 600 students were still enrolled who were academically ineligible to be enrolled—at least according to the probation policies defined in the catalogue. This, of course, meant that the institution had been drawing state formula funding (based on size and level of enrollments) beyond what it should have been awarded.

The Tennessee legislature passed a resolution requiring that the THEC conduct an enrollment audit on each of the twenty-one campuses in the state (to draw random samples of enrolled students' names from the state's student information system and dispatch teams to each campus to review the academic record of these students in the sample to see if they were eligible for enrollment). No other institution was found in violation.

Here was a classic case in which a violation by one institution brought disruption and suspicion to all institutions and caused the intrusion of legislative interest into a matter ordinarily the province of a campus faculty and administration. This illustration does not fit our definition of "program review" with preciseness, because the legislative and commission audits centered not on a degree program but on retention policy. It does reveal, however, how a breach of ethical and educational responsibility on a single campus can bring external interference to all campuses.

In the next section we examine the evolution of academic program review as an instrument of quality assurance and see how and why agencies beyond the campus have become so involved.

Evolution of Academic Program Reviews

American higher education was a growth industry in the early years of the past half century (1945 to 1985). However, enrollment patterns in recent years have been more stable, declining in some locales and states, and there have been serious vacillations in the patterns of both state and federal funding. For the most part, these have been more sobering than exhilarating. Adding to this social/political stew a few instances of ethical abuse within higher education and an occasional prostitution of integrity and abandonment of standards, the result described by Harcleroad (1980, p. 12) should come as no surprise: "In such a social, political, and economic climate, central agencies, whether in business, government, or education, tend to tighten controls and to move back from previous efforts to decentralize." In *AGB Reports* two contiguous 1988 articles carried titles and abstracts that capture the themes we are trying to emphasize. An article by Eisenberg (1988, p. 5) speaks of higher education's "crisis of confidence" and is abstracted in this sentence: "Public support of higher education has been shaken, and it will take more than a glitzy public relations campaign to restore it." In the same publication, Seymour (1988, p. 24) warns us: "In today's financially restrictive environment, developing and approving new academic programs can be a delicate business."

The emergence of interactive roles in the approval and review of academic programs is a relatively new trend with potential discomforting dimensions, especially when viewed from the campus and faculty perspective. In earlier days, if agencies external to the campus ventured into program evaluation, they were likely to examine indicators related to funding recommendations and allocations—enrollments, class sizes, faculty salaries. Questions raised by agencies beyond the campus tended to focus on "how much" rather than "how effective." The quality assurance efforts of both regional and professional accrediting agencies, as outlined in Chapter Two, were quietly accepted by state agencies. No longer is that the case, however.

In recent years, executive and legislative officers have increased their level of activity. In the late 1970s, for example, the governor and the legislature of Colorado proposed substantive changes in the programs of Colorado institutions, going well beyond analyses and recommendations related to size of budgets. In an accrediting visit to a campus in 1986, one of the authors observed three different legislative audit teams at work, even as the self-study visit was taking place. Apparently, the presence of these audit teams had resulted from an unfortunate combination of factors on the campus: the nonvoluntary departure of the president, dissent among the faculty, and questions about financial operations. The audit teams were examining not only financial operations of the college but also a series of personnel and other policy matters.

The point here is that institutions face rising interest in program, policy, and operations review from a variety of external agencies. Why is this so? Conrad and Wilson (1985) suggest three reasons: a widespread interest in improving program quality, the need to respond creatively to severe financial constraints, and expectations for accountability by institutions' external constituencies.

Another reason has to be that higher education has grown bigger, more expensive, and more complex. In addition, public confidence in a number of our social institutions has declined, the "crisis of confidence" alluded to in the earlier citation by Eisenberg. Yet another factor can be traced to the size and visibility of education budgets, which in many states account for 50 percent or more of the state budget—when one combines the expenditures for elementary, secondary, and higher education. Moreover, these budgets are often the major source of discretionary spending, because many state expenditures involve required transfer payments and expenditures tied to federal appropriations.

As our previous illustration makes clear, however, there is yet another reason for increasing numbers of reviews by external agencies: an emerging concern with the ethics of policy and practice at the campus level. The misuses of institutional funds, the failure to administer federal aid programs properly, the abuse of state resources such as cars and travel funds, the neglect of building and equipment maintenance, and abuses in intercollegiate athletics furnish the stimulus for increased external interest that goes well beyond quality assurance.

In 1979, the American Assembly published a paper entitled *The Integrity of Higher Education* that stated that "academic life carries for its members obligations of personal conduct (by trustees and administrators, faculty and students) that lift expectations of behavior beyond the ordinary" (1979, p. 5). Ethical suspicion of a social institution from which the public has the right to expect nobility of performance is particularly regrettable because, among other results, a breach of ethics often brings pressure for increased control.

We stand now more than a decade from the report by the American Assembly. Has much has changed? A recent book by Charles Sykes entitled *PROFSCAM* is unkind to both institutional and personal behavior within our colleges and universities. Sykes sets forth a "bill of indictments" ranging from faculties' "distorting curriculum to accommodate their own narrow interests" to "being overpaid, grotesquely underworked, and the architects of academe's vast empires of waste" (Sykes, 1988, pp. 5-7).

Killing the Spirit, a 1990 book by the well-known historian Page Smith, is equally devastating in its criticism of the American university. Smith indicates that faculties at the elite universities "are in full flight from teaching" (p. 6); that "there is a mad reductionism at work. God is not a proper topic for discussion, but 'lesbian politics' is" (p. 5); that what universities "are clearly pursuing with far more dedication than the truth is big bucks" (p. 13). Finally Smith accuses the modern university of "spiritual aridity": "By 1990 the university had cast out every area of investigation and every subject that could not be subsumed under the heading 'scientific' and had made all those that remained (like literature and philosophy) at least profess to be scientific. Excluded were such ancient and classic human concerns as love, faith, hope, courage, passion and compassion, spirituality, religion, fidelity—indeed one is tempted to say, anything that might be somewhat encouraging to young people eager to receive some direction, or, in the words of a student survey form, develop 'a philosophy of life.' If love could not be discussed, sex, of course was a lively topic" (Smith, 1990, p. 20).

Those who labor in our colleges and universities would not accept Sykes's bill of indictment as a totally accurate description of higher education today, nor would they believe that the deeper spiritual concerns listed by Smith are totally absent in student-teacher interactions. There is, nevertheless, truth in these criticisms; and we must bear the consequences of that truth. The conclusion is clear: Wrongdoing and irresponsibility have destructive costs and consequences. They include a loss of confidence, diminution of trust, and a narrowing of management discretion and flexibility, and these can have damaging effects on quality.

Our discussion thus far suggests varying levels of initiative and responsibility for academic program review and evaluation. A monograph by Craven (1980) pointed to evaluation activities by four actors: institutions, systems, state agencies, and accrediting agencies. We described the role of accrediting agencies in Chapter Two. In this chapter, we examine the levels of initiative at the campus level, the system/coordinating level, and the state agency level, which may include both executive and legislative involvements.

Campus-Level Program Review

From the campus or institutional perspective, academic program review or evaluation can be seen as one of several instruments of quality assurance. Program review can also be a useful instrument to link planning, resources, and performance. In the Craven monograph previously cited, Munitz and Wright (1980) describe campus-level review systems at three institutions: Michigan State University, the University of Michigan, and the University of Houston.

At Michigan State University, departmental reviews are embedded in an annual evaluation and report system (AER). The two major components of the AER system are evaluation and report materials that contain a variety of statistical and activity profiles describing faculty activity and accomplishments, staffing patterns, enrollments, graduation trends, and work-load profiles. The department also prepares a "qualitative assessment of its own performance during the previous year in the three categories of instruction, research and professional activities, and public service. The unit is also invited to address major problems and imperative needs which were not adequately conveyed by the comparative data schedules. Both strengths and weaknesses are assessed in these evaluations. Departments are encouraged to incorporate results from external evaluations into their summary of unit performance" (Munitz and Wright, 1980, p. 24).

The planning and budgeting materials furnish an opportunity for the department to forecast future goals, their priorities, and the funding needs associated with each. Two plans are involved: a change plan and a flexibility plan. The change plan calls for a listing of prioritized department goals, with the funds necessary to support each, projected for each of the next five years. "The flexibility plan specifies how the department intends to reserve from long-term commitments a marginal percentage of its budget in anticipation of possible future reductions in general funds available" (Munitz and Wright, 1980, p. 25).

A check with the provost at Michigan State University revealed that the AER system has been incorporated into a comprehensive long-range planning process entitled Academic Program Planning and Review (APP&R), a major institutional effort in which planning is linked to budgeting. The process was described by the provost as follows: "Planning for every academic unit and support service requires the definition of role and objectives for each major administrative unit, and of purpose and aims for each department/school/division; the means for achieving the objective or purposes; the analysis of programs and funding; the assessment of alternatives for meeting objectives or purposes and for sustaining and improving quality; and the development of at least three-to-five-year plans (David Scott, letter to the author, May 1989).

Planning questions and materials to be completed by each academic and administrative unit are built on a major university policy paper entitled "The Refocusing, Rebalancing, and Refining

of Michigan State University." These three processes are described
as a "new concerted effort to assure that the university is 'doing the
right things, doing things right, at the right time in our history'"
(Michigan State University, 1989b, p. i).

This approach to planning and program review at Michigan
State is intensive and extensive. The current three-year planning
cycle (1989–1992), built on the document cited above, requires each
unit to engage questions related to proposed new activity and suggested discontinued activities. Fiscal notes are required on both.
Among the more interesting planning questions: "In addition to
the rebalancing to a new base budget level, what will be done differently to look at innovations that either produce a *simplification
of work necessary to the operation* of the major administrative unit
and the units contained within the MAU, will produce *collaborative efforts* with other units extramural to the MAU, will *enhance
the academic distinction* or assure the quality of programs in both
the short and long run, and will effectively use all funds available
to the unit" ([italics in original] Michigan State University, 1989b,
p. 8).

Munitz and Wright (1980) also described review approaches
used at the University of Michigan and the University of Houston,
including a two-dimension evaluation matrix for all programs at
the University of Houston on the basis of (1) the extent to which
the program was central to the mission of the university and (2)
judgments of the overall academic quality of the program (emi-
nence/distinction, strength/better than average, and adequate/
sound but not distinguished). A recent inquiry revealed that "the
University of Houston has maintained a cost generated model as
one tool for reviewing departmental college costs." However, according to associate vice president Ezell (Shirley Ezell, letter to the
author, May 1989), the institution was then participating in a five-
year review of doctoral programs initiated by the Texas Higher
Education Coordinating Board. We will have more to say on the
Texas Review Plan later in this chapter.

While we are examining campus-based approaches to program review and evaluation, it can prove helpful to recall from
Chapter Four that the Educational Testing Service (ETS) offers the
program self-assessment service (PSAS) "to help colleges and uni-

versities carry out departmental or program reviews at the undergraduate level" (Educational Testing Service, n.d.). This service provides a participating campus with a series of three program assessment questionnaires to be completed by faculty, undergraduate students, and alumni, giving comparative data (means and standards deviations) on sixteen scales, incorporating students, faculty, curriculum, policies and procedures, and several other aspects of university life.

Considering again the basic issues concerning program review and evaluation at the campus level, we encounter the same questions as those likely to be posed for any effective educational evaluation:

> *Purpose:* What is the purpose of the review/evaluation?
> - To start or implement a new program
> - To assess the quality of an existing program
> - To revise or discontinue an existing program
> - To ascertain resource needs
>
> *Criteria:* What indicators of activity and performance will be used to judge the program (see Chapter One)?
> *Evaluators:* Who will make the judgments of quality?
> - External consultants or peer evaluators
> - Currently enrolled students
> - Alumni
> - Advisory panels
> - Deans or other administrators
>
> *Time:* When and how often will reviews be conducted? Will programs be reviewed every year, on some recurring multiyear cycle, or on the basis of some performance signal?
> *Costs:* How much will reviews cost and who will pay?

Governing and Coordinating Board Program Review

Governing and coordinating boards have been for many years primary actors in reviewing and approving new program proposals. Typically, such reviews provide various assurances: to demonstrate the need for a new program that is requested or to assure that the program will not be an unnecessary duplication. Sometimes the reviews concentrate on the institution's capability for mounting and sustaining the requested new program and the availability of funds. Reviews by governing and coordinating boards can also focus on how the requested new program relates to both institutional and system mission. Approval for new programs by agencies beyond the campus is not, however, our main concern in this chapter. Although governing and coordinating board involvement in the approval of new programs can certainly be seen as an instrument of quality assurance, our main concern is on reviews of existing programs.

Barak (1982) noted the extensive involvement of external agencies in program review. Bogue (1980) explored the roles of three state-level agencies in reviewing existing academic programs. One of the agencies, the Tennessee Higher Education Commission (THEC), then as now, had authority to review and recommend but not to terminate existing programs. However, the THEC regularly conducted reviews of low-producing programs, as a result of which campuses and their governing boards voluntarily agreed to terminate a number of programs. The Tennessee approach to review of existing programs called for cooperation among the commission, the three governing boards for higher education in the state, and their respective institutions.

Reviews conducted by the Washington Council for Postsecondary Education were similar to those in Tennessee, beginning with a review of programs that "evinced low chronic productivity" and centering on the goal of minimizing unnecessary duplication. As described in the paper by Bogue (1980), essentially, the Washington CPE staff conducted extensive research on the three key principles most often used by institutions seeking new programs and attempting to retain existing ones about which there may have been questions: (1) the essentiality of a certain complement of programs for an institution to remain truly comprehensive, (2) the essentiality of graduate programs in providing for the growth and satisfaction of faculty by providing for programs in research, and (3) the essentiality of graduate programs to undergraduate program quality. Bogue explains how extensive research by the CPE staff revealed the exaggeration of these three often cited arguments.

Also reported in the earlier cited paper by Bogue were the program review actions of the Louisiana Board of Regents, one of the oldest, most thorough, and most continuous state-level reviews in the nation. The Louisiana Board of Regents has reviewed over 900 programs since 1975–1976. These reviews are conducted as follows (Louisiana Board of Regents, 1984). Affected departments or programs complete a program self-review, after which out-of-state consultants conduct on-site visits and subsequently submit comprehensive reports. Affected institutions respond to the reports, after which the Academic Affairs Committee of the board holds public hearings. Following the hearings, the staff of the board of regents submits recommendations to the Academic Affairs Committee, which then sends recommendations to the full board for its action.

Between 1975 and 1979 the board of regents reviewed 108 doctoral programs in 45 disciplines. The board reviewed 325 master's and specialist's degree programs during 1983 and began a series of discipline-based reviews of bachelor's degree programs in 1984. Actions of the board of regents during the period from 1975 to 1983 resulted in 325 program discontinuations, 111 at the graduate level. The board also issued commendations for those programs that peer reviewers considered to be of exceptionally high quality. Of the 909 programs reviewed during this period, 24 were cited for excellence (Louisiana Board of Regents, 1984).

Mentioned earlier was the Texas Higher Education Coordinating Board, which initiated a review of doctoral programs in October 1987. Each review involves a three-stage procedure, with each stage requiring progressively more information. Doctoral programs are grouped into categories of related programs, and a separate panel of consultants with appropriate expertise is engaged to review the programs in each category (Texas Higher Education Coordinating Board, 1987). These reviews essentially rate the programs for continuation or for further review. The final or third-stage review places a program in one of four categories: adequate for continuation, adequate for continuation subject to specific limitations, inadequate for continuation unless specific improvements are made within a specified time, and inadequate for continuation and should be phased out.

Earlier in the discussion we stated that the purposes of program reviews were financial, educational, political, and ethical. We suggested that the essential questions centered on the relationship between purpose and performance and on the question of resource adequacy. But there is another question that often drives program reviews, especially those initiated external to the campus. This question centers on whether a state is offering too many programs within a given field and level—the question of "unnecessary duplication." This term appears frequently in the lexicon of American higher education and most often within the context of academic program reviews. To pause a moment and explore its different meanings may prove helpful.

We note first that the base term *duplication* is rarely found without its modifier *unnecessary,* as though all duplication were unnecessary. That all duplication is not unnecessary is patently obvious to anyone who thinks about the matter. For example, in most urban centers in the United States, one can find a public university and community college both offering lower-level instruction in such fields as English, mathematics, science, and history. Indeed, within a single institution we often see multiple sections of English and mathematics as well as courses in descriptive and inferential statistics taught in a variety of disciplines—mathematics, psychology, quantitative business methods, agriculture, education. Is such duplication "unnecessary"? The answer may depend upon one's academic discipline and responsibility. If each class section is filled to capacity, it can be argued that the duplication is necessary. But what is an optimal class size—25 for English and 250 for introductory psychology? Like a bad piece of taffy candy, the argument grows as it is chewed.

Historical factors are at work in our understanding of the definition of unnecessary duplication. In the early 1970s, the Tennessee Higher Education Commission conducted a statewide study on the need for master's of business administration (MBA) programs in the state. The conclusion at that time was that perhaps four might be the optimal number. Today, each of the nine senior universities in Tennessee offers the MBA degree, and each is considered basic to the programs of those schools. What has changed in the few short years since the original study was completed?

The historical unfolding of our understandings about unnecessary duplication may also have financial roots. In a word, our perspectives and attitudes turn more conservative when money is tight. In the last quarter century, almost every state in the South, and others over the nation as well, built a second medical school and a new veterinary medicine school—both highly expensive educational operations—accompanied by loud and passionate arguments that usually moved back and forth between the legislature and state-level coordinating and governing agencies. Once state resources began to shrivel, legislative and higher education officials began to scratch their heads about whether their decisions of earlier years were smart ones.

Another factor that has fanned the flames of discussion over program duplication is the growing pressure to make additional programs available to major urban population centers. Certainly this generalization will not hold for every state; but in many states, the early establishment of major universities, with their comprehensive array of educational programs, tended to be away from major population centers. In earlier years, citizens in Memphis, Tennessee, for example, could reach St. Louis and a number of other population centers with major universities more easily and quickly than they could Knoxville, where the University of Tennessee with most of the state's doctoral programs was located. On the other hand, citizens living in Knoxville and other parts of East Tennessee found the 400- to 500-mile trip to Memphis for medical school equally discomforting, a factor that accounts for some of the creation of new medical schools. In Florida, citizens living in Miami, Orlando, and Tampa, for example, are beginning to believe that they should have as much access to advanced graduate programs as those living closer to Tallahassee and Gainesville.

Combinations of educational and philosophical forces appear to be at work concerning duplication. For example, Georgia has a population base of approximately 6.2 million people but operates only one public engineering program, at Georgia Tech; Tennessee, with a population of 4.8 million, operates four public engineering programs; the state of Louisiana, with a population of 4.5 million, operates six public engineering programs. The point is that the question of unnecessary duplication is exacerbated by a variety of educational, historical, political, and financial factors.

We propose a rough definition: *Unnecessary duplication occurs when the number of programs available in a particular curriculum is producing more graduates than needed; the number of programs available is more than can be operated with high quality, considering the resources available; or the number of courses and/ or programs is not being delivered with the most efficient application of existing resources.*

Again, program and/or course duplication is sometimes necessary. Access, availability, and course delivery schedules are also important considerations. It is reasonable for students to have access to basic, core courses in their own college, even if these same courses are offered across town. Students who are limited to evening classes have a right to a full curriculum, even if the courses they need are offered earlier in the day for day students.

Another state coordinating agency active in institutional effectiveness policy and program evaluation is in South Carolina, which signed into law in June 1988 "cutting-edge legislation" declaring that "each institution of higher learning is responsible for maintaining a system to measure institutional effectiveness in accord with provisions, procedures, and requirements developed by the commission on higher education" (South Carolina Coordinating Commission, 1988, p. 3). Among the effectiveness components endorsed by the commission are many of those discussed in several of the chapters in this book, including assessment of student performance on measures of general education and major field, follow-up studies and licensure, and certification examinations. A component of direct interest to this chapter is this requirement: *"Reports of Program Changes That Have Occurred as a Result of External Program Review*—Evaluation and assessment of programs is expected to produce change that enhances student achievement. Change that takes place as a result of external program evaluations should be reported to the Commission" ([italics in original] p. 3).

Of additional interest in the South Carolina approach is the requirement that institutions report on the number of student athletes who fail to meet regular admissions requirements and the graduation rate for students by sport, race, sex, field of study, and degree earned. This state is clearly in the vanguard of attempts to bring order and integrity to what many believe to be a troubled sector of higher education.

System Roles in Academic Program Review

One of the better examples of multicampus or system-level program review efforts is found in the State University System of Florida. Policies, procedures, and philosophy for the nine universities in the State University System of Florida (SUSF) are outlined in SUSF "Procedural Guidelines for Review of Existing Programs" (n.d.). Program reviews in the state system are conducted on five-year rotating cycles. An outline of the program review cycles over a sixteen-year time period for each program area was promulgated, showing the year each program was to have its initial review.

The policy manual furnishes extensive outlines of responsibilities for both campus and consultant roles in the review process, guidelines for content and form of reports, special issues to be engaged in the statewide reviews, and criteria to be employed. The twelve criteria contained in the SUSF policy document are clear, concise, and comprehensive. They range from role and scope consideration to program costs, from quality indicators to characteristics of students to be served, and from the question of unnecessary duplication to the accessibility of the program via the Academic Common Market of the Southern Regional Education Board (State University System of Florida, n.d.).

These criteria are used by the system staff and external consultants to the board in their preparation of recommendations to the board of regents. In addition, the State University System of Florida furnishes consultants with a specific and detailed set of evaluative questions concerning the following elements of program activity and achievement: appropriateness of program goals, program quality, program resources, program priority, relationships with other agencies, equal access and equal opportunity, and personnel needs. Of more than passing interest in this list of review areas is "equal access and equal opportunity." Here, consultants are asked to review the sex, age, and ethnic composition of the faculty and student populations and the affirmative action activities of the program.

An excerpt on how the consultants viewed their evaluative responsibilities in a particular program area, psychology, may be instructive and is indicative of the role consultants can play in an external review: "The Committee attempted to review each program objectively and sympathetically. Committee members took the position that their task was to assess the quality of each program and to do so in a supportive and helpful fashion. The Committee further took the position that its role was to encourage and assist the programs in their efforts in improving quality and to provide suggestions and recommendations that were consistent with overall program objectives" (State University System of Florida, 1987, p. 3).

The psychology report reveals one of the major strengths of system-level reviews, namely, the opportunity to examine general issues in a discipline or program. The state legislature considered the review initiative by the State University System of Florida to be of sufficient importance that the program review responsibility of SUSF was enacted into law.

No discussion of academic program reviews would be complete without some reference to New York. In that state, the board of regents holds a historic and strong role in program and review and approval authority. It is currently the only state agency to be recognized by the U.S. Department of Education as an accrediting body. The board of regents approves and registers every new degree program and also conducts periodic reviews in different fields of study. This authority for program registration/approval and review also embraces programs offered by private institutions, including proprietary schools. The regulations of the commissioner of education and the guidelines published for the periodic self-studies present standards that are similar in content to those used by regional accrediting agencies reported in Chapter Two. With over 300 institutions of postsecondary education in New York, more than can be found in clusters of several states, it becomes easier to understand why New York has developed this comprehensive approach.

We close this discussion on system roles in program review with an example from outside the United States, an illustration helpful in exploring some of the potential pitfalls in academic program review. A contemporary and critical reviewer of program reviews is Skolnik (1989), who telegraphs his position with the title "How Academic Program Review Can Foster Intellectual Conformity and Stifle Diversity of Thought and Method." Skolnik emphasizes how our philosophical set conditions our worldview, our view of the university, and our view of how to gauge quality: "Many of the questions posed by the humanist would be dismissed by the scientist as metaphysical or mystical, thus of dubious legitimacy for the university. Scientists, on the other hand, are preoccupied with counting, and this explains, for example, their preoccupation with citation indices as measures of quality, reflecting what Lindsey describes as a logical positivist bias in evaluation" (p. 624).

Skolnik examines the program review policies and procedures used by the Ontario Council on Graduate Studies, an arm of the Council of Ontario Universities. He claims that the Ontario review process is heavily weighted in favor of the sciences, furnishes evaluative data to support his claim, and concludes that "what are purported to be measures of quality are, in reality, measures of the degree of conformity to the model of graduate programs which obtains in the sciences" (Skolnik, 1989, p. 633).

In what we believe to be an instructive exercise, Skolnik engages three issues that are important to any well-balanced and effective program review process, at least at the graduate level. The first issue centers on an adequate definition of research, one that goes beyond quantity of publication: "Besides stimulating a torrent of pedestrian publishing, the practice of assessing quality by counting inhibits work which has a long gestation period and penalizes those whose inclination to publish is when they have something highly significant and polished to offer" (Skolnik, 1989, p. 634).

The second issue concerns the balance of faculty effort devoted to instruction, research, and service. Skolnik claims that Ontario reviews focus almost entirely on research outputs and fail to consider the merit of the "reflective practitioner" model: "In many professions, a new paradigm of the 'reflective practitioner,' which emphasized the development of theory through personal reflection on experiences in practice, is replacing the older linear view of the relationship between theory and practice, which was rooted in logical positivism" (1989, p. 636).

Finally, Skolnik criticizes the reviews for not looking at student-development outcomes, which he claims, with legitimacy, should be as important as measures of faculty research productivity—however that productivity might be measured. Skolnik concludes that the system of program review now in place in Ontario "works to suppress diversity, innovation, and non-conformist approaches in the search of knowledge" (1989, p. 638).

Suppression of diversity, innovation, and nonconformist approaches to the search for knowledge are disappointing and unwelcome outcomes for any quality assurance exercise. Hence, Skolnik's concerns merit attention. We add these concerns about the appropriateness of evaluative model and evaluative criteria to those cited earlier in this chapter.

We conclude this chapter with an acknowledgment that, although external-agency involvements in program review are important and impressive, they are not without fault. Criticisms are numerous and often have foundation. We identify six frequently voiced criticisms of reviews by external agencies.

1. Reviews are top down, furnishing little involvement at the campus level in selection of review criteria and consultants.
2. The selection of consultants ignores mission distinctions (for example, faculty from research universities reviewing programs at primarily undergraduate schools).
3. Visiting consultants show little knowledge of institutions they are visiting, leaping to large conclusions on the basis of little data and time.
4. Agency staff show little sensitivity to campus concerns, institutional nuances, and distinctions.
5. Reviews have the appearance of a punitive rather than an improvement function.
6. Agency staff exhibit personal and sometimes unfair bias in selecting and briefing consultants or in interpreting consultant reports to fit their own biases and goals.

These criticisms notwithstanding, the contributions of state agencies to quality assurance via program review are many and significant. Bogue (1980) described them succinctly: "With artistic leadership, state agency roles in academic program evaluation can complement institutional and governing board roles and enhance the renewal function of evaluation" (p. 69).

Program Reviews—A Partnership Perspective

It is clear that program reviews, as instruments of quality assurance, have negative as well as positive potential. Both campus and external evaluations can emerge from contexts with a negative tone—fiscal austerity, enrollment declines, unnecessary duplication concerns, management and academic malpractice. It is also clear that academic program reviews involve several participants with whom the potential for tension is high—the role of faculty and administrators within an institution and the role of system, coordinating, and state agencies external to the campus.

The previously cited work by Conrad and Wilson (1985) points out that we currently lack an informed basis on which to judge the merits of program review. They comment that "the stubborn fact is that not much is known about the effects of program review" (p. 65). On this same point, Skubal (1979) earlier noted that many institutions and states involved in program review did not know whether resources had been saved or how much money had been spent in conducting program reviews.

Institutional, multicampus-system, and state-agency–initiated program review may, in some cases, then, be built as much on a foundation of faith as fact when it comes to the effect of program reviews in achieving the purposes we earlier cited: the improvement of quality, the improvement of resource allocation and application, the demonstration of accountability, and the improvement of decisions related to program revision and/or termination.

Human interactions will inevitably have both positive and negative valences. Review and evaluation done without care and competence can damage community, demoralize personnel, and promote prejudicial and parochial views. With artistic and sensitive leadership at every level, however, academic program reviews can realize a renewing purpose. Whether the stimulus is internal or external to the campus, systematic program reviews challenge the campus—interrupting our inertia and diffidence and causing faculty and academic administrators to ask questions of purpose, or priority, of performance.

Throughout the book we have emphasized the interactions among each of these approaches to quality assurance. Barak and

Breier (1990) illustrate the contributions of a well-conceived system of program review to accreditation and to institutional planning. As to assessment and student outcomes, these writers comment: "A good starting point for integrating assessment data into the planning and budgeting process is to include them as a criterion for program review. Thus student outcome data become one measure of program effectiveness, which in turn is one criterion in a program review's data set" (Barak and Breier, 1990, p. 123). We commend this book as a useful resource for those campuses interested in developing a systematic approach to academic program review.

For those interested in enhancing their knowledge and understanding of program evaluation, we also recommend *Educational Evaluation* by Worthen and Sanders (1987). They offer a comprehensive and informing resource on different approaches to evaluation. For example, they classify contemporary models (they prefer the term *conception* to *model*) of evaluation into those that are objectives oriented, management oriented, consumer oriented, expertise oriented, adversary oriented, and naturalistic and participant oriented. The diversity of the philosophical and technical bases of these evaluation conceptions makes clear that program evaluation is not a totally rational exercise that unfolds by following simple and sequential steps but rather an activity complicated by ethical and political considerations. The concepts and illustrations offered in this helpful treatment will enhance the artistry and effectiveness of those responsible for the conduct of program reviews at the collegiate level.

Achievement of the renewal potential of academic program review will be enhanced if all parties to the process—whether internal to the campus or external—build on the following principles:

1. Reviews should be built on consensus agreements concerning evaluation criteria, standards, and model.
2. Reviews should reveal appropriate sensitivity to campus and program mission in selection of consultants and/or review panels.
3. Reviews should reflect a consensus among those involved in the review as to the decision purpose of the exercise.
4. Reviews should respect diversity of models for scholarship in

different fields, models that respect the many different avenues by which we search for and advance truth.

5. Reviews should furnish adequate advance preparation and on-site time for consultants and evaluators, with the realization that short visits cannot possibly bring consultants a totally adequate knowledge of the policy and personality history of a program or of the complex environment in which the program may exist.

6. Review results should be made a matter of public record and offer the programs and institutions being evaluated an opportunity for response.

SEVEN ⧉

College Outcomes:
The Test
of Results

Resources, reputation, results—our discussion of quality assurance approaches in American higher education has unfolded within a primary emphasis as suggested in these three words, though the simplicity there is overdrawn. The early standards of accrediting agencies, as outlined in Chapter Two, centered primarily on resources—faculty, library, financial, and so forth—though that chapter also pointed to the shift in emphasis to institutional effectiveness and student outcomes. And in Chapter Three, we noted that college reputations had not yet been fully linked to hard evidence on student growth.

This chapter explores college outcomes as primary indicators of both program and institutional quality. We will examine the history of outcomes assessment, take a look at several outcomes models, and then examine the decision issues that associate with this quality assurance approach.

The Emergence of Outcomes Assessment

The current emphasis on outcomes and questions of educational and managerial effectiveness in American higher education was predicted almost twenty years ago by Kenneth Mortimer (1972), who wrote in his monograph *Accountability in Higher Education* that "there will be more concern about the management of higher education and attempts to relate managerial efficiency to educational effectiveness" (p. 48). He also predicted the focus on results: "Accountability accentuates results—it aims squarely at what comes out of an educational system rather than what goes into it" (Mortimer, 1972, p. 6).

What exactly do we mean by the term *college outcomes*? Put simply and directly, college outcomes, at least in terms of student outcomes, center on student growth—on changes in knowledge, in skill, in attitudes, and in values. The question is whether there are differences in knowledge, skill, attitudes, and values from college entry to college exit. This is the "value-added" question of quality assurance.

Why the emphasis on outcomes? We explored some of those reasons in Chapter One. To reaffirm, we have this note from Stephen Spangehl (1987): "In industry after industry, we've discovered that we are not competitive, that other countries can make higher quality products more quickly and cheaply than we can. It should surprise no one that these concerns have spread to academe, where, for nearly a thousand years, we have organized ourselves on a pre-capitalist, pre-technological, pre-management science model" (p. 36).

As evidence of the decline in higher education quality, some critics point to declining test scores on a variety of standardized examinations. In his monograph on the standardized test scores of college graduates from 1964 to 1982, Clifford Adelman (1985) reports: "Of 23 examinations, performance declined on 15 (principally GRE subject area tests), remained stable on 4, and advanced on 4. The greatest decline occurred in subjects requiring high verbal skills. The performance and participation of U.S. students from different undergraduate majors appear to offer the most convincing explanation of observed changes. Students' majors in professional and occupational fields (the most rapidly growing group among both grantees and test takers) underperform all others" (Adelman, 1985, p. iii).

In a 1987 article appearing in *Change* magazine, New Jersey governor Thomas Kean wrote: "You are understandably attentive to your critics. What do they say? They say that higher education promises much and delivers too little. They say you are too expensive and inefficient. They say your graduates can't write clearly or think straight. And they say you dare not assess your work, evaluate your product, or validate your claims. The public wants you to prove the critics wrong. You can" (Kean, 1987, p. 11).

Here, by the way, is an interesting example of a case where a critic and a friend of higher education has an opportunity to take his own advice. In 1989, Governor Kean was appointed president of Drew University in New Jersey, where presumably he has the leadership opportunity to grapple with his own challenge to American higher education. This combination of attack and assurance describes the debate that swirls about outcomes today.

In a 1988 monograph entitled *Goals for Education: Challenge 2000*, the Southern Regional Education Board recommended that "the quality and effectiveness of all colleges and universities will be regularly assessed, with particular emphasis on the performance of undergraduate students" (p. 14).

In a thoughtful article appearing in the November/December 1989 issue of the *Journal of Higher Education*, Patrick Terenzini offered these reasons for the emergence of outcomes assessment: "Now that the costs of a college education are identifiable and measurable, important people (for example, legislators, parents, students) now want to know what the return is on their investments. What does one get out of a college education? The question forces a fundamental introspection on the part of both individual faculty members and institutions" (Terenzini, 1989, p. 645).

There can be little doubt that campuses have become more involved in assessment. In *Campus Trends, 1990*, published by the American Council on Higher Education, Elaine El-Khawas reports that eight of ten colleges and universities indicate that they are involved in some form of assessment. Do administrators believe that all this assessment will improve education? The results by institutional sector are revealing. More than six of ten community college administrators believe the results will prove helpful. However, only four of ten comprehensive college administrators and only three of ten doctoral university administrators believe that assessment will help improve undergraduate education.

Not everyone is convinced, obviously, that this goal is the right prescription or that we have a correct diagnosis. In an article appearing in the October 19, 1988, issue of the *Chronicle of Higher Education*, Jon Westling posed this question: "In short, assessment is based on a fundamental misdiagnosis of the malaise of American higher education. Does anyone really believe that the failure of colleges and universities to produce adequately educated young people is the consequence of our failure to develop precise instruments to measure what we are doing? Or that true education requires elaborate technical writers to evaluate its effectiveness?" (Westling, 1988, p. B1).

Another dissenting voice is Ernst Benjamin in the March/ April 1989 issue of *AGB Reports*. Benjamin accuses campus administrators of acquiescing to the current demand for accountability through assessment and suggests that this is one of the major reasons why faculties are often unhappy with campus administrators. Benjamin also holds the opinion that "measurement of student performance will not itself improve learning. In fact, it may inherently interfere with learning if standardized or intrusive measures shape teaching and curriculum" (p. 14). Thus, Benjamin highlights the limiting effects of "teaching to the test."

In the preface to his 1991 book *Assessment for Excellence*, Alexander Astin, one of the more thoughtful and thorough contributing scholars in this field, concludes that "although a great deal of assessment activity goes on in America's colleges and universities, much of it is of very little benefit to either students, faculty, administrators, or institutions. On the contrary, some of our assessment activities seem to conflict with our most basic education mission" (Astin, 1991, p. ix). This challenge of making our quality assurance efforts more penetrating and more "faculty friendly" to an institution is one that we will take up again in Chapters Nine and Ten.

Benjamin's comments can also perpetuate the perspective that faculty and academic administrators are adversaries rather than partners in the learning enterprise. We make no argument that the values and behaviors of some academic administrators offer unhappy evidence of the former rather than the latter. We emphasize, however, the power of partnership throughout this book.

What of trend and momentum? One of the better known national authorities on college outcomes and assessment, Peter Ewell, points out that assessment in higher education is not new. He cites early examples where assessment was directly tied to instruction and learning at the University of Chicago and in General College at the University of Minnesota; the early uses of the Graduate Record Examination (GRE), ACT, and SAT; and attempts such as the Pennsylvania General College Test Program in the late 1920s and early 1930s. Ewell suggests, however, that these assessments were intended primarily "to serve as an additional mechanism for gauging an individual student's mastery of a particular body of knowledge in order to provide guidance for future development" (Ewell, 1985a, p. 32). Early efforts, then, centered on the student as the unit of primary evaluative interest; contemporary efforts may center on curriculum, program, and institution.

What can we say about what is happening over the country in outcomes? A 1987 Education Commission of the States (ECS) survey furnished a summary view of state activity. Opening comments in the report state that "a year or two ago, only a handful of states had formal initiatives labeled 'assessment.' Now two-thirds do" (Boyer, Ewell, Finney, and Mingle, 1987, p. 1). Several states have mandated statewide testing programs, including Florida's College Level Academic Skills Test (CLAST), Georgia Regents' Rising Junior Examination, South Dakota's Higher Education Assessment Program, and New Jersey and Texas programs for basic skill assessment.

Current news on state activity related to assessment is available in *Assessment Update*—a newsletter on "Progress, Trends, and Practices in Higher Education," published by Jossey-Bass and edited by Trudy Banta. In the summer 1989 issue, Peter Ewell reported, for example, that the Virginia legislature had made assessment a permanent responsibility of the State Council of Higher Education for Virginia. In Colorado, institutional accountability plans are required by House Bill 1187 (Ewell, 1989). We explore state-level initiatives in quality assurance throughout the book; there can be little doubt that institutional management boards, state-level coordinating agencies, and legislatures are becoming more active partners in assessment and outcomes measurement and thus in quality assurance.

Some scholars of higher education are concerned that higher education assessment may take on the characteristics of assessment in elementary and secondary education. The University of California, Los Angeles scholar Eva Baker (1981) predicts: "To the extent that student assessment measures become widespread, I will predict that their original purposes will be transformed and that they will also drive out other indicators used to evaluate comprehensively the quality of higher education institutions. Simply look at precollegiate education as relevant history. Mandated large-scale testing occurred because the precollegiate system had no convincing information about its quality. No information was available to refute the claim that kids couldn't read and write, let alone do fractions and analyze Shakespeare" (Baker, 1981, p. 40).

Campus administrators and faculties are understandably anxious about and disquieted by this external interest. The fear is that the rush to testing will dampen the rich diversity of American higher education and encourage the fiction that colleges are another form of American factory whose product is a competent student. The important concern is whether outcomes assessment will constitute just another exercise in busywork that will cause a momentary ripple on the surface of higher education and pass on, leaving the depths undisturbed. Also of concern is whether campuses will discover instructional, learning, and renewal value in outcomes assessment—as claimed by some writers and scholars. D. W. Farmer (1988) places the issue nicely in these notes: "If faculty approach assessment as being divorced from learning and as simply being a bureaucratic hurdle for students to overcome, assessment will lose its credibility and be treated by faculty and students as busy work" (Farmer, 1988, p. 151). The jury is still out on this question and may remain out for a number of years. There are, however, encouraging models where institutions and their faculties have discovered that effective outcomes assessment exactly parallels good teaching, where the effectiveness of impact on student knowledge, skill, and attitudes and values can be enhanced by intervention in the instructional process.

There are also institutions on the other side of the fence, whose posture is described by Spangehl as follows: "Pitted against this rush to assess are a host of universities that have traditionally viewed their missions as more complex than simply turning out students who can outperform other schools' graduates on tests. Their philosophies, funding and budgetary structures, and organizational folkways are ill suited to assessment; they will be hostile to any attempt by a state board or accrediting agency to measure their worth on a simple minded, one dimensional scale" (Spangehl, 1987, p. 35).

The fascination of the profile is that one can find the same diversity of institutions taking the initiative on outcomes assessment: the small private liberal arts college, Alverno; the large doctoral university, the University of Tennessee; the comprehensive state university, Northeast Missouri State University; and the public community college, Miami-Dade Community College.

An advocate of the constructive promises of outcomes assessment, President James Daughdrill of Rhodes College in Memphis, wrote in the January 27, 1988, issue of the *Chronicle of Higher Education* that "asssessment is doing more for higher education than any other development in recent history" (p. 52). He offers two reasons for institutions such as his—the small private liberal arts colleges—to get involved. "First, assessment will enable them to find out whether what they're doing in the classroom is really working. Second, by having their own plans, they may escape the disastrous consequences of a national assessment program, which would subject all institutions—no matter how different—to the same standardized testing procedure" (p. 52). These are reasons for an offensive agenda in quality assurance for higher education. Let us turn now to exemplary work already in place.

Operational Definitions of College Outcomes

The term *assessment* historically implies more than one measurement or approach to evaluation. An assessment of college outcomes, then, requires that we acquire multiple evidences of those outcomes. First, however, we may need some common understanding of just what we mean by the term *outcomes*. Given the diversity of some

3,000 campuses over the United States—their missions, histories, and environments—we would be surprised to find a single model of college outcomes to fit all of these colleges. It is appropriate, however, to ask whether there are fundamental knowledges, skills, and attitudes/values that might associate with completion of the bachelor's degree, whether one is graduating from West Point, Oberlin, or the University of California, Los Angeles.

Writing in a 1985 paper, assessment and evaluation scholar Peter Ewell outlined a four-element model for college outcomes:

- Cognitive development: an assessment of general education and major field knowledges expected of the college graduate
- Skills development: an assessment of basic skills such as communication, critical thinking, and analytical skills
- Attitudinal development: an assessment of students' values and changes in those values
- Behavior after college: an assessment of student performance in work or further study after the first degree is received (1985a, pp. 32–36)

Ewell emphasizes the potential for enhancing the learning and instructional process via assessment of these four elements. Asking questions of ends inevitably forces us to focus on questions of beginnings. Questions of performance call us to questions of purpose.

For a more extensive model of college outcomes, we turn to Howard Bowen's earlier book-length treatise *Investment in Learning* (1978). Bowen opens his book with two comments that place us in an immediate tension: "Higher education has a clear responsibility to operate efficiently and to report its costs and results to the American people in ways that transcend the tired rhetoric of commencement speeches and slick brochures" (p. 22). This is an argument in favor of outcomes assessment. But then, Bowen reminds us that "Learning—like liberty, equality, love, friendship, charity, and spirituality—carries qualitative connotations that defy numerical measurement" (p. 24).

Bowen suggests a two-factor model or catalogue of college goals. Individual goals include these: cognitive learning, emotional and moral development, practical competence, direct satisfactions, and avoidance of negative outcomes. Societal goals embrace advancement of knowledge, discovery and encouragement, advancement of social welfare, and avoidance of negative outcomes (Bowen, 1978, pp. 31–59).

Because avoidance of negative outcomes is a concept not found in most other outcomes models, a brief word on Bowen's ideas may prove useful. He suggests that higher learning may produce men and women who are more informed, but they may apply their talents for both integrity and duplicity. Some outcomes of higher education may produce dissent rather than conformity, controversy rather than community. Whether a specific outcome is considered positive or negative may well depend on the values of those sitting in judgment, or on the timing or the circumstances involved. Bowen's cautions remind us of the arguments on the ethics of means and ends found in Saul Alinsky's volume *Rules for Radicals* (1971). Alinsky concludes, for example, that if America had dropped the atomic bomb on Japan immediately after Pearl Harbor, there would have been little ethical argument over the rightness of that decision.

In *Assessment for Excellence* (Astin, 1991), Alexander Astin presents a double-entry table for college outcomes classified by two types of outcomes and two types of data. Table 7.1 is taken from that presentation. Again, we are made to realize the complexity of collegiate outcomes. A further complexity may be added, as suggested by Astin, if we consider a third dimension of time. For example, we may want to assess student satisfaction with college during enrollment and immediately after graduation. Satisfaction with job and career is a longer interval measurement, which may or may not correlate with the earlier satisfaction variable.

One of the more comprehensive institutional models of college outcomes is the one developed at Alverno College. A small, private, liberal arts college, Alverno decided in the early 1970s to develop a competency-based liberal arts degree program. Faculty were involved in the definition of general goals, the identification of assessment techniques, and the development of validation methods for each of eight outcomes finally adopted: communication skill, analytical skill, problem-solving skill, facility in value judgment, facility in social interaction, understanding individual and environmental interactions, understanding world events, and re-

Table 7.1. A Taxonomy of Student Outcomes:
Type of Outcomes by Type of Data.

	Type of outcomes	
Type of data	Cognitive	Affective
Psychological	Subject-matter knowledge	Values
	Academic ability	Interests
	Critical thinking ability	Self-concept
	Basic learning skills	Attitudes
	Special aptitudes	Beliefs
	Academic achievement	Satisfaction with college
Behavioral	Degree attainment	Leadership
	Vocational achievement	Citizenship
	Awards or special recognition	Interpersonal relations
		Hobbies and avocations

Source: Reprinted with permission of Macmillan Publishing from p. 45, *Assessment for Excellence,* by Alexander W. Astin. Copyright © 1991 by the American Council on Education and Macmillan Publishing Company, a division of Macmillan, Inc.

sponsiveness to arts and esthetic awareness (Mentkowski and Doherty, 1984). Each of these eight outcomes or competencies is further segmented into attainment levels. For example, outcome seven, understanding world events, begins with the simple expectation of awareness of world events, moves to a knowledge of their historical and cultural antecedents, and then goes on to the expectation that the student will take a personal position on the issue.

It is obvious that these speak to more than cognitive outcomes. The strengths of the model are that it is specific to the educational goals of the institution, that it involves the allegiance of the faculty in development and implementation, and that it is directly linked to the curriculum and instructional processes of the institution.

An earlier developmental model for collegiate outcomes is one furnished by Arthur Chickering in his award-winning volume *Education and Identity* (1969). Chickering lists seven major "developmental vectors" for the intended outcomes of a college education:

- Achieving competence: intellectual, physical, social
- Managing emotions: increased awareness of emotions—aggres-

sive and sexual impulses—and learning effective modes of expression
- Becoming autonomous: achievement of independence and recognition of our interdependence
- Establishing identity: discovery of those experiences that resonate with our personality, development of purpose, and personal integrity
- Freeing interpersonal relationships: less anxiety and defensiveness and more tolerance and trust; development of friendships and love that transcend time, separation, and disagreement
- Clarifying purposes: development of direction for life and discovery of activity that furnishes a foundation of meaning
- Developing integrity: moving from rigid to the discovery of ethical choice, bringing behavior into consistency with values

Any collegiate educator looking at these potential outcomes quickly realizes the poverty of our measurement and assessment approaches if we are to be serious about determining whether we are successful in producing these outcomes in our students.

One of the earliest and most comprehensive approaches to the study of college outcomes was the work completed at the National Center for Higher Education Management Systems (NCHEMS), reported by Lenning and others (1977). A descriptive profile of the NCHEMS outcomes can be found in Exhibit 7.1.

An earlier report by NCHEMS researchers Sidney Micek and Robert Walhaus (1973) suggested a three-dimensional model concerned with college impact on students, college impact on graduates, and college impact on society. The time dimension is incorporated into the Micek and Walhaus work, which served as a predecessor to the more extensive model reported by Lenning, Lee, Micek, and Service.

Though most of these early scholars have long since departed NCHEMS, their research is counted as a pioneering effort in the United States, one that had a stimulus effect on both thought and action. The concern for outcomes remains active at NCHEMS today through the work of Peter Ewell, which is referenced throughout this and other chapters.

**Exhibit 7.1. The Major "Type-of-Outcome"
Category Names and Definitions.**

Economic Outcomes — Maintenance or change in economic characteristics and conditions of individuals, groups, organizations, and communities, such as, in economic access, in economic mobility and independence, in economic security, and in income and standard of living.

Human Characteristic Outcomes — Maintenance or change in human makeup and characteristics (other than knowledge and understanding) of individuals, groups, organizations, and communities, such as, aspirations, competence and skills, affective characteristics, perceptual characteristics, physical and physiological characteristics, personality and personal coping characteristics, recognition and certification, and social roles.

Knowledge, Technology, and Art Form Outcomes — Maintenance or change in the knowledge and understanding, technology, or the art forms and works possessed or mastered by individuals, groups, organizations, and communities, such as, discoveries and inventions, technical developments, syntheses and reformulations of knowledge, new schools of thought in art and work created in those new traditions, renovation of art works.

Resource and Service Provision Outcomes — Maintenance or change in the direct resources and services (other than those included above) provided to individuals, groups, organizations, and communities, such as, providing facilities, events, advisory assistance, analytic assistance, teaching, health care, and leadership.

Other Maintenance and Change Outcomes — Examples would be: maintenance or change in the format, arrangement, activity, or administrative operation of an organization or institution; maintenance or change in the asthetic/cultural level of the local community; maintenance or change in family or community activities, practices, and traditions.

Source: Lenning, Lee, Micek, and Service, 1977, p. 23.

Their work encourages the observation that, with any good idea or practice, effective quality assurance does not happen overnight. We are now two decades beyond this conceptual trailblazing at the National Center for Higher Education Management Systems. We are sure that many of these scholars must take pleasure in seeing the range of assessment and outcomes activity currently under way, as they reflect on their stimulus roles in producing the early points of this trend line. However, they were without that reinforcement in their early work; those who sow are not necessarily those who reap. Many of the more active and visible scholars cited in this chapter and others stand on the shoulders of those who built this pioneering foundation at NCHEMS.

Predating all of these outcome models are the taxonomies of educational objectives developed by Benjamin Bloom (1956). Three monographs outline taxonomies for cognitive, affective, and psychomotor objectives—knowing, valuing, and acting, matters of head, heart, and hand. To illustrate the nature of these, we briefly explore the taxonomy of cognitive objectives here. In this domain, Bloom and colleagues suggested a hierarchy of intellectual skills: knowledge, comprehension, application, analysis, synthesis, and evaluation.

Here is where knowledge enlivens the art form of instruction. For the amateur teacher, and for many who would not be classified as amateurs, teaching is simply a business of spooning out facts and figures; testing amounts to the regurgitation of those facts and figures; and this exchange defines the teaching-learning process. This, however, works on the most elementary level of educational practice.

Knowledge is defined as those activities that emphasize recall; the storing of information; and the later presentation of facts, terminology, trends, classification, or principles. For example, we may expect the student to learn the parts of speech, which is a primary level of educational objective.

Comprehension involves the understanding of what has been presented and encompasses the skills of interpretation, translation, and extrapolation. Here we may expect the student to take these parts of speech, his knowledge of their relationships, and the principles of good grammar and not only recall these definitions and relations but also construct sentences that reveal understanding.

Application emphasizes the ability to show understanding and application by putting ideas and concepts to work in solving problems. At this point, we ask students to write a basic business letter, a résumé, a short essay, and a book review.

Analysis emphasizes the ability to break problems and materials into constituent parts and relationships, for example, to distinguish fact from opinion. Here is a newspaper advertisement for a new product or a political advertisement. We want the student to write an analysis of the appeal or argument used in these materials.

Synthesis recognizes the abilities needed to take the parts of knowledge and put them together into a whole. One may know, for example, the parts of speech and be able to write and diagram a sentence. Synthesis involves putting together words, thoughts, and sentences into paragraphs and essays.

Evaluation is the ability to make judgments of merit or worth, to discriminate. Here we will have students evaluate an essay, using these criteria: grammatical correctness; effective use of supporting materials such as illustration, quotes, statistics, and logic or argument; and effectiveness of transition.

The Bloom taxonomy is a useful instrument. It not only makes us think about the levels and types of instructional goals and outcomes, but it also gives us a useful instrument for doing so. Finally, it furnishes an instrumental link to the final and perhaps most critical part of the teaching process—that of evaluating learning.

Since we have used the Bloom taxonomy to focus on the nature of teaching and learning, let us note in passing an informing and provocative book entitled *Open to Question* (Bateman, 1990). Bateman urges teachers to move past the "empty bucket" theory of dishing out content to the art of teaching by inquiry. His book is rich in conception and illustration. If, for example, we add to the ideas furnished by the Bloom taxonomy the developmental stages of learning advanced by Perry (1970) and illustrated by Bateman, we can begin to understand college teaching as something more than an amateur's occupation. Bateman's book is more than informing; it is fun. It also reveals the "discovery" pleasure enjoyed by those willing and equipped to ask good questions. Curiosity about purpose and performance thus can lead us to curiosity about the activities that link the two—the nature of teaching and learning.

We close this section on outcomes models with a citation not directly related to college outcomes per se but containing concepts worthy of our reflection. We have noted that the work of Benjamin Bloom enlarges our understanding of the nature of human abilities and levels of performance within each of the three major taxonomies that Bloom developed: cognitive, affective, and psychomotor.

An equally provocative work, and a current one, is the model of multiple intelligences developed by Howard Gardner and reported in *Frames of Mind* (1983). This paragraph in the early pages opens us to the limitations of single-factor views of intelligence:

> But what if one were to let one's imagination wander freely, to consider the wider range of performances that are valued throughout the world? Consider, for example, the twelve year old male puluwat in the Caroline Islands, who has been selected by his elders to learn how to be a master sailor. Under the tutelage of master navigators, he will learn to combine knowledge of sailing, stars, and geography so as to find his way around hundreds of islands. Consider the fifteen year old Iranian youth who has committed to heart the entire Koran and mastered the Arabic language. Now he is being sent to a holy city, to work closely for the next several years with an ayatollah, who will prepare him to be a teacher and a religious leader. Or, consider the fourteen year old adolescent in Paris, who has learned to program a computer and is beginning to compose works of music with the aid of a synthesizer.
>   . . . It should be equally clear that current methods of assessing intellect are not sufficiently well honed to allow assessment of an individual's potentials for achievements in navigating by the stars, mastering a foreign tongue, or composing with a computer [Gardner, 1983, p. 4].

The remainder of Gardner's book then centers on the empirical and experiential basis for the identification of six intelligences: linguistic, musical, logical-mathematical, spatial, bodily-kinesthetic, and personal intelligence.

A second contemporary work that opens up our curiosity on the nature of talent diversity and intelligence definition is Robert J. Sternberg's book *The Triarchic Mind* (1988). Sternberg offers a critique of Gardner's work, suggesting that intelligence be defined as the capacity for selecting new environments, adapting to new environments, and shaping our environments. On the basis of that definition, Sternberg argues that musical ability should not be considered an "intelligence," that a person can function quite adequately in most environments without musical ability. Sternberg also demolishes some of the more conventional and narrow notions of intelligence: to be quick is to be smart, to have a large vocabulary is to be smart, and to solve problems with a fixed strategy is to be smart. As an example, we take the case of the person who operates on the assumption about vocabulary and intelligence, who spends time memorizing from the dictionary—a person who knows many big words with little comprehension of their meaning or their application.

In summary, Sternberg offers the theory that there are three forms of intelligence: analytical skill, synthetic skill, and practical or applied skill. His work is helpful in distinguishing between problem solving that may occur in structured climates such as schools and colleges and the more complex climates of applied and practical settings.

In school and college, there is a tendency to compartmentalize problems so that they fit the framework of our discipline. There is also a tendency to suggest that every problem has a solution, which can be found at the back of the book. Finally, there is a tendency to teach about methods of inquiry independent of the personal, cultural, and ethical factors that often attend the pursuit of truth.

In the world of practice, problems often involve elements from many different fields of thought and impose agonizing choices that defy the black and white neatness of computer solutions. The pursuit of what is right—intellectually and ethically—may pit us against the power of popularity and the inertia of the status quo. The history of men and ideas makes clear that new ideas often make a bloody entrance, that they require a level of character and perseverance not always reflected in the simplicity of a grade point average.

As we engage questions related to the definition and measurement of student learning and development outcomes, we are led on unexpected and serendipitous learning journeys. When we ask questions of results, we are eventually moved to consider questions of beginnings (of intent) and style (of method). Thus, our efforts to assure quality in collegiate settings will be a journey in learning

and discovery. In any field of inquiry, there will be found interesting and illuminating interactions between knowledge and
technology, and we believe this learning bridge exists for our ventures in quality assurance as well.

What can we learn from the variety of these models for student outcomes? Among the primary fears of faculty is that governmental policymakers will impose a unitary model on higher
education, or that accrediting agencies might do so. As shown in
Chapter Two, the regional accrediting agencies have not thus far
insisted on common measures. They have, instead, held institutions
to a standard of effectiveness of their own election—but insisting
that the standard and the evidence be both public and measured
against the goals of the institution.

What of governmental decision makers? There are, of course,
some states that have insisted on common measures, for example,
the rising junior examination in Georgia and the CLAST program
in Florida. In a study of five states, however, Ewell and Boyer (1988)
reported: "Contrary to wide belief, we found state leaders more than
willing to listen to a range of local options in assessment—if intel-
ligently sold. Harder for state leaders and policy makers to accept
was institutional silence on the issue" (p. 47). To return to an earlier
theme, the absence of an offensive agenda concerning educational
effectiveness often leaves higher education on the defensive.

Assessment Issues

We will not attempt in this chapter to furnish an inventory of
current instruments available for assessing college outcomes. There
is a wide diversity of such institutional and commercial instruments—some in final form, such as the American College Testing
Program (ACT) Comp; some still in developmental or pilot stages,
such as the Educational Testing Service (ETS) Academic Profile, or
the ACT Collegiate Abilities Assessment Profile (CAAP); the College Base (Osterlind, 1989); some specific to states, such as the College Level Academic Skills Test (CLAST) in Florida; and some
specific to institutions, such as the Alverno Competency Assessment
efforts. Readers interested in an inventory of available instruments
are referred to excellent articles by Harris (1985), a report by John

Centra for the U.S. Office of Education (Centra, n.d.), and a mono-graph by Jacobi, Astin, and Ayala (1987). A more recent resource is the helpful book by Erwin (1991), *Assessing Student Learning and Development*, which offers specific guidance in such areas as iden-tifying student learning objectives, selecting assessment methods, collecting information, analyzing and evaluating information, and reporting and using assessment results.

What we want to accomplish in this section is to place before the reader some of the decision issues related to the design and development of a college outcomes assessment process.

Matching Assessment to Outcomes Definition

The most obvious question is whether a given assessment instru-ment or approach matches the outcomes desired and defined by the faculty of an institution. Given the diversity of outcomes models previously outlined, it is obvious that the transport of an instru-ment from one institution, such as Alverno College, to another, such as the University of Michigan, may be neither feasible nor desirable.

Because the involvement of faculty in the definition of out-comes is a tedious process, there is an unhappy tendency to let the instrument define the outcomes. This approach is like that of the neophyte graduate student who has found a useful questionnaire and goes in search of a research problem to which he or she can affix the questionnaire, rather than vice versa. Here is a commercial in-strument: It purports to assess writing skills, mathematical skill, and critical thinking skill; its cost is modest. Let us adopt it for the assessment of general education outcomes that will satisfy the board or the regional accrediting body, and so forth. Besides, it saves us the pain of having to think about what outcomes we really want in our students.

McMillan (1988) cautions us to remember the trade-offs that may be necessary if an institution decides to use a commercially published instrument: "Consequently, if an institution decides to use general measures like the GRE or National Teacher Examina-tions, there should be a recognized trade-off between the advantages of psychometric quality and institutional comparisons with the disadvantage of a possibly weak correspondence between the test content and content objectives of a curriculum. Without a sound judgment about content-related evidence, however, it may be easy to overlook this disadvantage and make invalid inferences about the results" (McMillan, 1988, p. 567).

Ensuring Validity and Reliability

Measurement theorists tell us that a good measurement instrument will have high validity and high reliability. There are technical definitions for both terms, but the basic idea is that a high-validity instrument measures what it purports to measure, and it does so consistently and with low error (reliability). As noted, locally developed instruments have the advantage of responding more directly to institutionally defined outcomes and decision needs, but this possible absence of validity and reliability information is a liability of locally developed instruments.

Selecting Score Options

Another decision concerns score options. An institution interested in a comparative standard of performance beyond the institution might be more effectively served by a nationally developed test that offers comparative score profiles from other institutions.

Other issues here turn on whether decision makers need data for individual or group decisions. If an assessment instrument is being used to make decisions about a program, a sampling of students and total scores may prove adequate. If, however, the decision affects the counseling, placement, or certification of a particular student, then item and scale scores are necessary. Criterion scores reflecting levels of proficiency and not just comparison with other students may be needed.

If, for example, an institution wants each of its students reaching the junior year to have mastered a certain level of mathematical proficiency before the student is admitted to a major field or upper-division study, then normative or comparative scores will be of less utility than criterion or proficiency scores. Many national companies are starting to recognize this decision need. The Academic Profile developed by ETS offers both a normative and a proficiency or criterion score.

Evaluating Time and Money Costs

Institutionally developed assessments will generally take large investments of time and money for design, field test, scoring, and administration. Only the institution can evaluate the trade-offs involved in local development vis-à-vis the selection of an "off-the-shelf" instrument whose costs are relatively modest and whose development already includes the extensive field tests necessary to produce an instrument of proven reliability and validity.

Another question of cost centers on who will pay for the assessment. Some institutions are sufficiently well funded that the institution or the state recognizes costs through the general fund budget. In other institutions, individual students will be asked to pay the cost, just as they are asked to pay breakage, laboratory, or graduation fees to help defer selected costs beyond basic instruction.

A part of the cost question turns on the amount of time needed for test administration. Assessments whose primary decision needs are for the evaluation of programs may allow testing strategies of greater simplicity and brevity than those whose decision purposes relate to individual students.

Terenzini (1989) examines the cost issue from a different perspective. He suggests that the costs of not assessing outcomes must be considered: "Important opportunities may be missed, including, for example, the chance to clarify institutional goals, to review and revise (or reconfirm the value of) existing curricular purposes and structures, and to examine the successes and failures of current policies and practices. The costs of rejecting or deferring assessment may be substantial, if difficult to calculate" (Terenzini, 1989, p. 654). The associated beneficial outcomes cited by Terenzini affirm the discovery potential of quality assurance, a point we earlier emphasized.

Isolating Sources of Bias

One of the major criticisms heard of standardized and commercial assessments in the United States is that they are insensitive to differences in experience, language, culture, and sex. Normative data, it is asserted, tend to encourage labeling and the maintenance of cultural prejudice. In a word, we are told that tests and assessments are often biased and discriminatory.

A complication on this issue turns on whether the bias is in the test, in the culture, or in the use of the test. Often, there are confounding effects. Flaugher (1974) defines these sources of test bias:

- Test content: Is the assessment insensitive to differences in experience or language?
- Test administration: Is the atmosphere of the assessment (the time, the place, the sex or race of the test administrator) or the attitude of the test taker (an expectation of confidence vis-à-vis an expectation of prejudice) a source of bias?
- Test use: Is one group systematically favored in selection, classification, or benefit?

Although the existence of bias on all these points can be demonstrated, curious and equally unfortunate scenarios are played out by those hoping to avoid bias. One of the authors knows of a state in which the validity of a state assessment used to make decisions about licensure of teachers was decided by whether the assessment yielded equal pass rates by race and sex.

As Diamond (1976) suggests, the options are to declare a moratorium on all tests until any and all biases can be rooted out, or to use assessments with discretion as we attempt to control for the three sources of bias identified. Diamond then indicates that "to declare a moratorium on the use of tests requires a corresponding but unlikely moratorium on decisions—employment decisions, selection decisions by colleges and universities, and decisions based on the evaluations of various educational and social programs" (1976, p. 35).

Diamond also observes that "if tests are guilty of reflecting middle class values, will the judgments of the middle class teachers, counselors, administrators, and employers necessarily be less so?" (1976, p. 35). Diamond's conclusion centers on the need for multiple sources of data on an individual, a principle whose importance is celebrated throughout each of these chapters. Finally, Diamond offers a series of steps designed to remove or alleviate sources of bias. They include a number of statistical and technical devices, the use of representative groups (to include minorities) in reviewing test content, and the application of advances in computer capabilities.

Examining Levels of Difficulty

Clifford Adelman (n.d.) suggests that it may be possible for an assessment instrument to be valid (a technical criterion we earlier explored) and still leave some question as to difficulty level. He uses in illustration an example taken from Northeast Missouri State University.

Northeast Missouri State University used the mathematics subtest of the National Teacher Examination (NTE) to test the mathematics knowledge of seniors graduating in teacher education. This subtest is a twenty-five-item test. Adelman reports that in the twenty-five items "virtually identical questions are asked of college seniors (on the NTE) and high school juniors (on the CEEB)" (p. 188). Adelman concludes: "The NTE/Math may be very valid— hence "appropriate"—for NMSU though one would hope that prospective high school math teachers also know trigonometry, intermediate algebra, solid geometry, elementary functions and analytic geometry, set theory, elementary statistics and probability" (Adelman, n.d. p. 188).

Adelman proceeds to explore several schemes for evaluating the difficulty level of assessments. For example, the Foreign Service Institute uses a scale comprising four criteria to rate language proficiency in terms of speaking, listening, reading, and writing. There are levels of performance on each of these four language skills in eleven intervals from "0" to "5." Adelman also suggests the Bloom taxonomy, previously discussed, as a means of judging difficulty level in intellectual tasks.

A correlate problem of assessment difficulty levels is described by Jacobi, Astin, and Ayala (1987) as "the likelihood that students will bottom out on a pretest or top out on the posttest" (p. 35). If a test is too difficult, scores may show little variance, and there is a concomitant danger that students may begin academic careers with anxiety and frustration in trying to deal with an assessment that is well beyond their capacity. And, as the authors suggest, "these negative effects may be particularly acute when such tests are administered to incoming freshmen, many of whom are already uncertain about their ability to succeed in the new more demanding college environment" (p. 35).

Reconciling Value-Added Issues

In knowing whether its instructional program has made a difference in student knowledge, skill, or attitude/value, an institution is interested in the "value-added" question. There are, however, lively debates on the difficulties in developing adequate value-added assessments.

Among these issues are those that reveal that changes in student performance can often be assigned to variables outside the instructional process. Here are examples.

- *Maturation:* Did the improvement in performance occur simply by virtue of student maturation rather than the instructional intervention?
- *Other experience:* Can improvement on a particular set of questions or assessment experiences be more properly assigned to an extracurricular experience (for example, foreign travel, summer camp, computer gaming, and so on) rather than instruction?
- *Pygmalion effect:* Do the expectations of those making judgments bias the actual performance or perception and evaluation of performance?
- *Regression effect:* Does the statistical tendency for low scores to increase and high scores to regress affect the observed change in scores in value-added exercises.

Readers interested in one of the more lively debates centered on value-added assessment can refer to two articles appearing in the bulletin of the American Association for Higher Education. Jonathan Warren (1984) fires the first shot in an article entitled "The Blind Alley of Value-Added," opening with these notes: "In the abstract, the logic of value-added gives it great appeal. In practice,

I'll argue, it seldom leads anywhere. Its results are often trivial, difficult to make sense of, and peripheral to most instructional purposes" (Warren, 1984, p. 10). Warren refers to value-added as the reigning gospel of contemporary higher education assessment. In a follow-up article entitled "The Value-Added Debate . . . Continued," Alexander Astin (1984) responds to Warren with these criticisms: "Value-added assessment, as Warren suggests, is not a panacea to be applied mechanistically or insensitively in every situation. But my experience has been that institutions are smarter than Warren gives them credit for. A far greater danger is that which Warren's position itself exemplifies: of trivializing a powerful concept to the point that institutions are unwilling to experiment with developmental outcomes assessments of *any* kind" (pp. 11–13).

Finally, Leonard Baird (n.d.) warns us about the limitations of value-added. After touching on some of the issues already outlined in this discussion, Baird concludes that "perhaps the greatest practical problem with assessing gain on a common criterion is that the method allows (and in some cases may encourage) invidious comparisons" (p. 213). He is concerned with comparison of average gain scores across disciplines, colleges, and institutions.

These concerns bring us back to questions of financial support levels and ultimately, as Baird suggests, "lead an institution to lose sight of its educational purpose" (p. 214). On that point, let us now examine an assessment issue that may prove fundamental to all others.

Focusing on Decision Purposes of Outcomes Assessment

How exactly do we intend to use assessment data? Essentially, we face two decision domains—that of the individual student and that of the program or institution—and in each of these two domains are two additional decision applications:

Student Decisions	*Program Decisions*
Counsel or place	Accept or improve
Certify	Retain or terminate

Readers are referred to Millman's (n.d.) informing discussion on decision purposes. Millman clusters the assessment decision purposes, for example, under the following: placement decisions, certification decisions, course and program evaluation decisions, and institutional evaluation decisions. Two other reports that will prove useful to those interested in identifying and improving campus decision utility of outcome results are those prepared by Peter Ewell and published by the National Center for Higher Education Management Systems (1985b). In both volumes, entitled "Using Student Outcomes Information in Program Planning and Decision Making," Ewell (1985b) outlines five lessons:

- "Lesson One: Information about student outcomes is generally available on campus if you look for it—but rarely in the form you want it" (p. 34).
- "Lesson Two: Address your data utilization effort to a particular commonly recognized issue or problem" (p. 35).
- "Lesson Three: Involve as many kinds of people from as many parts of the campus as possible" (p. 36).
- "Lesson Four: Efforts to utilize outcome information are often positively influenced by external forces and individuals" (p. 37).
- "Lesson Five: When raising questions about student outcomes, be prepared for discussions to turn eventually to broad issues of institutional mission and effectiveness" (p. 38).

In more recent work (1988), Ewell furnishes an informing and thorough treatment of three themes: the identification and assessment of college outcomes; the attribution of outcomes, or linking outcomes to educational experiences; and valuation, or deciding what the results mean and to whom they apply. In a concluding section of this excellent paper, Ewell engages the decision question of "getting there: using outcomes information as a change agent" (p. 85). His analysis of institutional attempts to make more effective decision use of outcomes and assessment information provides a sobering but useful counterpoint to Astin's note, cited earlier, that much of the current assessment is having little impact. Ewell's paper makes clear that many institutions are struggling with the decision application issues. Ewell closes his paper with a comment on what he calls the classic academic dilemma: the requirement to know everything before attempting anything. He then emphasizes a point that we salute throughout this book: the call to act on what we already know.

Let us cite a really simple example of how quality assurance ventures can begin to have an impact on institutional policy. A large research university opened an inquiry on how it could more effectively measure the results of its required general education curriculum. The question of how to assess the outcomes of the general education sequence eventually led the faculty-and-staff task force back to the university catalogue to see what educational goals and rationale had been offered to support the forty-eight-semester-hour requirement in English; mathematics; and discipline clusters in the humanities, social sciences, sciences, and health and physical education. Did they find there an educational rationale that made sense to students—such as developing skill in written and oral communication, facility in numerical analysis, and acquaintance with modes of thought by which we advance on truth? No. What they did find was a single lead sentence indicating that the purpose of the general education curriculum was to "facilitate transfer" of credits among institutions in the system. The task force concluded that this was an empty and inadequate rationale for the university faculty to offer its students, and they set about fashioning a more meaningful educational preamble.

One might argue that this result is of small moment. It is, however, an improvement that might not have been made had the university been about business as usual. We have already given other examples, in Chapter One as an instance, in which the simplest attention to quality assurance might have assisted in preventing educational neglect and abuse of student potential. We certainly encourage the kinds of conceptual and action research outlined by Ewell in his 1988 paper, but we are impatient with those who want to stand around wringing their conceptual hands. Improved impact for our students and our institutions is possible with the knowledge we have at hand now.

Evaluating Other Assessment Options

An inclination obvious in previous commentary on assessment issues is that some of these concerns relate to more conventional assessment approaches—predominantly those of the paper-and-pencil variety. However, many institutions are trying more imaginative models, among them senior capstone courses, portfolio assessment, assessment centers, external examiners, connoisseurship, and disguised observers.

For example, at King's College each student participates in a capstone course designed to strengthen and ultimately assess a student's transfer of liberal arts skills to his or her major field (Paskow, 1988). Colleges participating in the Appalachian College Assessment Consortium have developed a senior exit interview process in which a faculty member conducts an interview with a group of three students, each with a different major, using questions to draw on all areas of their general education. These interviews serve the dual purpose of obtaining student perceptions of their institution and their experience there and their judgment of its quality (Paskow, 1988).

Lehman College of the City University of New York evaluates student portfolios, which consist of essays written in different courses over a wide range of subjects. This assessment procedure was developed to ascertain the effectiveness of a recently instituted revised general education curriculum. Lehman is using a control group of students to evaluate this program (Paskow, 1988).

Some campuses are using "assessment center" approaches. An example is the teacher education program at the Indiana University of Pennsylvania, where a series of simulations and other activities test student teaching mastery and simultaneously develop additional competence. Activities in the teacher education assessment center call for students to analyze and evaluate short video tapes of classroom episodes, to prepare a short lesson plan and present the lesson, to organize a district-wide education, and to plan an educational museum exhibit (Paskow, 1988).

Other colleges are using the "external examiner" approach. Alverno College calls upon professionals external to the college to serve as volunteer assessors. Another example is at Berea College, which uses external faculty examiners to assess learning in the students' major fields, via written and oral examinations given by these external faculty (Paskow, 1988).

One of the more creative concepts being applied to assessment of academic programs is that of Eisner's connoisseurship model at the University of Nebraska, Lincoln, where program review involves a team that includes students and faculty—both external to the department and to the university. Indeed, Eisner's book (1985a) *The Act of Educational Evaluation* furnishes an excellent reason for the utilization of multiple approaches to evaluation: "To fish for trout in a stream using bait designed to catch salmon and to conclude from our failed efforts that no trout are there, is to draw what might very well be an erroneous conclusion. Our nets define what we shall catch. If there is one message I would like to convey in this book it is the desirability of weaving many types of nets" (Eisner, 1985a, p. 7).

Now, finally, we mention one other approach to program evaluation, just to illustrate that the assessment of collegiate outcomes furnishes a splendid opportunity to utilize our imagination. Several years ago, one of the authors was involved with pilot assessment projects in a variety of colleges in Tennessee (Bogue and Brown, 1982). The College of Pharmacy at the University of Tennessee Center for Health Sciences decided to evaluate some of their recent graduates with a "disguised observer" approach in which graduate pharmacy students posed as customers. The purposes of the evaluation were to ascertain whether practicing pharmacists could recognize customer description of symptoms that needed referral to physicians, to ascertain the accuracy of prescription fillings, and to ascertain pharmacists' ability to spot fraudulent prescriptions.

Defining the Outcome

Earlier we noted that any attempt to evaluate performance inevitably brings up questions of purpose. Asking "how good a job are we doing?" certainly requires that we have some notion of "what did we hope to achieve?" The decision challenge for American higher education is nicely placed by L. J. Benezet as follows: "What is to be learned in college is judged differently according to whether one sees college as a place to absorb man's heritage of knowledge and culture, or to sharpen already superior intellectual talents, or to prepare for a graduate profession, or to become a discoverer of new knowledge or creator of new arts forms, or to mature as a thinking, feeling, and rationally acting person, or to relate better to other human beings, or to start on any of a hundred different careers requiring skills beyond the high school, or to learn what needs to be learned in order to attack the most urgent problems of mankind" (Benezet, 1973, p. 11). Obviously, some choice is necessary, because most colleges and universities will not find it possible or even desirable to assess all possible outcomes—especially the longer-range and social/economic outcomes suggested by some of the models previously outlined.

If, for example, we elect to restrict our focus to student outcomes, we are still left with a formidable set of questions. Let us for the moment say that we want to elect the apparent simplicity of the first three elements of Peter Ewell's model and center our assessment on student knowledge, skills, and values/attitudes. Let us look at the questions that might follow.

Knowledge

Perhaps we might decide early that we should assess student knowledge in both general education and the major field. But exactly what model of "general education" do we select? Most general education curricular requirements are implicit in what we might call a "mode-of-thought" model. That is, asking our students to sample courses in a variety of disciplines—humanities, science, and so on— we apparently are asking that they know something about how humans advance in their search for the truth. Certainly, it is a highly legitimate general education goal for our students to take an epistemological journey—to know that truth may emerge from the objectivity of science, the heat of adversarial arguments, the rationality of analysis, the interpretative and passionate moments of art and music, the revelatory moments of literature and religion, and the quiet moments of history.

There are other models to choose from, however. Instead of a "mode-of-thought" model for general education, we might select one with a cultural/historical bent. The historian Will Durant, for example, says that if we hope to understand the flow of history and culture, we must examine the ways in which society deals with economics, education, religion, art forms, and political/governance issues (1954). One might also choose, for example, to build a general education model on the multiple intelligences outlined by Gardner or Sternberg. This question leads to yet another decision challenge. How might we elect to distinguish between knowledge and skill?

Skill

Presumably, we move here from cognitive acquisition to acting, from knowing to doing. But precisely what skills do we wish our students to acquire? Which of the following skills might fit within our outcomes model: communication—oral and written, analytic/problem-solving, judgment/evaluative, interpersonal, creative/artistic, psychomotor/physical? There are some who say that contemporary education neglects the education of the intuition. See, for example, Robert Ornstein's important work *The Psychology of Consciousness* (1972). Western intellectual traditions tend to be verbal/intellectual in their emphasis. The reflective and contemplative traditions of the Orient offer realities that are often disturbing to the Western mind, yet provoking to our curiosity as well. Might the education of what is described as intuition find its way into our general education skill considerations? Here we find ourselves moving into the realm of philosophy and religion, which bridges nicely to our third element, that of values.

Values and Attitudes

Nothing is plainer in its truth than that many college graduates place themselves, their customers and clients, and their organizations and institutions in harm's way, not because of technical incompetence but because graduates abandon their integrity. No college or university would subscribe to the notion that they sought to nurture no values in the education of their graduates. Well, then, what are the values we wish to impart to our graduates and what role do assessment and outcomes play in the ethical makeup of our students? And how many colleges are explicit about the values they hope to impart and the methods used to develop these values?

There are surely some fundamental values we can salute—dignity, courage, responsibility, and so forth. In one of the more impressive displays of commitment, the board of regents for the State University System of Florida adopted a set of fifteen values in their master plan for 1988–1989 through 1992–1993. We take the liberty of reproducing them here in their entirety:

- Personal integrity that is rooted in respect for truth and love of learning
- A sense of duty of self, family, and the larger community
- Self-esteem rooted in the quest for the achievement of one's potential
- Respect for the rights of all persons regardless of their race, religion, nationality, sex and age, physical condition, or mental state
- The courage to express one's convictions, and recognition of the rights of others to hold and express differing views
- The capacity to make discriminating judgments among competing opinions
- A sense of, and commitment to, justice, rectitude, and fair play
- Understanding, sympathy, concern, and compassion for others
- A sense of discipline and pride in one's work; respect for the achievements of others
- Respect for one's property and the property of others, including public property
- An understanding of, and appreciation for, other cultures and traditions
- A willingness to perform the obligations of citizenship, including the right to vote and the obligation to cast an informed ballot, jury service, participation in government and the rule of law
- Civility, including congenial relations between men and women
- A commitment to academic freedom as a safeguard essential to the purposes of the university and to the welfare of those who work within it

- The courage to oppose the use of substances which impair one's judgment or one's health [State University System of Florida . . . , 1988, pp. 10, 12].

We might note that this discussion of values and attitudes in the assessment of outcomes and the quest for quality offers a perspective in some contrast to the quality definition assigned to Mayhew, Ford, and Hubbard (1990) in Chapter One. It may be remembered that Mayhew and his coauthors were not enthusiastic that colleges could have a significant impact on student values and attitudes.

Addressing the question of what outcomes to assess, then, can be an exercise of some majesty. The quest for quality offers a journey of philosophical and technical complexity. It is, however, a journey with significant learning potential as well.

Linking Knowledge and Practice

Before we issue a concluding note about the renewing impact of outcomes assessment, we provide this reflection about promoting public confidence in higher education. As suggested in our opening chapter, collegiate educators need not believe that quality assurance for colleges is more complex than that for corporations. Both are multifactor enterprises where the evidence can and should be varied. The nature of a performance guarantee in our colleges and universities also is no more complex than in many other professional fields. Indeed, there are few clinical professions whose history will not reveal imperfect and inadequate links between knowledge and practice—and equally serious questions about links between expenditures and outcomes. We think of medicine and law as two examples.

It has been scarcely a hundred years since the largest medical issue facing the nation of France was how to import several million leeches when the domestic supply was exhausted. Quinine was used in the treatment of malaria, successfully so, long before we understood the causal relations involved. There is some question as to whether future perspective might make some of today's surgeries—

tonsillectomies, radical mastectomies, and heart by-pass surgery—
look rather barbaric.

As physician-researcher-author Lewis Thomas recounts in
The Youngest Science: Notes of a Medicine Watcher (1983), the
medical literature of the turn of the century makes horrifying reading today: "Paper after learned paper recounts the benefits of bleed-
ing, cupping, violent purging, the raising of blisters by vesicant
ointments, the immersion of the body in either ice water or intol-
erably hot water, endless list of botanical abstracts cooked up and
mixed together under the influence of nothing more than pure
whim and all these things were drilled into the heads of medical
students" (Thomas, 1983, p. 19). Thomas reports that as late as the
middle of 1930 "we didn't know much that was really useful, that
we could do nothing to change the course of the great majority of
the diseases we were so busy analyzing, that medicine, for all its
facade as a learned profession, was in real life a profoundly ignorant
occupation" (p. 29). The scientific base of the art of medicine is for
the most part a development of the past fifty years.

Even now, with all the scientific and technical advances of
modern medicine, the philosophy and values of the contemporary
practitioner continue to have a powerful impact on the health and
well-being of patients. Consider the practice of medicine represented in the following illustrations shared recently by a physician
friend. An elderly man had been operated on by an orthopedic surgeon for a fractured hip. Following the surgery, the patient failed
to regain consciousness and remained in a comatose state. Given the
patient's age, the surgeon and one other attending physician were
not optimistic about his recovery. However, friends of the patient
asked a physician friend to come by and look in on him. His diagnosis was that the man had contracted pneumonia with attendant
high fever causing the comatose state, apparently not an unusual
matter in older patients. Treatment for the high fever brought the
patient back to consciousness in short order, producing what appeared to be a miracle in the eyes of the patient's family. In the first
diagnosis, the narrowness of the surgeon's interest prevented him
from seeing other options, whereas science and art were both at
work in the second, more constructive, one.

As for the profession of law, we were well into the latter half of this century before the poor of this nation stood before the bar with a court-appointed attorney to represent them. It took a prisoner in a Florida penitentiary—see *Gideon's Trumpet* (Lewis, 1964)—to bring about that change. If we are to break the logjam in today's courts or lighten the weight of frivolous and unnecessary lawsuits, the probabilities are that someone other than a lawyer will be the author of ideas to achieve those changes.

It took farmers twenty-five years to accept hybrid corn and equally as long to accept other empirical and scientific principles concerning the raising of other crops. The distance between the activities of yesterday and recent advances in catfish and crayfish farming, for example, is long indeed. Developing an educated human being is far more complex than developing a better breed of corn or catfish.

In his informing book entitled *Knowing and Acting: An Invitation to Philosophy*, Stephen Toulmin (1976) concludes with this note: "Rather than prolong this survey any further, therefore, let me simply invite you to put this book aside, face the philosophical problems that you find most perplexing in your own mind and begin tackling them for yourself, and in your own ways" (Toulmin, 1976, p. 310). Those collegiate educators interested only in armchair philosophy, in a wringing of hands over the liabilities and limitations of collegiate outcomes assessment, will surely have a more restricted and less advantageous journey of learning than those who are willing to act on the possible while awaiting perfection.

In a word, our potential for understanding and improving our impact on our students is not enhanced by passive and argumentative modes of thought *alone*. We develop no muscles as spectators; the harnessing of action and reflection is the beginning of discovery, and adventure in learning. We will languish in both intellectual and emotional poverty, as will our students, if we are unwilling to pose and answer the question: "What has been our impact on our students and how do we know?"

Part Two

Enhancing Quality

EIGHT 🐟

Forming Partnerships for Quality Enhancement

In earlier chapters we offered a glimpse into the emerging role of the state in quality assurance and enhancement—in outcomes assessment and academic program reviews, for example. The more active participation of state governing boards, coordinating agencies, and legislative and executive bodies on questions of collegiate quality is clearly a trend of the past twenty to twenty-five years. If we were to summarize the nature of that trend, we might do so with three words: equity, effectiveness, and excellence.

Most states adopted a formula funding approach for their colleges and universities in the 1960s. Funding formulas were designed to promote *equity* of resource allocation by awarding funds based most often on a double-entry enrollment matrix by program level and program field. In the next stage of development, states began to add incremental funding for special programs and quality efforts, emphasizing *effectiveness*. The performance funding project begun in Tennessee during the late 1970s fits this mode (Bogue and Troutt, 1980).

In the last decade, states have taken a more proactive role in both quality assurance and enhancement. They have adopted policies that encourage and require institutions to become more aggressive in quality assurance. Many states have gone beyond quality assurance to quality enhancement, fashioning an array of funding incentive and policy efforts designed to emphasize *excellence*. These initiatives include endowed chair programs, program enhancement grants, equipment endowment programs, and research enhancement programs.

Consider this evidence of state incentive actions, in a report of the Forum for College and University Governance entitled *State Incentive Funding: Leveraging Quality* (1990). A research effort of the National Center for Postsecondary Governance and Finance, this particular report furnishes clear evidence on the extent to which states have moved into incentive funding. The report reveals that states have supported a variety of categorical, competitive, and mixed category programs for a total of approximately $1.25 billion over the decade of the 1980s.

The purpose of this chapter is to offer the reader a perspective on contemporary policy and trends in quality assurance and quality enhancement at the state level—illustrating a uniquely American partnership between campus and state. Readers interested in a helpful analysis on the nature of the partnership between higher education and state government will find Edward Hines's monograph (1988) on that theme informative. Encouragement or intervention: What is the most effective form of that partnership when it comes to governance, funding, economic development, quality assurance? A productive partnership is one in which campus and state join their strengths in seeking mutual goals.

As we examine this trend of state-level involvement on questions of quality assurance and enhancement, we will see two familiar themes emerge. First there is the continuing tension of identifying appropriate minimal performance standards—in general education, for example—while promoting diversity in institutional mission. We will note a variety of state approaches that range from direct statutory requirement for assessment and quality assurance activity to more permissive policies that allow considerable discretion to campuses. A second theme concerns two different goals of quality assurance and enhancement efforts—goals that are announced by the words "assurance" and "enhancement." We will see state policies that center heavily on the improvement or enhancement goal while others focus on the accountability or assurance goal. Two different motive forces, then, drive assessment and quality assurance policies and programs: the internal need for improvement and the external need for accountability.

In slightly oversimplified terms, then, it is possible to conceptualize state programs in a two-by-two matrix built on style and motive, as in Table 8.1. And, as the previously cited report from the University of Maryland Center for Postsecondary Governance and Finance (Forum for College and University Governance, 1990) suggests, the incentive programs can be further classified into categorical grants, competitive grants, and mixed models. We will give examples of the state programs in the table above as the chapter unfolds.

The majority of states now require some campus assessment of student learning outcomes. Beyond these assessment and quality assurance initiatives, many states have implemented financial incentive programs that embrace the following approaches:

- Eminent scholars/endowed chairs
- Centers of excellence/program recognition and enhancement
- Equipment and capital trust funds/scientific and computing equipment enhancement funds
- Grant programs for program/curricular innovations
- Research and public service enhancements
- Library enhancement
- Economic development
- Faculty recognition programs

Table 8.1. Style and Motive in State Programs.

| | Program motive | |
Program style	Quality assurance	Quality enhancement
Regulatory	Maryland—Performance Accountability Plan	South Carolina—Cutting-Edge Program
Incentive	Tennessee—Performance Funding Project	Louisiana—Endowed Chairs/Professors

We begin with the most fundamental policy area, that of outcomes assessment.

Performance Accountability—The State Role

An interesting and informing opening to this discussion on the extent of state-level initiative in assessment and performance accountability can be found in a 1990 paper prepared for presentation to the Education Commission of the States by Peter Ewell. In this paper, Ewell said that "today, the majority of assessment activities occurring at American colleges and universities is due to state initiatives" (p. 1). To back up that opinion, Ewell cited a Fall 1989 survey indicating that over three-fourths of the states reported some student assessment planned or in place.

Ewell pointed out, however, that this state-level conversation on, and interest in, assessment and accountability should not be seen as "a rhetoric of disinvestment" (1990a, p. 4). Indeed, he suggested that an enhanced demonstration of performance accountability is the key to further increments in state-level funding. Moreover, Ewell later noted that information on performance results might produce a greater readiness for states to grant additional management flexibility.

Now let us examine what some states have been doing to promote performance accountability among colleges and universities. State initiatives range all the way from statutory requirements for basic skill mastery, as in the Texas Academic Skills Program (TASP) to Florida's College Level Academic Skills Test (CLAST), which operates at lower-division or sophomore level. We cannot completely outline these various state initiatives; however, we can furnish some perspective on the diversity of those policy initiatives by examining four states.

Sections 11-303 through 11-307 of the Annotated Code of Maryland (1989) require each college in Maryland to prepare a performance accountability plan. The code makes provision for relating this plan to campus mission but, as specified in Section 11-305 (abstracted in Exhibit 8.1), requires the campus to present evidence of performance on a variety of indicators: student academic performance, student retention and graduation, and regional and profes-

Exhibit 8.1. Content of Maryland Accountability Plan
Section 11-305.

Performance accountability plans developed under this subtitle shall:

1. Be based on the institutional mission statement and shall include a statement of the outcomes which each institution expects to achieve;
2. Include multi-year studies which shall include quantifiable indices of student academic performance and development including graduation and retention rates and the results of academic program reviews;
3. Identify institutional performance objectives appropriate to the mission of the institution in addition to those related to student learning and include reports based on regional and professional accreditation and certification;
4. In the case of senior public higher education institutions, designate a set of peer institutions to which the institution's performance will be compared; and
5. Make provision for improvements, as needed, as a result of the performance accountability report. (1988, ch. 246 < 2.)

Source: Annotated Code of Maryland: Education, 1989, p. 271.

sional accreditation. The code also requires the identification of peer institutions, a report each year, and improvement action to be taken as a result of the performance accountability report.

The Texas Charter for Public Higher Education, adopted in 1987, requires the Texas Higher Education Coordinating Board to develop a multifactor program of college funding that includes base, incentive, special initiative, and research and technology funding. Exhibit 8.2 shows the variety of campus efforts to be recognized through the incentive funding program. Note the inclusion of student performance in general education and specialized fields or majors.

Some states are obviously using the requirement of law to move campuses into assessment and accountability planning; other states have created an accountability stimulus via financial policy. Two examples are Tennessee and New Jersey. Work on the Tennessee Performance Funding Project was begun in Fall of 1974 when one of the authors became an American Council Fellow with the Tennessee Higher Education Commission, with responsibility to design, develop, and direct this project. The purpose was to explore the feasibility of allocating some portion of state funds on a perfor-

Exhibit 8.2. Texas Charter for Public Higher Education.

Incentive Funding shall be established to reward institutions achieving specific goals, including but not limited to:

1. Achievement of minority recruitment and retention goals while keeping standards high;
2. Attainment of specified graduation rates while keeping standards high;
3. Demonstrated commitment to liberal arts core curriculum;
4. Demonstrated commitment to continuing education programs;
5. Improvements in energy conservation;
6. Improvements in use of campus buildings;
7. Demonstrated commitment to renovation and maintenance of existing facilities;
8. Development of articulation arrangements;
9. Accreditation of a specified proportion of eligible academic programs;
10. *Assessment of the performance of graduates as a measure of general education outcomes (for example, assessing performance of a sampling of graduates on an appropriate standardized test);*
11. *Assessment of the performance of graduates on a measure of specialized field outcomes (for example, assessing performance of a sampling of graduates on professional licensing examinations);*
12. Evaluation of instructional programs through a survey of students, recent alumni and the community/employers;
13. Peer evaluation of academic and research programs by scholars from other institutions on a continuing, systematic basis; and
14. Attainment of, or progress toward, academic goals established by the institution in its long-range plan.

Source: Texas Higher Education Coordinating Board, 1987, p. 10.

mance criterion rather than an enrollment criterion. Motives for the project included the desire to encourage campus initiative on performance accountability rather than to have this accountability legislatively imposed or mandated. The complete story is told in the project's final report (Bogue and Troutt, 1980) and in a shorter journal version appearing in the *Harvard Business Review* (Bogue and Brown, 1982).

The project involved the acquisition of $500,000 in grant funds from federal and private foundations, the use of campus-based pilot projects, and the use of both state and national advisory panels comprising faculty, state political leaders, and national experts in higher education leadership and finance. Originally, campuses could earn up to 2 percent additional dollars on their base budget recommendation, dependent upon their record on five performance variables:

1. Percentage of accreditable programs that were accredited
2. Performance of students and programs in major fields (including licensure exam performance, exit exams in major fields, and external review of graduate programs)
3. Performance of students on measures of general education
4. Alumni satisfaction indices
5. Corrective policy and practice steps taken as a result of performance improvements identified above

In addition, campuses could earn additional performance credits by developing and piloting new assessment instruments.

This policy was adopted in Tennessee in 1979, following a five-year pilot and developmental effort in which campus and state political involvements were cultivated to ensure its operational acceptance. The policy has now been in operation for over twelve years, and the percent of funding dedicated to the performance funding feature of the Tennessee formula has grown from 2 percent during the first year to 5.45 percent.

The College Outcomes Evaluation Program (COEP) in New Jersey represents a major step taken in performance accountability by the New Jersey Board of Higher Education. The report of the committee on COEP contained ten recommendations, as outlined in Exhibit 8.3 (Advisory Committee to the College Outcomes Evaluation Program, 1987). The board is now moving to implement these, with special assessment emphasis on entry-level basic skills (college readiness skills) and college outcomes at the sophomore level (general education outcomes).

In a slightly more permissive mode, the State University of New York System (SUNY) is beginning to encourage its campuses in assessment. A recent address by provost Joseph Burke (n.d.) of SUNY suggests a set of principles of undergraduate assessment for the SUNY system, which are shown in Exhibit 8.4 and are worthy of review.

Exhibit 8.3. Recommendations on College Outcomes
Evaluation in New Jersey.

---

1. A common statewide assessment of general intellectual skills should be developed for use by each institution.
2. Each institution should assess the specific outcomes of its general education program.
3. Faculty in each program, department, or discipline should assess students' learning in each major course of study prior to graduation.
4. Student development should be assessed at each institution using common statewide definitions for each of the following indicators:

   - Retention rates
   - Program completion (including graduation) rates
   - Grade point averages
   - Credit completion ratios
   - Licensure/certification exam results
   - Post-collegiate activities, including:

        job/career information
        further education
        community/professional involvement

5. Each institution should assess both the personal development of its students and the degree of their satisfaction/involvement with their institutions.
6. Each institution should assess the outcomes of its efforts in the areas of research, scholarship, and creative expression.
7. Using common statewide definitions, each institution should assess its success in providing access and meeting the human resource needs of its population, as well as appraising its economic impact on the community.
8. Based upon its mission and goals, each institution should assess its particular impacts on the community it serves.
9. Provide all institutions with additional funding, guidelines and criteria, and technical assistance needed to carry out these recommendations.
10. In all of these matters, involve faculty and administrators intimately in the process with a goal of commitment, not mere compliance. In this regard, create a standing broad-based COEP Council to continue the development of these efforts, oversee the collection and analysis of the information, and report regularly to the Board of Higher Education.

Source: New Jersey, 1987, pp. iv–v.

**Exhibit 8.4. Principles of Undergraduate Assessment
for the SUNY System.**

Any approach to the assessment of undergraduate education for the State University of New York, the largest and most diverse system of higher education in the world, must be comprehensive, comprehensible, complex, cost effective, collegial, constructive, and campus based.

1. Comprehensive. Campus plans should assess institutional and student performance in the following areas of undergraduate education: communication and computation, general education, academic majors, and student social and personal development.
2. Comprehensible. Campus plans and assessment reports should be clear and comprehensible to internal and external constituents and publics. Annual assessment reports should indicate the current level of institutional and student performance in the areas outlined in #1 as compared with the levels recorded in previous reports.
3. Complex. The plans should use multiple approaches to assessment and multiple indicators of effectiveness that reflect the complexity of the goals of higher education and the diversity of SUNY campuses.
4. Cost Effective. The plans should be cost effective and use, where appropriate, existing data bases and evaluation processes and sampling techniques.
5. Collegial. Campus plans should incorporate active faculty and student participation in the development and implementation of assessment programs.
6. Constructive. Assessment should be used not to compare or grade campuses or students but to demonstrate current levels of achievement and to improve future performance. The appropriate comparison is not with other institutions but with a campus's own past performance. The goal of assessment for students and institutions is to help them become the best they are capable of being.
7. Campus Based. Guidelines for assessment will be issued from the Central Administration for the System as a whole, but development and implementation of assessment plans that suit the needs of each of the State-operated Campuses and Community Colleges of SUNY require that assessment be campus based. In effect, assessment should be "owned" and "operated" by the campuses (Burke, undated).

Source: Burke, 1988. Reprinted by permission.

Quality Enhancement Initiatives

Over the nation, state-level initiatives to promote quality assurance and performance accountability are clearly evident and widespread. Beyond the accountability motive, however, many states have set in motion an array of quality enhancement programs. Selected illustrations described below show the diversity and power of these programs.

Eminent Scholar/Endowed Chairs

The most frequently adopted options for quality enhancement are those that state financial policies have designed to attract and hold widely recognized scholars in various fields. A relatively simple financial mechanism is used to create the incentive. Private dollars raised by institutions to support endowed chairs are matched on some incentive ratio by state funds.

In Ohio, for example, the eminent scholars program is an investment in world-class scholars in which the state matches private donations dollar for dollar. Nine distinguished professorships have been funded for each of the past four years. In operation since the 1970s, a similar program in Florida has resulted in the funding of almost seventy full chairs and fifty partially funded professorships. Tennessee has established an endowed chair program as well (Tennessee Higher Education Commission, n.d.). The power of that incentive is evidenced in the University of Tennessee Center for the Health Sciences, which over the past ten years has secured funding for over thirty endowed chairs.

Beyond the provision of fully endowed chairs, typically in the range of $1 million, several states also furnish matching funds for distinguished professorships in which state dollars are matched with private dollars to furnish salary supplements to base salaries. These salary supplement policies are often attractive to smaller and newer state schools that find it easier to raise smaller sums rather than the $500,000 to $750,000 required for fully endowed chairs. Since 1964, the New York state regents have funded ten endowed chairs in a visiting-scholar program known as the Einstein and Schweitzer chair program. Designed to emphasize both the rich and diverse nature of human inquiry and creativity, these ten chairs annually bring to SUNY institutions an imposing cluster of talent in humanities and science ("Einstein and Schweitzer Chair Program," 1986).

Centers of Excellence/Program Enhancement Grants

Several states have developed funding policies designed to enhance excellence within specific programs. Ohio, for example, appropriated $3 million over each of the past four years for one-time enrichment grants aimed at strengthening undergraduate programs. This quality assurance venture is titled Program Excellence (Ohio Board of Regents, 1988). These awards are made in a statewide competition and allow competitive proposals with a variety of goals: faculty and student development, teaching improvement, and facility and equipment improvement.

Tennessee adopted a Centers of Excellence Program in 1984, funding some thirty-two centers over the state for a total of $45 million. An intriguing feature of the Tennessee program is its requirement for measurable benchmarks of performance over a five-year period: increase in faculty publications and invited presentations, student aptitudes and performance, increase in external funding, and so forth. Operated under the auspices of the Tennessee Higher Education Commission (THEC), the centers of excellence were subjected to a comprehensive evaluation by external consultants in 1987, which set the stage for additional five-year proposals solicited for 1989 (Tennessee Higher Education Commission, n.d.).

In 1980–1982, Virginia established the Funds for Excellence Program to promote innovation and excellence. This is also a competitive grant program with broad purposes. In 1988–1989, for example, Virginia funded projects on such themes as building skills across the curriculum, faculty development, academic advising, integrating race and gender issues into the curriculum, international education, and educating a diverse student population. Thus far, Virginia has invested over $10 million in some 120 projects (Council of Higher Education for Virginia, n.d.).

Equipment and Library Enhancement

Recognizing that both institutional and research equipment can quickly become outdated and that few states have a plan for amortizing and replacing this equipment on a regular basis, some states have developed special-funding support initiatives to update instructional, computing, and other special research equipment—with a special focus in science and engineering.

These funding enhancements can take the form of special requests in annual budget requests. A different approach is the creation of an equipment trust fund, such as the one established in Virginia. The trust fund program involves a cluster of approaches designed to acquire and replace equipment on a rotating schedule. Among the features of the trust fund program are issuance of debt instruments with payback from both student fees and legislatively appropriated general fund money, contributions of equipment to take advantage of tax incentives and deductions for manufacturers who donate equipment, and sale leaseback to furnish both cash and long-term lease.

Research and Economic Development Enhancement

As the United States attempts to strengthen its posture in scientific and advanced technology leadership, renew its manufacturing base, and maintain a strong economy in the face of significant international competition, there are few states that are not looking to their own welfare as well as the national welfare on these same themes. Economic development and the creation of new jobs are even more critical to states that have been hit with economic slumps in recent years. Here, then, is another area into which many states are pouring incentive funds.

Among those states that were hard hit by the 1980s slump in the oil industry is Texas. The Texas legislature established two competitive grant programs in 1987 designed to focus university research and technology transfer on state economic development and competitiveness (Texas Higher Education Coordinating Board, 1988). Two programs were implemented as a result of this legislation: the Advanced Technology Program (funded at $40 million) and the Advanced Research Program (funded at $20 million). The goals were the promotion of basic research and the commercialization or technology transfer of existing ideas. Over 3,200 proposals were received in competition for the $60 million allocated during the first biennium.

Another state active in this form of incentive program is Utah. Among the fields of technology development supported by the Utah program are those in computer-aided manufacturing and artificial heart (the Jarvik heart) and hearing technologies. Seven technology areas were targeted with the initial $5.2 million state appropriation: biomedical, manufacturing, engineering, natural resources, communications, space engineering, and biotechnology. The Utah Board of Regents' report claims that over fifty companies have emerged from this program (Utah Board of Regents, n.d.).

The state of New Jersey enacted a science and technology bond act in 1984 to establish and support a network of advanced technology centers at both public and private colleges and universities. The bonded amount was $90 million. The size of this financial commitment, those cited above, and other state initiatives not described here reveal the seriousness that states attach to technology transfer efforts (New Jersey, 1984).

A slightly different source of state funding, but with similar application, is the Louisiana Education Quality Support Fund (Public Affairs Research Council of Louisiana, 1989). Over a period of fifteen years, Louisiana is scheduled to receive a total of $640 million derived from the 1978 amendment to the Federal Outer Continental Shelf Lands Act (the 8G Act). These funds are received in a series of escalating payments over the years and are invested with the interest income split evenly between higher education (the Louisiana Board of Regents) and elementary/secondary education (the Board of Elementary and Secondary Education). At present, the board of regents is expending $15 to $20 million each year on the following program elements: carefully defined research efforts of Louisiana public and private universities; endowment of chairs for eminent scholars; enhancement of the quality of academic, research, or agricultural departments (but not athletics) within a university and recruitment of superior graduate students.

Quality—A Comprehensive Agenda

Although many states have one or more of the previously described quality assurance and enhancement initiatives in place, few have well-integrated packages. Among the states that seem to be active in both quality assurance and quality enhancement are Florida, Ohio, South Carolina, Tennessee, and Texas. (This notation of states is meant to be representative, not exclusive).

Ohio, for example, publishes its initiatives in a brochure entitled "Ohio Continues Its Investment in Excellence," which includes a cluster of seven initiatives: (1) program excellence, (2) academic challenge, (3) productivity improvement challenge, (4) eminent scholars, (5) research challenge, (6) super computer center, and (7) independent college challenge (1963–1988) (Ohio Board of Regents, 1988). South Carolina outlines "the cutting edge initiatives for research and academic excellence in higher education" by outlining programs in five major areas: (1) excellence for students, (2) excellence in instruction and educational services, (3) excellence in research for economic development, (4) improving accountability through planning and assessment, and (5) excellence through enhancement of the effectiveness of the Commission on Higher Education. The South Carolina approach thus integrates program elements that involve both policy and funding actions (Elliott, 1988).

The Accountability-Autonomy Tension

As we move to the end of these chapters on quality assurance in American higher education and to the conclusion of this particular chapter, we can see the insertion of new actors and the emergence of new partnerships. Peer involvement was and is the principal instrument of quality assurance—as expressed in accreditation, reputational studies, and academic program reviews. It is clear, however, from the programs and policies described in this and in other chapters, that the state has become an active and, we believe, an essential partner in both quality assurance and enhancement. There are, however, aspects of the partnership between campus and state worthy of our vigilance. In *The Aims of Education*, Whitehead wrote: "The faculty should be a band of scholars, stimulating each other, and freely determining their various activities. You can secure certain formal requirements, that lectures are given at stated times and that instructors and students are in attendance. But the heart of the matter lies beyond all regulation" (Whitehead, 1929, p. 99).

Agencies external to the campus—governing and coordinating boards, legislators, and executive officers—can play stimulating, leveraging, and regulating roles in quality assurance and enhancement. But the most fundamental and operational expression of academic standards will always reside in the heads, hands, and hearts of the faculty.

Few would argue with the ideological necessity of campus autonomy. Can it be, however, that campus administrators and facilities invite external intrusion? In *Choosing Quality* (1987), Newman presents case illustrations of the more pernicious forms: examples of bureaucratic, ideological, and political intrusion. Newman offers this comment: "There is indeed a tendency for states to intrude and, in fact, for the universities to cause or invite that intrusion. What becomes clear is that the real need is not simply for more autonomy but for a relationship between the university and the state that is constructive for both, built up over a long period of time by careful attention on the part of all parties" (p. xiii).

In an earlier work, one of the authors (Bogue, 1985) also furnished disguised case illustration of both ethical and educational malpractice, the results of which invite external scrutiny of campus practice, both educational and managerial. The truth is that those living in higher education cannot neglect their leadership and educational responsibilities without expecting and getting some external attention.

In summary, effective campus-state partnerships are built when campus and state leaders hold a shared vision of quality for the state's system of higher education. These leaders value differential missions and do not create what Newman calls a pyramid of prestige in which research universities occupy top billing on the quality/prestige ladder, state colleges are left in a kind of confused no-man's-land, and community colleges are treated as places to do what is left over from the research universities and state universities. Campus and state leaders avoid arrogance in their public values and move to treat both persons and organizations with dignity and trust; and they behave in an ethically responsible manner, willing to dare and to take risks but avoiding prostitution of personal and institutional integrity that would breach the public trust.

A final reflection has to do with the nature of the incentives furnished by the state and the nature of the university and its role in our society. One cannot miss the economic development emphasis in many of the state quality enhancement efforts. In our national race to maintain a competitive international economy, few cities and states are not using their universities as major engines of economic development. Developing new technologies and translating these technologies more quickly and directly into commercially profitable enterprises has become a major goal of both local and state policy. As the major developed nations compete, the emphasis on science and technology is to be expected.

However, Ernest Schumacher cautioned in his book *Small Is Beautiful* (1973): "There is measure in all natural things—in the size, speed, or violence. As a result, the system of nature, of which man is a part, tends to be self-balancing, self-adjusting, self-cleansing. Not so with man dominated by technology or perhaps I should say: not so with man dominated by technology and specialization" (Schumacher, 1973, p. 57). Schumacher then points out the three major negative outcomes that are so apparent in our contemporary society: Man becomes the servant of technology, often in a debilitating and suffocating sense; the environment becomes damaged by the waste products and processes of technology; and the nonrenewable resources of our planet become endangered, to say nothing of some living species.

Here is another note from Schumacher worth remembering (1973, p. 139): "What is quite clear is that a way of life that bases itself on materialism, that is on permanent, limitless expansionism in a finite environment, cannot last long, and that its life expectation is the shorter the more successfully it pursues its expansionist objectives."

Incentive programs and policies aimed at quality assurance and enhancement should embrace and serve the broader purposes of college and university education. As Bertrand Russell once observed: "Men who boast of being what is called 'practical' are for the most part exclusively preoccupied with means. But theirs is only one half wisdom. When we take account of the other half, which is concerned with ends, the economic process and the whole of human life take on an entirely new aspect. We ask no longer: What have the producers produced, and what has consumption enabled the consumers in their turn to produce? We ask instead: What has there been in the lives of the consumers and producers to make them glad to be alive?" (Russell, 1989, pp. 72–73).

Questions of purpose and principle, meaning and value: This is the business of philosophy and the most enduring occupation of the university. Here lie questions and inquiries worthy of state incentive efforts as well.

NINE

Promoting
Campus Renewal
Through
Quality Assurance

In the early history of American higher education, lay boards of visitors often attended and participated in senior examinations. This examination of graduates by a group independent of the faculty constituted an interesting beginning of quality assurance practices. Coulter describes the origins of this practice at the University of Georgia: "Examination times were tasting times and this tasting should be done by more than the cooks only. In the original charter a board of visitors was established 'to see that the interest of this institution is carried into effect,' but its duties were so intangible that it never got out of the charter until someone discovered that attending examinations would be a benefiting work for such a board" (Coulter, 1928, p. 52). The principle of subjecting the results of our teaching to a panel of judges independent of the faculty remains under active discussion in our search for quality and is one that we will address in this chapter. To this early practice of the senior examination have been added the practices and policies outlined in previous chapters.

Clearly, American higher education has fashioned a diverse cluster of quality assurance instruments, which possess interesting theoretical and value foundations. Whatever allowances we may make for the philosophical and technical frailties associated with any one of them, we must remain impressed with the energy and the thought devoted to quality assurance—and to the finding that American higher education is one enterprise in our national life that enjoys a favorable balance of attention when it comes to international exchange.

The title of this chapter anticipates our theme and our hope. We continue to emphasize quality assurance practices in our colleges and universities as instruments of decision, which enable us to improve service to students and society, and as instruments of discovery, which encourage us to learn more about the nature of the enterprise in which we are engaged. Through these practices comes campus renewal.

To achieve these purposes, we first propose to glean from our review of existing quality assurance practices a set of principles by which we may build a philosophy of quality. Second, we will review a few institutions that are models of action and discovery. Third, we will present a minimal-element quality assurance model that we think will help deliver on the quality definition offered in Chapter One: conformance to mission specification and goal achievement within publicly accepted standards of accountability and integrity. And, finally, we intend to describe the renewing and learning outcomes that can associate with our search for quality.

A Philosophy of Quality

As we reflect on the quality assurance approaches described in previous chapters, several principles appear on which an effective quality assurance effort might be constructed. These constitute a useful test for building quality assurance efforts where none exist and for evaluating those already in place.

Partnerships

To the important quality concerns of purpose and performance in our opening chapter, we add the concept of partnership. Effective quality assurance is a partnership journey of caring and daring. In *When Giants Learn to Dance,* Kanter (1989) tells of the leadership styles and attitudes that American corporate executives need for competing in today's international business Olympics—the need for teams and partnerships rather than corporate cowboys and corporate czars. We believe that team efforts are important to collegiate quality as well.

No one who has taken the journey toward improved quality concludes that journey without acknowledging the need for partnership. In his book describing the development of a new core curriculum and associated assessment system at King's College, discussed later in this chapter, D. W. Farmer notes: "A condition of trust is the first ingredient required on a college campus to create a positive attitude toward change. Trust is not simply the result of rhetoric but more importantly the result of deeds. Actions are what help to define interpersonal relationships and expectations. Faculty and administrators need to see themselves as partners in higher education, not as adversaries" (Farmer, 1988, p. 16).

What is true for parties within the academy is also true for those external to the campus. Governing boards, state coordinating agencies, legislative and executive officers, and media professionals—the list of stakeholders in the quality of colleges and universities has been growing over the past few decades, particularly in the last quarter century. We have noted the potential discomfort and the liabilities that associate with the entry of these new partners.

We do not diminish the premier role of the faculty in defining, evaluating, and improving quality in our colleges and universities. Any quality assurance program that does not directly affect the quality of teaching and the quality of what happens in our classrooms, studios, laboratories, and other learning settings is an empty exercise. We believe, however, that in their best and most effective expression, the quality concerns of those external to the university constitute acts of friendship rather than enmity. Why do we need that external vigilance? Throughout these chapters, we have referred to one or more critiques of colleges and universities. Indeed, for the past few years, we have been averaging a critical commentary almost every year.

Cahn suggests in *Saints and Scamps: Ethics in Academia* (1986) that the unethical practices of college professors endanger the very academic freedom so important to their work. The subtitle of

Allan Bloom's best seller *The Closing of the American Mind* (1987) reads: "How Higher Education Has Failed Democracy and Improverished the Souls of Today's Students." Writing in his polemic *PROFSCAM*, Sykes (1988) describes the faculty as follows: "The modern academic is mobile, self-interested, and without loyalty to institutions or the values of liberal education. The rogue professors of today are not merely obscurantists. They are politicians and entrepreneurs who fiercely protect their turf and shrewdly hustle research cash while they peddle their talents to rival universities, businesses, foundations, or government" (Sykes, 1988, p. 7).

The latest of these major critical commentaries is Smith's book *Killing the Spirit* (1990), which describes the flight from teaching, the pedestrian nature of some research, the integrity problems of big-time sports, and the unhappy alliances of the university with arms of government and with corporations. Smith suggests that the last thing anyone wants to do within the contemporary collegiate climate is to ask questions about the nature of the enterprise. Those who have lived, loved, and labored in our colleges and universities—as the authors have—would not accept these critiques as descriptive of the entire reality of collegiate life. There is, however, sufficient validity to critics' and cynics' claims to illustrate that, though it is painful, we can profit from their friendly concerns.

Gardner's often quoted and paraphrased comments about uncritical lovers and unloving critics (made originally in a commencement address at a New England university) fit nicely here and help make our point: "All too many of our institutions are caught in a savage crossfire between uncritical lovers and unloving critics. On the one side, those who love their institutions tend to smother them in an embrace of death, loving their rigidities more than their promise, shielding them from life-giving criticism. On the other side, one finds a breed of critics without love, skilled in demolition but untutored in the arts by which human institutions are nurtured and strengthened and made to flourish" (John Gardner, letter to the author, August 1984).

Linkage to Teaching and Learning

Having validated the merit of quality assurance partnerships, we emphasize a second principle: the importance of tying quality assurance efforts to teaching and learning. Reporters for *U.S. News and World Report* or *USA Today* will, for the most part, not be teaching in our classrooms, nor will members of governing boards or legislators. A moment's reflection and a search of our memories will remind us of who is the premier architect of quality. As students, we do not remember the policy studies and critiques that have swirled about colleges and universities; the activities in state, regional, or national settings; members of the board; or perhaps even the president. Rather, we remember faculty members who cared about us, who lifted our spirits and our vision, who challenged our intellectual apathy and fired our curiosity, who helped us escape the poverty of the commonplace and lifted us to new horizons of discovery and meaning. The quality of a college or university is quite simply found in the quality of its caring for students.

Improvement-Centered Atmosphere

Colleges and universities that care for their students are interested in ascertaining the impact they have on students and society and in improving that impact. As we stated in our opening chapter, our first accountability is to our students. Admission, placement, retention, graduation, and certification: Each educational decision we make and assist our students to make is fundamentally an act of caring. It is not an act of caring when low standards and unimaginative teaching allow our students to cheat their own potential. In this sense, then, our quality assurance instruments should tell us something about the climate of caring in our colleges and universities.

In the spring of 1990, Louisiana State University in Shreveport used the ACT Student Opinion Survey to obtain the reactions of a random sample of currently enrolled students to university programs and services. This survey form provided a means to obtain structured responses on a five-point scale to many dimensions of services and support. In addition, however, students had the opportunity to furnish open-ended comments at the end of the form. Students were invited to comment on "what they liked best" and "what they wanted to see improved," and thus they had a lot to say about the climate of caring at the university.

The open-ended comments yielded easily to an informal factor analysis. The quality of advising services, the quality of support services available to evening and part-time students, and the attitude and spirit of service on the part of some faculty and staff stood out as lively improvement targets. In its planning and goal-setting activities, the university committed itself to the principle of treating its students with dignity and rendering instructional and administrative service with courtesy and competence. The student comments offered a useful test about the extent to which the university honored that commitment and identified specific places where improvement work could be undertaken.

Unobtrusive Practices

A few years ago, Webb, Campbell, Schwartz, and Sechrest (1966) wrote a book called *Unobtrusive Measures,* to suggest that our assessment of performance and quality can often be approached along novel paths. To measure the attractiveness of art exhibits, for example, one can measure the wear on floor tiles in front of those exhibits. However, what we have in mind with this term is that our quality assurance programs should be so woven into the educational fabric of the institution that their influence on the quality of what happens to teaching and learning is guaranteed. At Louisiana State University in Shreveport, faculty members from all disciplines are involved in the evaluation of the written essay that is a part of the long form of the academic profile test published by Educational Testing Service. This sharing of evaluative responsibility tends to create a sense of community among these interested faculty members and enhances their sensitivity to the importance of good writing as they return to their classrooms in different departments over the campus. The assessment is linked to improvement through the faculty.

Unobtrusive quality assurance practices are not heavily laden with publications and reports that burden our storage shelves, nor are they of interest to institutional research officers only. Unobtrusive systems do not necessarily require a director or office of quality assurance. What they do require is an intellectual and emotional commitment on the part of everyone in the collegiate community.

This commitment will ensure that the concern for quality is expressed as much in the passions as in the policies of the institution.

Varieties of Excellence

No principle is more central to our philosophy of quality than this one. Beginning with the definition of quality presented in Chapter One, we have continued to affirm the importance of recognizing and rewarding diversity of institutional mission and individual talent.

Quality is not a single-factor attribute of personal or organizational performance. Every dimension of collegiate life sings to the beauty and power of diversity. Begin with the cold chills that run up and down our spines when we sit in the recital hall of the music building and know that we are in the presence of a great talent singing or playing. Experience the touch of wonder as we study the power of simplicity carried in the message of a short poem in a literature review published by the English faculty. Marvel at the integrating power of the mind that has just produced a new history. Stand amazed at the biology graduate student who has replaced a complex machine for splitting embryos (costing several thousands of dollars) with a razor and microscope slide roughened by diamond dust (costing just over a dollar). Be impressed with the physicist and the theologian discussing the nature of reality, each recommending to the other Zukav's *The Dancing Wu Li Masters* (1979) and Jastrow's *God and the Astronomers* (1978). The hallway linking science and religion may be shorter than we thought. Who can stand next to this exciting array of experiences, ideas, and inquiry— to say nothing of the diversity of institutional climates that furnish homes for them—and say that quality can be captured in a single factor or indicator?

Creating a larger vision of excellence is a theme to which we will return in our closing chapter. Let us acknowledge here, however, that we require a larger vision not only of student performance but of institutional performance. Just how difficult a challenge this is for our universities, many of whom remain wedded to a single-factor expression of excellence as shown in faculty research productivity, is made clear in a 1990 *Change* article by Lewis Miller, Jr.

We were impressed with the power of an illustration in Miller's article, related to integrity issues earlier cited. Miller reported that a West Coast university anxious to improve its national image took steps to recruit what Miller calls a "superprofessor" of chemistry from another campus. The academic courting was intense but had little effect until the superprofessor indicated that it would be difficult for him to move unless his wife, a Ph.D. in sociology, also found employment. The West Coast university thereupon offered her a tenured contract in its sociology department, which she promptly accepted. The superprofessor, however, remained at his original institution. It seems that the couple were in the process of getting a divorce, and the university became the unwitting and unfortunate partner in this marital solution. Thus, narrow definitions of excellence may have more than one unhappy outcome.

Multiple Indicators

We have emphasized throughout the book that no single indicator of measurement of quality can stand without some criticism. Outcome measures may not tell us about the value-added contributions of the collegiate climate. Student options do not tell us whether students have learned anything. Reputational and ranking studies are sometimes viewed as "quantified gossip" and often do not furnish useful information for improving programs and policies. Accreditation can be an exercise in professional back-scratching, a cost-and-time burden serving only the interests of various professions and disciplines. Licensure examinations can be subject to the changing interests and standards of a profession and its own self-interests. Academic program reviews can be punitive instruments of external agencies more interested in cost than quality. Alumni opinions can mellow and modify with time.

Obviously, then, we need multiple indicators for this conceptual challenge and for other reasons as well, because individual and institutional performance are, as we have noted, too complex to be captured in a single point of evidence. The artist/scientist physician does not look at a single indicator of our physical or emotional condition to ascertain our state of health; diagnosis and prescrip-

tion are built on analysis, evaluation, and interpretation of multiple
indicators. We will suggest an educational diagnostic profile in this
same spirit.

Public Disclosure

Colleges and universities are built to stimulate and sustain our
search for truth. An essential feature in that search is our willingness to expose both our ideas and our personalities to the test of
public disclosure, both within and outside the institution. The
transmission and the testing of ideas confer upon publication an
essential role in the academy. How can we lay claim to a concept
or to a value until we have tested that idea or that value in the
crucible of practice or publication? The student of science or music
will have his or her knowledge of both science and music greatly
enlivened by reading the biographies of Galileo and Stravinsky.
Both of these creative minds were exposed to unhappy public recep-
tions of their works, as is true with so many scholars.

In a recent visit to a state university, we had the opportunity
to examine the progress of a faculty struggling with the adequacy
of its general education curriculum and the appropriate means to
assess the effect of the general education core. The institution had
employed a director of assessment and had appointed a representative committee of faculty and staff to work with the director of
assessment. The minutes of the committee were instructive; at one
point, it debated the merit of any assessment and the selection and
development of an assessment procedure, because this would offer
the prospect of the results becoming public and perhaps being carried in local newspapers. The minutes recorded no conversation or
commentary on the contrast between this value disposition and that
on which the academy is built: the sharing of perspective, process,
and products with those external to the community as a means of
testing our advance on truth. To the credit of this faculty, we must
report that the initial suspicions and concerns were overcome, and
the campus has moved forward in the best spirit of the decision-and-
discovery journey we are trying to emphasize in this chapter.

What we expect our students to learn about the search for
truth can also be found in our search for quality. How can we

furnish effective models of curiosity and courage for our students unless we are willing to submit the nature of the collegiate enterprise to the test of public scrutiny? The journey from knowledge to wisdom begins with performance—when we lay open the workings of mind, heart, and hand to the critical review and standards of others. The journey of institutional learning begins in the same fashion, in a performance test that brings us to our next principle.

External Standards

The principle of public disclosure also assumes that we are willing to place the performance of our students and services against standards external to the campus. When we seek accreditation and conduct academic program reviews as instruments of quality assurance, we are making use of this principle. When we use assessment instruments that offer comparative performance profiles from other institutions and student populations, we recognize the merit of an external standard. When we make use of student performance on licensure examinations, we use this standard.

When graduates of the University of Georgia were first examined by the Board of Visitors, this principle was placed in action. Writing of this early practice, Boyer indicates that "the almost universal practice of asking outside examiners to question students rested on the notion that, beyond the scrutiny of each teacher, it was the responsibility of a third party—a scholar removed from the process of instruction—to certify that graduates were truly equipped to enter the world of educated men and women" (Boyer, 1987, pp. 252–253).

A philosophical and conceptual tension is inherent in this principle. Some contemporary views of quality assign the responsibility for quality to those involved in the development of the product, rather than to a third party. Is it a misplacement of responsibility and trust to insist on this independent check on performance? We believe not, and for reasons just cited in our discussion of the "public disclosure" principle. An essential nature of the collegiate enterprise, in the search for truth, is the testing of conviction and findings against the community of scholars, for there may be elements of insulation and solitude in creative acts of scholarship. That this is indeed true is made apparent by biographical illustrations found in Storr's 1988 book *Solitude*. The results of creativity must come into public forum and public test at some point.

Unresolved Tensions

We are not sure whether this next point qualifies well as a principle, but it is surely a matter of reality and merits our attention. We speak of certain tensions among the principles cited. In the previous discussion, for example, we cited the tension between internal responsibility and external standards in our search for quality. The call for recognizing diversity of talent and variety of excellence will argue with the call for minimal standards for our credentials and degrees. It seems reasonable to ask that the musician, the engineer, the accountant, and the teacher master certain communication skills—but at what level and standard? The role of competition argues with the role of cooperation in learning, but where is the balance point? We emphasized in our definition of quality the essential requirement of tying quality judgments to the mission of a campus. How can we reconcile this emphasis on internal standards to the use of external standards? We hold up for salute the premier role of faculty in quality assurance but admit to legitimate roles for other partners external to the campus. Living with the comfort or discomfort of these ambiguities is a legitimate learning exercise in our search for quality.

Learning by Doing

In our roles as teachers we daily embark upon the delicate obligation of judging human talent. As consultants we are willing participants in the task of judging organizational performance in cultural, civic, and corporate settings. For our students we conceive performance tests that will give us public access to private mastery and growth. Our students must demonstrate concept or skill mastery through some behavioral and overt expression.

Thinking about quality is certainly a reasonable first step in its delivery—no matter what the organizational setting. But thinking must be linked to action if we are to realize the full fruits of learning about quality. Thinking about writing will not release that parade of friendly thought that will march across the page when we begin the "doing" of writing, when our fingers hit that first key or our pen carries that first word to paper. Similarly, only those institutions that have married argument to action will experience the discovery potential of the search for quality. Let us turn our attention now to some of those institutional models of discovery.

Models of Discovery

Six brief illustrations of institutional quality assurance programs allow us to emphasize the points made above. Each of the campus models described below illustrates long-term investments in time and talent devoted to quality assurance. We examine here the results of that journey, but we will not be able to appreciate fully the combinations of initiative and impedance, of passion and prejudice that are reflected in current campus status. The campus models illustrate the decision focus of effective quality assurance efforts— the application of data for improvement and accountability. Additionally, these models represent integrated approaches that embrace a variety of performance indicators for both students and programs.

Enhancing Student Learning at King's College

A first example comes from the experience of a private college, emphasizing again the contributions of diversity in our system of American higher education. In a comprehensive development effort, King's College, Wilkes-Barre, Pennsylvania, reworked its planning, curriculum, and assessment activities and produced a model core curriculum that defines the educational outcomes that the college expects of its students. The core curriculum is built on four learning areas (Farmer, 1988, pp. 149-187):

1. The transferable skills of liberal learning: critical thinking, creative thinking and problem-solving strategies, effective writing, effective oral communication, quantitative analysis, computer literacy, library and information technology competency,

values awareness, comprehension skills, writing and language skills, and basic speech

2. Knowledge, traditional disciplines, and interdisciplinary perspectives: civilization—historical perspectives, foreign cultures, human behavior and social institutions, literature and the arts, natural sciences

3. Responsible believing and responsible acting: Catholic perspectives on believing; fundamentals of philosophy; New Testament perspectives on believing; Old Testament perspectives on believing; philosophy of human nature; basic Christian ethics; Christian marriage; ethics, business, and society; faith, morality, and the person; and rights, justice, and society

4. Electives

This comprehensive core curriculum is combined with a comprehensive assessment program that includes pretests and posttests on the knowledge and skill outcomes, a sophomore-junior diagnostic project, standardized assessments, a senior-level integrated assessment, and alumni follow-up surveys. Parents and students examining this linkage of outcomes, curriculum, and assessment are certain to have more confidence in the educational experience than are parents and students looking at core curriculum patterns that reflect the outcome of faculty and curriculum politics rather than the learning needs of students. As we noted above, the smaller and private schools often lead the way—another contribution of diversity.

The Value-Added Program at
Northeast Missouri State University

One of the older and better known models of quality assurance among public colleges and universities is that of Northeast Missouri State University (NMSU). This nationally recognized model has been developing since 1972 under the leadership of former president Charles McClain, who is now serving as state commissioner of higher education for Missouri.

The NMSU program is described more specifically in the monograph *Degrees with Integrity,* published by the American Association of State Colleges and Universities in 1984, following

NMSU's selection to receive the prestigious Mitau award for their value-added program. The NMSU program is well integrated and comprehensive. Academic and attitudinal data are gathered on prospective students, currently enrolled students, and alumni. Surveys and tests are employed in obtaining data. For example, entering-student abilities are measured by the American College Testing (ACT) examination and the College Outcomes Measures Program (COMP) battery, also published by the American College Testing Program. These two exams are also administered at the end of the sophomore year. In the senior year, students in various majors take the Graduate Record Examination, the National Teacher Examination, the field tests in the Undergraduate Assessment Program from ETS, and other measures of knowledge and skill in specific majors.

Nationally recognized scholar Alexander Astin had this to say of the NMSU program in his preface to the American Association of State Colleges and Universities (AASCU) monograph: "Basically, the pursuit of excellence, for most institutions, is equated with the mere pursuit of resources: money, facilities, highly trained faculty, and bright students. Those institutions that succeed in amassing a disproportionately large share of such resources are generally regarded as excellent while most of the others tend to be regarded, at best, as mediocre. The value added approach to excellence represents a highly promising departure from this view. Rather than focusing on the mere acquisition of resources, the value added view emphasizes how existing resources are used to enhance student learning" (Northeast Missouri State University, 1984, p. xi).

Indeed, it is the decision application and decision utility of the NMSU program that constitute its most interesting feature. The use of data from this quality assurance effort to improve both the general education program and programs in such fields as psychology and nursing at NMSU is one of the more attractive features of the program and the monograph describing the program.

When reviewing this exemplary effort, it is tempting to forget that we are reviewing the arrival and not the journey it took for the university to come to the arrival: the construction of a vision, the investment of talent and caring, the persevering moments and the disappointing moments, the hostile and suspicious attitudes, and the building of ownership and partnerships among faculty and staff of the university. It has taken almost twenty years for NMSU to move from the inception of this program to its place in the national spotlight.

Planning and Evalution at
Louisiana State University in Shreveport

A moderate-sized comprehensive university in an urban setting, Louisiana State University in Shreveport (LSUS) was one of seven institutions in the South that participated in the field test of the new Southern Association of Colleges and Schools Criteria on Institutional Effectiveness (see Chapter Two on accreditation). What the university has attempted to accomplish in its quality assurance program is to link planning (purpose) and evaluation (performance), as shown in Figure 9.1. (Note that the emphasis of the planning effort is on decision.) At LSUS the focus, then, is on those two leadership questions with which we opened the book: purpose (What do we hope to accomplish?) and performance (How good a job are we doing and how do we know?).

Let us take a look at a specific decision feature of the LSUS program. The use of alumni follow-up data was cited in Chapter Four for its value in making improvements in the general education component for one of the university's degree programs, the bachelor's degree in general studies. The university has also been pilot testing the general education skills assessment test published by Educational Testing Service—the Academic Profile. The decision intentions of this assessment at the sophomore level are as follows: "To ensure the satisfactory mastery of such fundamental skills as composition, critical thinking/problem solving before graduation—and before student is admitted to more rigorous work of upper division . . . To encourage students to take fundamental and required courses in general education instead of putting them off until junior and senior year . . . To assemble data for diagnosis and evaluation of the general education requirements. To ensure that transfer students, at whatever point of transfer, master the same general education skills before receiving the LSUS degree" (Louisiana State University in Shreveport, 1990, p. 69).

Figure 9.1. Planning Products and Philosophy at LSUS.

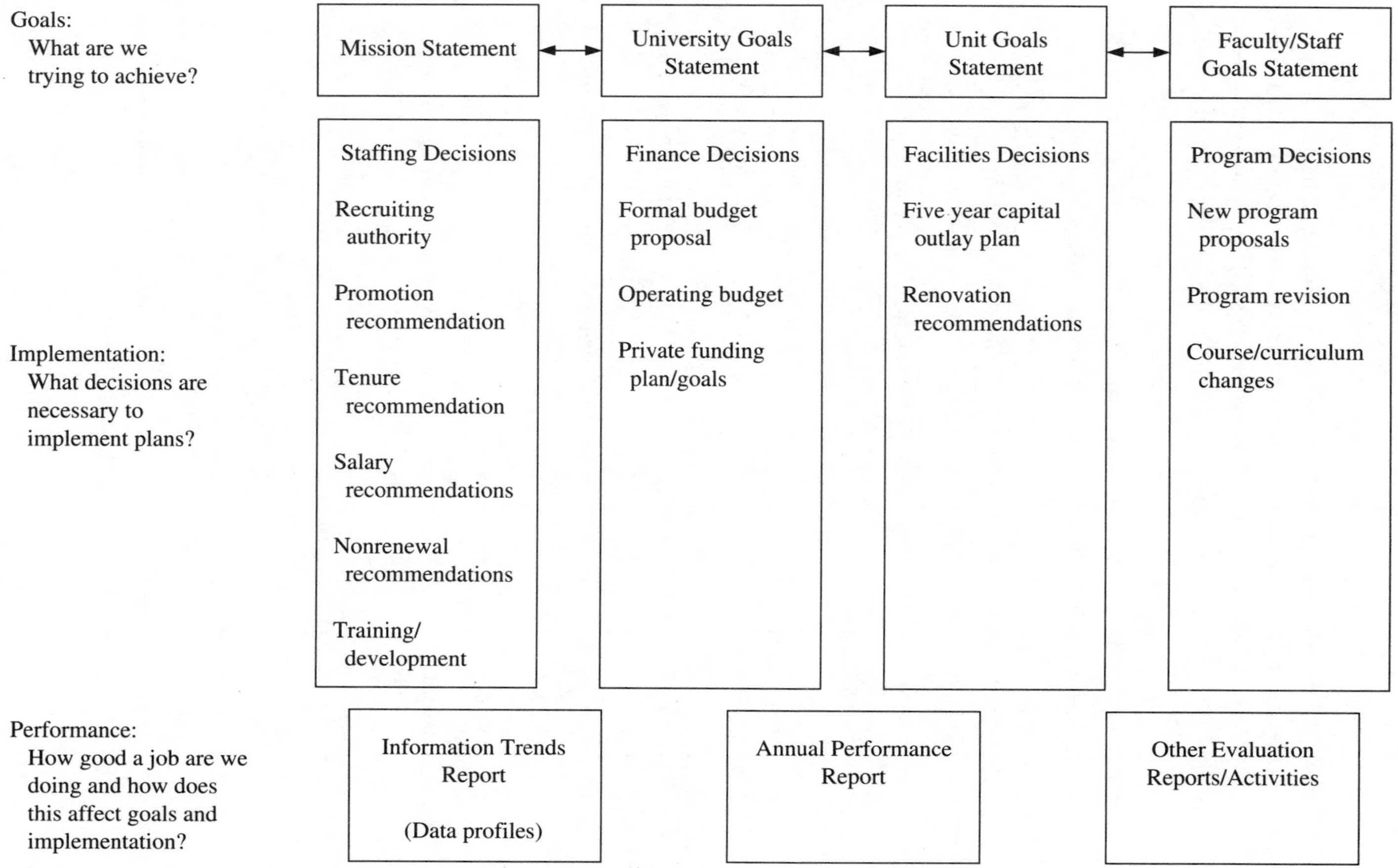

Goals:
What are we trying to achieve?

Mission Statement

University Goals Statement

Unit Goals Statement

Faculty/Staff Goals Statement

Implementation:
What decisions are necessary to implement plans?

Staffing Decisions

Recruiting authority

Promotion recommendation

Tenure recommendation

Salary recommendations

Nonrenewal recommendations

Training/ development

Finance Decisions

Formal budget proposal

Operating budget

Private funding plan/goals

Facilities Decisions

Five year capital outlay plan

Renovation recommendations

Program Decisions

New program proposals

Program revision

Course/curriculum changes

Performance:
How good a job are we doing and how does this affect goals and implementation?

Information Trends Report

(Data profiles)

Annual Performance Report

Other Evaluation Reports/Activities

Source: Louisiana State University at Shreveport, 1989, pp. 4, 5, 6.

Table 9.1 displays the range of evaluation activities. Under "Curricula and Programs" is an instrument called Community Satisfaction Survey, which was commissioned by the university and conducted by an independent management consulting company in the Shreveport metropolitan area.

Table 9.1. LSU Shreveport Evaluation Activities and Reports.

Student Performance Measures	Curricula and Programs	Personnel Reviews
Admissions/placement	Retention studies	Annual review of executive administrators (MBO)
American College Testing (ACT)	Placement report	
	Community Satisfaction Survey (3–5 years)	Faculty evaluation of academic administrators
Nelson Denny Reading Test	Alumni survey (3 years— ACT Questionnaire)	annual (P.S. 2 08.00)
English Composition (local test and essay)	Enrolled student survey (every year)	Faculty evaluation of administrative services (P.S. 1 09.00)
Mathematics Test (local test)	ACT Student Opinion Questionnaire	
General education assessment (between 45 and 60 semester hours)	Entering student survey Phone	Chairman annual review of faculty (P.S. 2 04.01)
Academic Profile—long form with essay (ETS)	SACS accreditation (10 years)	Student evaluation of instruction
Graduation	Professional accreditation	
National Teachers Examination	Education (1989–1990)	
	Business (1989–1990)	
Graduate Management Aptitude Test	Computer science (1990–1991)	
Graduate Record Examination (GRE)	Journalism (projected 1991)	
	Chemistry ( )	
Jury Review of Writing (English)	Academic program reviews (as scheduled by board of regents)	
Jury Review of Art (art)	Biology (1989–1990)	
	Computer science (1988–1990)	
	Chemistry (1990–1991)	
	Journalism (1988–1989)	
	Graduate program reviews (every four to five years)	

Source: Louisiana State University in Shreveport.

A Commitment to Excellence at James Madison University

The Southern Association of Colleges and Schools published a helpful monograph by Folger and Harris entitled *Assessment in Accreditation* (1989). Three models of action and discovery are outlined in the closing pages, and readers are encouraged to review this book. Among the exemplary institutions whose programs are described is James Madison University (JMU) in Harrisonburg, Virginia. Table 9.2 outlines the elements of the JMU program and shows the comprehensive approach to quality assurance involving both cognitive and affective dimensions of student life and development. Once again, the decision utility of quality assurance is featured. Consider this report: "In economics, the faculty determined that the ability of students to critically analyze a position paper in written form as a fundamental skill for all students to possess. As part of their assessment procedure in the major, faculty developed an exercise to test this skill. Results from the pilot exercise suggested that students failed to meet faculty expectations. Thus, the curriculum has been modified to provide for assignments which specifically address this area of interest" (Folger and Harris, 1989, p. 20).

An impressive feature of the JMU quality assurance effort is that the campus makes public its purposes and performance achievement on these purposes. In the Virginia Plan for Higher Education 1989, for example, the university presents ten statements of purpose and discusses the relative balance of attention to, and emphasis on, each of these purposes. This section is followed by a discussion of the institutional assessment program in four areas: alumni follow-up, high-risk students, general education assessment, and major field assessment. Instruments used and results obtained are described for each of these four areas. The university has committed to a major assessment effort in its student affairs division as well and presents in this publication some initial descriptive and activity data from the student affairs division.

We have been using the term "discovery" to lead this discussion. The use is deliberate. Although the beginnings of quality assurance discussions on any campus inevitably bring moments of anxiety, suspicion, and hostility, the latter will almost surely deliver

Table 9.2. Quality Assurance at James Madison University.

Assessment Dimension	Assessment Instrument	Time to Administer (Approximate)
1. Liberal studies	1. ACT-COMP	2 3/4 hours
	2. Academic Profile	3 1/2 hours
2. Objectives across the curriculum	1. Watson-Glaser Critical Thinking	45 minutes
	2. The Cornell Critical Thinking Test, Form 2	45 minutes
	3. Essay	
3. Functional skills	1. Essay	1 hour
	2. Local Math Placement Test	1 hour
4. Degree of student challenge	1. The College Student Experiences Questionnaire	30 minutes
	2. JMU specific questions added to questionnaire	10 minutes
	3. Parallel survey of faculty	30 minutes
5. Affective	1. Erwin Identity Scale	20 minutes
	2. Scale of Intellectual Development	30 minutes
	3. Defining Issues Test	45 minutes
	4. Student Development Task Inventory	30 minutes
6. Major	1. Graduate Record Exam	3 hours
	2. National Teacher Exam (core)	6 hours
	National Teacher Exam (specialty area)	2 hours
	3. CLEP	1 1/2 hours
	4. Locally developed instruments	
	5. Rating scales	
7. Alumni	1. General portion	30 minutes
	2. Major portion	15 minutes

Source: Folger and Harris, 1989, pp. 118–119.

moments of pleasure, surprise, and satisfaction, as faculty and staff members discover the power of assessment for improvement.

A Venture in Quality Assurance at the University of Tennessee

Can any campus be more difficult to move than a research university? These institutions are highly complex in their histories of organizational structures, size, and internal academic and political interests. An interesting exchange between the University of Virginia and the State Council for Higher Education for Virginia (SCHEV) is reported by Pat Hutchings and Ted Marchese in the October/November 1990 issue of *Change* magazine. That article illustrates the challenge of change faced by research universities. It does more than this, however. It also illustrates the power of partnership—even though the partnership initially may be forged in moments of anxiety and anger. When partners are willing to learn from one another, which is one of the messages in the Hutchings and Marchese report, the cause of quality is more effectively served.

Some of these huge institutions have made noteworthy progress. One that has made a major investment in quality assurance over the past fifteen years and that now has in place a positive model of action is the University of Tennessee at Knoxville (UTK). Complete descriptions of the UTK quality assurance effort can be found in a paper presented by Banta and Fisher to the 1989 meeting of the American Educational Research Association, in an article by Banta and Moffett in a 1987 issue of the Jossey-Bass monograph series New Dimensions for Higher Education, and in an article by Banta appearing in the Spring 1990 issue of *Assessment Update* (Banta, 1990b).

At UTK, a research university, fifteen years of investment in quality assurance have produced one of the nation's leading assessment programs. Stimulated by the development of the Tennessee Performance Funding Project described in Chapter Eight, UTK has developed an assessment program with three major elements. To ascertain the extent to which student development objectives are being met in general education skills, the university uses the American College Testing Comp instrument. For assessment in major fields, faculty in over 100 programs employ a variety of standardized examinations, locally developed instruments, and exercises, and two faculty were contracted for development of a student satisfaction survey described in Chapter Five. A series of these survey instruments is used for obtaining feedback from enrolled students (undergraduate and graduate), alumni, and dropouts. Banta and Moffett report that the surveys ask respondents about the use and quality of various campus services, programs and services provided by academic departments, and dimensions of classroom experience (Banta and Moffett, 1987).

The decision and improvement payoffs to these quality assurance ventures are described in the paper by Banta and Fisher (1989). For example, reviews of the student ratings led to a series of institutional ventures designed to produce more personal contact between students and faculty. Student internships were implemented and strengthened. Catalogue copy of courses and policy was reviewed and clarified. Assessment in major fields led the College of Business to reduce course requirements in economics and enhance those in business law. The renewal improvement outcomes derived from both the assessment process and quality assurance outcomes are apparent in the work at UTK. Most important of all, the application of the results for improving the educational process and the impact on students is apparent.

Here, then, is another institution that has established itself as a model of quality assurance initiative. It was not always so. The University of Tennessee has taken an interesting journey. One of the authors was involved in a visit to UTK in the Fall of 1975, a visit associated with the early development of the performance funding inventive project described in Chapter Eight. The purpose of the visit was to see if UTK would be willing to become a pilot institution in testing several approaches to quality assurance, as the state of Tennessee explored the policy question regarding the feasibility of allocating a portion of state funding support on some educational performance basis, as contrasted to an enrollment basis.

The conversation involved a dozen academic deans along with colleagues from the office of the vice chancellor for academic affairs, which had convened the meeting at the request of the author and his assistant director from the Tennessee Higher Education Commission. On that day, the deans of the university were unable to agree that there were any common intellectual expectations for each of their bachelor's degrees, even though all had the UTK catalogue in front of them showing that there were several courses—English, American history, mathematics—required of every bachelor's degree recipient at the university.

Anyone who has participated in a similar discussion on general education ceases to be amazed at occasional flashes of irrationality in the house of intellect and becomes more patient with the paradox that we can be smart and dumb at the same time. There was, more importantly, a good bit of attitudinal distance between that opening discussion among the university deans in the Fall of 1975 and the significant and exemplary accomplishment reported by Banta and Fisher.

What made the difference in this journey was that one dean in the group, the dean of engineering, was willing to engage in the pilot effort and that the university administration was willing to support him. When the performance funding policy was finally adopted and placed in action in 1979-1980, the university, which began this experiment so cautiously, became one of the more aggressive institutions in the state, until it reached its current level of national visibility for its quality assurance efforts—a salute to leadership flexibility, commitment, and competence.

Student First Quality Quest at Samford University

This final institutional example allows us to emphasize several points not treated in the five previous illustrations and also prepares the way for the development of a strategic and unifying vision of quality in Chapter Ten. Our descriptions of the five institutions treated quality assurance primarily in the area of educational programs, but their quality concerns by no means stop with the quality of these programs.

One institution, however, that is clearly developing the concept of total quality management is Samford University in Birmingham, Alabama, a private university of approximately 4,000 students with an array of educational programs, including schools of law, pharmacy, nursing, and divinity. In designing training programs for faculty and staff at Samford, and for other quality assurance forums, Dr. John Harris, leading scholar in assessment and quality assurance in higher education, builds on the fourteen-point quality assurance approach outlined by W. E. Deming (1986). Deming is considered the American pioneer in quality assurance thought and the progenitor of the dramatic Japanese improvements in quality in the latter half of this century. Harris also includes in the Samford training program other analytical tools associated with total quality management: flowcharts of production processes (educational and administrative), cause-and-effect (fishbone) diagrams, pareto charts, histograms, and scatter diagrams (Harris, Hillenmeyer, and Foran, 1989).

The total quality management approach culminates in the plan-do-check-act cycle. The "plan" step calls for the analysis of operational issues and the design of an improvement plan. The "do" step constitutes the implementation of the design plan. The "check" step compares the performance of the improvement design to a baseline performance criterion that allows evaluation of the design. And the "act" step completes the quality assurance cycle by making the new design an operational reality.

To illustrate the application of total quality management at Samford University, we can explore the results of teams at work in several noneducational areas. Quality assurance teams have reduced utility costs by installing room motion sensors that automatically turn lights on and off, have enhanced the illumination levels of fluorescent light fixtures and simultaneously reduced the number of bulbs from four to two in those fixtures, and have dramatically reduced the response and completion time for emergency maintenance in student housing.

Among the process and cost improvements produced on other campuses with the total quality management approach is a significant reduction in the admissions and records office staffing pattern (a reduction in operation budget by one fourth), with concomitant service improvement. Another campus has improved its approach to scheduling facilities renovation projects, and still another has developed a co-generation electricity facility that has not only reduced utility bills but produced revenue for the campus.

Samford University president Tom Corts emphasizes the importance of the customer/client in quality assurance by naming the Samford program the "student first quality quest" (Harris, 1990). Corts also emphasizes that a concern for students is not a new issue with him by referring to his May 14, 1973, article in the *Chronicle of Higher Education* entitled "College Should Be Consumer Minded." In addition to "student first," Corts also nicely illustrates a number of other internal and external "customers" of the university, including donors and other supporters.

At Samford University, the total quality management program illustrates that a concern for quality is a concern to be cultivated throughout the university in both educational and administrative support activities, that training involving both philosophical and analytical components is an essential foundation for performance improvements, that understanding often comes with action, and that quality improvements can be realized even as we continue to learn. Harris uses the term "collaborative quest" (Harris, 1990, p. 1) to describe the journey of learning, application, and partnership associated with quality assurance. Thus, the Samford University approach to quality assurance also illustrates the "decision and discovery" spirit we mentioned earlier in this chapter and the renewal outcomes that we will explore in the closing discussion.

An Integrated Quality Assurance Model

As we reflect on the various tests of quality presented in the previous chapters and the principles cited in the opening reflections of this chapter, we are led to another question: Is it possible to conceive a model of quality assurance that would furnish a minimal base for a campus thinking about its students and its programs—a model that would speak to both improvement and accountability motives?

One liability of presenting such a model is that it might prove limiting in its effect. We do not want to encourage a dependent spirit that can be linked to "looking in the back of the book for answers" before we try to solve the problem. We believe, however, that this potential liability is a modest one and that there is merit in thinking through this question. Reflected in our definition of quality and in the principles we have outlined is our intent to encourage individual campuses and their faculties to define and describe their own varieties of excellence—the features of purpose and performance that mark the perimeters of distinction for a given campus.

Tables 9.3 and 9.4 present the suggested elements of this model. The elements of Table 9.3 center on student performance and attitude indicators, whereas the elements of Table 9.4 describe program and service assessment. In Table 9.4 we want to draw attention to a cluster of performance indicators associated more with

**Table 9.3. A Minimal Element Quality Assurance Model
of Student Assessment.**

Assessment	Decision focus
Upon admission	
College readiness skills inventory	To ascertain student readiness for college work
Interests inventory	To explore student personal and career interests
Values inventory	To establish baseline student values disposition
End of sophomore year	
General education knowledge skills	To ensure that each student has mastered acceptable skill knowledge
Communication skill	
Problem-solving/analytical/ critical thinking skill	
Reading skill	To ascertain changes (value-added) in student knowledge and skill
Familiarity with modes of thought	
Cultural/historical awareness	
Health/nutrition/exercise awareness	
At graduation	
Major field assessment	To ensure that each student has achieved acceptable mastery of concepts in major field
Value inventory	To chart major changes in values disposition
Senior thesis/project portfolio	To ensure student ability to conceptualize, implement, and report on inquiry
Postgraduation	
Alumni follow-up surveys	To obtain alumni evaluation of programs/services and establish baseline and trend data on satisfaction

**Table 9.4. A Minimal Element Quality Assurance Model
of Programs and Services.**

Activity	Decision focus
Annual	
Review and evaluation of newspaper/media coverage	To evaluate evidence of educational/management integrity
Review and evaluation of governing board/executive/legislative audits or other	
Special reports	
Periodic	
Sampling survey of enrolled students (phone, interview, and/or questionnaire)	To evaluate programs and services as seen by "customers and clients" of the campus
Sampling survey of alumni	
Sampling survey of service-area constituents	
Sampling survey of employers and schools receiving graduates or transfers	
As required	
Regional accreditation	To ensure that program service units and institution reflect on goals and performance
Professional accreditation	To subject programs and services to external perspective/standard
Academic program reviews by peer teams, advisory boards, or board of visitors	To encourage renewal moments

the quality of leadership and support than the quality of educational programs and services. Here we list the acquisition and evaluation of media coverage profiles and financial/performance audit reports.

These evidences of performance reflect a conviction that the educational and leadership integrity of a campus is also related to its quality. We recognize the danger of depending upon newspaper and media coverage, for example, as a reflection of campus performance. However, a campus that is frequently cited in the press and media for integrity questions related to its personnel, its policies, and its programs invites questions about quality. We do not believe that quality exists independent of integrity. A campus periodically cited by the inspector general or legislative auditor for poor judgment, sloppy practice, or obvious criminal activity will at the very least have a more difficult time keeping public attention on its educational quality.

The Renewal Outcomes

Quality assurance efforts constitute a discovery venture, an adventure in learning. Learning about the nature of our goals (what we thought they were, what they really are, what we want them to be), learning about the nature of performance and how to define performance so that it adequately reflects both individual and institutional diversity, learning about the nature of truth and more about how we access truth: These are renewal outcomes worthy of an educational enterprise. Here is a brief and closing exploration of the nature of those outcomes.

Discovering Purpose

To suggest that we can evaluate the quality and effectiveness of any educational program without knowing the goals of that program seems the height of illogic. There is, however, more than a little merit in a "goal-free" evaluation. As faculty and staff ask questions about results (How good a job are we doing?), they are inevitably forced to address questions of intent. Asking questions of ends forces us to address questions of beginnings.

Academics are fond of the notion that one of the purposes of a college education is to develop in students the ability to think critically. Now how do we go about developing that facility? Do we simply throw students into a smorgasbord of courses from different disciplines and trust—not really know—that this feast will, in fact, develop the capacity to think critically?

Suppose that developing critical thinking skill is a legitimate goal for our general education program and we decide to assess the extent to which that skill is being developed in our students. Does critical thinking involve more than just problem solving? Does it involve the ability to exercise judgment? What about the ability to analyze and synthesize? What about the practical intelligence suggested by Sternberg to which we referred in Chapter Seven? What instrument might we employ to assess the mastery of critical thinking skill? The Watson Glaser Test of Critical Thinking is available, and the Academic Profile Test of ETS claims to measure reading and critical thinking skill. Will a historian, a literature scholar, a musician, an engineer, an economist, and a chemist agree on whether these instruments do, in fact, measure this skill?

In his preface to Richard Paul's book *Critical Thinking* (1990), Gerald Nosich describes critical thinking as more than the acquisition of knowledge and skill. It involves the ability to examine without prejudice points of view that are directly opposed to those we hold. The person who thinks critically does not just entertain differing points of view; he or she actively seeks opposing perspectives and ideas. The key point to this partial definition of critical thinking is that it involves elements of mind and heart. Critical thinking will not exist in the absence of a passion—a sustaining and driven curiosity harnessed to habits of judgment and evaluation. Paul's book proposes that critical thinking is not just cognitive but also moral and affective.

Does the Watson Glaser Test of Critical Thinking or the ETS Academic Profile Test meet this measurement challenge? To engage the question of how to assess the presence or absence of critical thinking in our students takes one on an interesting and exciting conceptual journey concerning learning goals, concept definitions, and measurement.

Defining Priorities

Putting first things first is an act of leadership. When Robert Hutchins took over the presidency of the University of Chicago, he found that "the great depression conferred marked benefits upon the university, for it forced a reconsideration of the whole enterprise. The first thing I had to contend with was the demand that I cut everything 25 percent. This made no sense to me. I thought what was important should be supported and what was trivial should be dropped" (Hutchins, 1966, p. 182).

We now know enough about mind–body interaction and the importance of nutrition and exercise in our lives that it would be reasonable to find some moment in our general education programs for knowledge of our physical selves. We should also consider new knowledge emerging as biologists explore the genetic factors related to disease. Is it important for this kind of self-knowledge—knowledge of nutrition and kinesthetic intelligence as described by Gardner—to be a goal of our general education programs? If so, what priority position should it occupy? And should there be a value-added assessment just as we might insist on for communication and critical thinking skills?

A serendipitous outcome of quality assurance exercises is that they often lead those working on the exercises—faculty and students—to an improved sense of what is important in a college education.

Enlarging Our Vision of Quality

One of our more obvious convictions is that when faculty and staff begin to struggle with the philosophical and technical questions of quality, effectiveness, and evaluation, they will appreciate more fully the variety of meanings associated with quality.

When faculty and staff begin the exercise of developing an applied philosophy of quality, new understandings will emerge. In a community of learning, this is an important and appropriate outcome to model before our students because it demonstrates an institutional commitment to curiosity and courage.

The exercise before our students and our colleges exemplifies one other important idea. Of all the pleasures enjoyed by educated men and women—learning, loving, serving, creating—learning is perhaps one of the most fundamental. Our willingness to escape disciplinary boundaries—indeed, to apply the truth tools of our disciplines—in a venture of common interest sends a happy message to our students, who learn not only from what we say but from what we model.

Extending Value Sensitivities

An extension of the previous renewal outcome is that the values of those who undertake journeys of discovery will be tested. As we confront questions of measurement and meaning, we discover again that not all that is meaningful, not all that is real, and not all that is important yield to measurement: the smile of an awakening mind, the satisfied grin of mastery, the courage of men and women with ideas in advance of their time, the payoff of perseverance, and the inventing force of knowledge in action.

A ray of sunlight falling through an early morning mist will reveal something about the nature of light that cannot be found or expressed in the physics of reflection and refraction. An orchestra performing Dvorak's New World Symphony will reveal something about music and humankind that cannot be found in the laws of musical intervals. The beauty of a painting or a poem can define the limits of the rational. Explorations in modern physics invite us to consider the reality of "antimatter" and "dark matter" and reveal again the short half life of "common sense." Here is a note from now-deceased Harvard scholar Stephen Bailey: "I have a fairly simple theory: It is that what students take away in a positive sense from institutions of higher education is little more than the spillover of excitement and commitment they observe in the adult models about them. If administrators, faculty and support staff are made up of contentious cynics and spiritual zombies, students will develop a notion of the life of the mind that is finally expressed in the phrase 'who needs it.' If, on the other hand, they find themselves surrounded by human beings who exude excitement about their own lives, an invaluable role model is created as young people are induced to recognize the possibilities of joy in the options of continued growth" (Bailey, 1974, p. 4).

Thus, in quality assurance efforts are to be found lovely discovery moments: wondering about the richness of human experience and talent, valuing a diversity of realities, experiencing humility and anxiety in the face of the unknown, and knowing the power of decision and daring.

Promoting Personnel Development

This renewal outcome is really embedded in a number of those already outlined. It is worth, however, a more specific mention. Rightly orchestrated, quality assurance efforts open yet another avenue for personnel development and growth, perhaps as useful as a good sabbatical.

Physicists will learn about the Delphi Technique. Historians will argue about normative and criterion standards. Accountants will debate not numbers but the merits of contrasting goals. Economists will stray from their regression analyses and explore adversary methods of evaluation. Literature scholars will examine the meaning of the standard error of measurement. Psychologists will teach literature scholars what the standard error means. All of this can take place on a journey of learning and developing.

In the decade of the seventies, one of the authors directed a statewide quality assurance venture designed to explore the feasibility of allocating some portion of state funds to colleges and universities on a performance rather than an enrollment criterion, on a criterion of achievement rather than one of activity. A bright and energetic colleague in that venture was an accomplished literature scholar from the state's research university, who began the venture as the project's resident critic. This scholar, however, played no small role in keeping the entire five-year discovery process both honest and productive. He brought not only intelligence and a reasoned suspicion to the venture but also curiosity and intellectual stamina that other, more agreeable "friends" often lacked. No person participating in this statewide venture became a more informed and passionate advocate of quality assurance than did this friendly critic.

Quality assurance and evaluation ventures will present opportunity, then, for all to explore new conceptual and personal frontiers, to investigate and challenge biases, and to fashion friendships on a community venture. This last note carries us to a final renewal outcome.

Strengthening Community

Few instruments of human construct fail to have both positive and negative valence. We have cited what we believe to be the positive and the renewal outcomes of quality assurance ventures. There is intent. There is style. There is result. Obviously, poor or mean judgment in any one of these steps can work against all of the renewal outcomes cited here, can obscure purpose, can divert energy, can nurture cynicism and suspicion.

Rightly conceived and rightly prosecuted, however, the renewal benefits can strengthen community by bringing colleagues together in the spiritual strengthening that comes from working on a common goal, from translating difficulty and disappointment into achievement, and from fashioning consensus out of conflict. Why is this so important? We restate a point made in Chapter One: There can be no quality in any educational enterprise without caring, and there can be no caring without community.

Community Renewal: A Journey of Decision and Discovery

What kind of community? We outlined the dimensions of community, as suggested by a 1990 Carnegie report, in the concluding pages of Chapter One. Here we offer this brief note from one of the nation's leading scholars and academic administrators: "Universities are a very special kind of place. They are fragile as truth itself is fragile. They exist by public sufferance, and it is a marvel that the public at large supports with its dollar an institution that is independent, free standing. Openly critical of the conventional wisdom, enchanted with controversy, hospitable to those who 'think otherwise.' May it always be so" (Enarson, 1973, p. 16).

Critical of the conventional wisdom, friendly to disputation, enchanted with controversy, hospitable to those who think otherwise—we should be willing to model within higher education what we hold as a model before society. Asking questions of purpose and

performance—the search for quality—offers an unparalleled moment to demonstrate the best features of a learning community. To
those elements of community character cited by Enarson, we ap-
pend those of curiosity, caring, and courage. The search for collegiate quality is a journey of caring and daring, an exercise in reason
and passion: an adventure in decision and discovery.

TEN

Developing a Strategic Vision of Academic Quality

For anyone who writes, a 1990 book titled *Rotten Rejections* will prove a delightful companion. It is a compilation of rejections received by authors great and small. Surely one of the more interesting comes from a Chinese economic journal: "We have read your manuscript with boundless delight. If we were to publish your paper, it would be impossible for us to publish any work of lower standard. As it is unthinkable that in the next thousand years we shall see its equal, we are, to our regret, compelled to return your divine composition, and to beg you a thousand times to overlook our short sight and timidity" (Bernard, 1990, p. 44).

This lighthearted introduction on matters of quality standards launches our concluding reflections. In the previous chapters, we have explored and evaluated contemporary approaches to quality assurance. In this chapter, we will not revisit the advantages and liabilities of those quality assurance instruments—having already done so to our satisfaction and, we hope, to the reader's. In Chapter Nine we proposed a set of principles that are essential in the design and implementation of an effective quality assurance effort and we pointed to some of the renewing benefits that may derive from that effort.

In this concluding chapter, our purpose is to examine systemic concerns associated with the construction of an effective quality assurance program and to aim toward the future. We hope to build a vision of quality that will prove strategic and unifying in its effect.

We use the descriptors *strategic* and *unifying* with careful intent. In the January-February 1991 issue of *Assessment Update*, Daniel Seymour contrasts collegiate perspectives on quality to those of the corporate sector. In the corporate sector, Seymour suggests that "quality has evolved from a narrow technical discipline, focused on the detection of manufacturing flaws, to a broader field that encompasses all stages, from design to production to market" (p. 1). His view reinforces that of Garvin, whom we cited in Chapter One. In contrast to the corporate perspective, Seymour observes that "higher education continues to view quality as a problem to be solved" (p. 1).

From previous chapters we can identify a number of systemic liabilities. First, we have several approaches to quality assurance, not always with clear and effective interactions among them. Second, we have a variety of partners, on and off campus, interested in quality assurance, not always united in motive and tactic. Third, we have a range of perspectives on the purpose of quality assurance efforts. Some look on quality assurance with an eye to civic accountability, others for the improvement of teaching and learning, others as a means for student development, others as a tool for management, and still others as an occupation for research—all legitimate purposes. Fourth, our concerns for quality may be myopic, an occupation of the moment. And finally, there can be a serious question on many campuses as to whether the concern for quality has penetrated the institution, residing not in the hearts and minds of those who give life and meaning to the institution but too often resting only on the administrative surface.

Strategies and Scholars

In our lead-in comments, we indicated that the use of the terms "strategic" and "unifying" would carry particular meanings. Although we hope to make those meanings clear in this discussion, we admit to a bit of apprehension. Too often concepts and terminology are plucked from corporate-sector commentary and put to work in collegiate settings. Such usage constitutes a kind of "buzzword" vocabulary, a surface mentality, that shows we have read the latest works in business management. That such terminology often enters and exits collegiate conversation with modest impact is apparent if we look back on such terms as program budgeting, networking, information systems, and other phrases that have occupied our attention over the past quarter century. The current terms include *strategic, downsizing,* and *environmental scanning.*

We have even borrowed the concept of bankruptcy from corporate friends and now make place for *academic bankruptcy.* Whether bankruptcy appropriately conveys our concerns for justice and mercy in either financial or academic settings is a matter open to question. And what contribution does it make to the cause of personal responsibility, which we take to be a legitimate mark of an educated person?

The discomfort with the transfer of corporate and business management concepts to higher education settings has a long history reaching back to the *cult of efficiency* concerns raised years ago by Callahan (1962). A contemporary expression of this concern can be found in Barzun's March 20, 1991, opinion piece in the *Chronicle of Higher Education,* "We Need Leaders Who Can Make Our Institutions Companies of Scholars, Not Corporations with Employees and Customers" (p. B1). The college president is described by Barzun as one who "travels all over the land to address alumni clubs and assure them of the splendid health of their alma mater, whose pulse he has not really taken since he and she first shook hands" (p. B1). Barzun further refers to college presidents as "galley slaves running to stay in the same place" (p. B1). The point here is not that collegiate America cannot learn from corporate America. It can. There is room for two-way traffic in the learning exchange, however; some sensitivity to the nature of the enterprise is necessary in either exchange.

Galley slaves, congenial fund-raisers, absentee executives— these and other unflattering terms applied to college presidents rival the negative descriptors of faculty found in critiques cited earlier, such as those by Sykes, Cahn, and Smith. This criticism from within and without, by the way, constitutes one of the climate concerns in which our search for quality must take root, a contextual matter to which we now turn.

The Leadership Context

There are multiple realities to every time and place. Whether we have an accurate grasp of the environmental variables affecting higher education, we leave the reader to judge. Here, however, are reflections on ethical, economic, and educational factors at work.

Americans continue to demonstrate their support of higher education. The evidence of that trust and support is visible, for example, in the array of incentive programs that have been funded in recent years, as outlined in Chapter Eight. And what is the investment of faith and finance represented in the development of our research universities, the rapid expansion of state colleges and universities, and the unparalleled growth of community colleges in the last half of this century? It is impossible to traverse the collegiate landscape of this nation without being impressed by the extraordinary investment that Americans have made in opportunity and quality.

The 1987 Carnegie Foundation technical report, *A Classification of Institutions of Higher Education*, revealed, for example (even in a decade of retrenchment), a net gain of 317 new institutions of higher education in the period 1976 to 1987. The number of institutions granting doctorates increased in this eleven-year period from 184 to 213. Although the number of comprehensive universities and colleges remained relatively stable, the number of two-year institutions increased from 1,146 to 1,367.

However, comments throughout this book make clear that American higher education may not continue to enjoy unquestioned loyalty or financial support in the future. We may have entered a period in which more intensive questioning of purpose and performance is expected. The spirit of the times is plainly captured in sources such as Newman's book *Choosing Quality* (1987) cited in Chapter Eight and in some of the book-length critiques cited in Chapter Nine. To these we add the commentary of Robert

Atwell, president of the American Council on Education (ACE), who, in a March 26, 1990, letter to college presidents of ACE member institutions cautioned: "Gone are the days in Washington when our virtues were self-evident and our faults nearly invisible. Whatever we think of the national educational goals, and however long they remain a focus for policy making, our job over the next few years is to show that we are using our resources wisely, that we are making tough decisions about priorities, and that we are facing up to the needs of a changing population and a changing world. Only by dealing with the substance of our problems can we refurbish the public image of higher education and restore confidence in our ability to advance the national interest" (Atwell, 1990, p. 4).

Current events do not always make pleasing or productive contributions to the problem of image and confidence. According to several stories from the *Chronicle of Higher Education* (Cordes, 1991a, 1991b), Stanford University president Donald Kennedy was put on the griddle by a congressional panel for alleged irregularities in federal research grant overhead charges. These included among other things questionable practices in assigning expenditures related to the president's home to federal research grants. These stories were followed shortly by the story of a presidential colleague who went from president to "potential inmate" within a few months— a slide of occupation and domicile of no small moment. Former University of South Carolina president James Holderman has been indicted for allegedly using his presidential post for personal gain. The story of his indictment was carried in the April 3, 1991, issue of the *Chronicle of Higher Education* ("Ex-President Is Indicted for Illegal Payments," 1991), with a follow-up story of the mixed results in the April 24, 1991, issue (Leatherman, 1991b).

In an earlier issue of the *Chronicle* ("Minn. Legislature Audits . . . ," 1988), two other college presidents were placed in public pillory. A Minnesota legislative audit inquiry reportedly was examining the expenditures of $1.45 million to refurbish the home and $200,000 to renovate the office of president Kenneth H. Keller, who later resigned from the office. These expenditures included approximately $16,000 for a desk and credenza in the president's office (p. A22). In the same issue appeared a story of West Texas State University president Ed Roach filing a libel lawsuit against two professors. Consider the ethical and social plain of activities associated with this institutional ferment: "Anonymous individuals also have sent cards purportedly smeared with excrement to those known to support the president, said George Whittenburg, Mr. Roach's attorney. The cards accuse the recipients of being 'brown noses' for T. Boone Pickens, the oil magnate who chairs West Texas State's Board of Regents. Someone also had a black cake and black balloons delivered to the president, Mr. Whittenburg said" ("West Texas President Files Lawsuit . . . ," p. A13).

Certainly, these illustrations do not represent the reality of goodness that one can find among the majority of administrators and faculty who invest their time and talent in caring performance in higher education. But just one behavioral departure from the track of nobility and integrity in our colleges and universities mars our image for quality. And, unfortunately, these ethical concerns are occurring at a time when the possibility of cost containment is getting more play in both the public and professional press; thus ethical contextual concerns are linked to economic concerns.

An article in the March 6, 1991, issue of the *Chronicle of Higher Education* is entitled "Increasing Productivity at Colleges Is a Hot Topic for the 1990's." The national symposium on strategic higher education finance and management issues in the 1990s apparently produced a leading concern on "getting more bang for the buck." This article cites the growth in administrative staffs in recent years and traces some of that growth to the transfer of tasks, such as advising, once done by faculty members (McMillen, 1991).

The provocative pieces emerging from the Pew Higher Education Research Program are welcome additions to higher education policy discussions. Two recent issues of *Policy Perspectives,* a publication of that program, center on cost-containment themes. The visuals attending these policy papers always carry a quick meaning. For example, in June 1990 the article entitled "The Lattice and the Ratchet" treats the issue of enlarging administrative staffs with a cartoon depicting capital additions to the university. A small "classroom wing" is shown attached to larger wings described as "committee interface and dialogue wing, faculty talk show booking wing, papercup tracking wing, grant writing wing, and safety compliance wing" (p. 1).

The February 1991 issue of *Policy Perspectives,* entitled "The Other Side of the Mountain," carries a cluster of discussions on cost containment. A front-page cartoon depicts an overweight administrative officer standing before a blackboard on which the theme "University Shape Up Class" is written. Before the "administration" teacher are a variety of folks representing different departments—some obviously fat and others suffering from serious malnutrition. The teacher is saying to the class: "Just to keep things absolutely fair, we'll each be asked to lose ten pounds" (p. 1).

In one of the internal papers entitled "Cost Containment: Committing to a New Economic Reality," Zemsky and Massey identify three factors that have contributed to cost increases in higher education: the practice of setting tuition to cover current programs and new initiatives, the proliferation and entrenchment of administrative staff, and the shift of faculty interest away from institutional goals such as teaching toward scholarship and publication. Anyone who has walked the halls of some colleges and universities and seen there the range of administrative offices, heard there the complaints of students about poor teaching and poor service, and noted there the empty offices of professors teaching one or no courses in the current term can testify to the accuracy of this analysis.

For Zemsky and Massey the essential message is that "the 1990's are shaping up to be a period of unprecedented austerity in post-World War II history of the nation's public sector. No matter what the source of concern—the economy, declining tax revenues, or institutional inefficiencies—the message is the same: institutions need to live more effectively within reduced means. . . . Most of all, the message is that colleges and universities must learn to decrease or cut some, but clearly not all, expenditures in order to continue doing well—perhaps even better—what they have done well in the past" (Zemsky and Massey, 1991, pp. 1, 2A).

For other evidence of this environmental ferment concerning the financial future of American colleges and universities, we can turn to the May 27, 1991, issue of *Forbes,* which featured an interview with Nobel Laureate economist Milton Friedman. After a discussion in which Friedman explores the "products" of the contemporary college and university (schooling, research, and monuments), reflects on the inefficiencies of the collegiate sector, and points to notable independent research units such as Battelle Memorial Institute and Bell Labs, Friedman says: "Let's set up some taxable liberal arts colleges and see how they compete" (Spencer, 1991, p. 304).

Accompanying these ethical and economic issues are educational challenges. Accommodating and nurturing the increased diversity of those seeking access to higher education remains a matter of high priority. Finding ways to reconcile and reward good teaching is a topic of lively conversation. Respecting and nurturing forms of scholarship beyond that of discovery, which is the aim of basic research, is yet another educational issue. The Carnegie Foundation for the Advancement of Teaching report *Scholarship Reconsidered: Priorities of the Professoriate* (Boyer, 1990) urges an enlarged definition of scholarship to include scholarship associated with teaching, with the integration of knowledge across disciplines, and with the public service applications of knowledge. The monograph reminds collegiate educators that many contemporary issues—of environment, of social and economic justice, of health—were first and forcefully engaged by writer/critics moving independent of the academy. Where scholars of the contemporary American college and university can be found on these and other issues is illustrated nicely by an issue of *Policy Perspectives* from the Pew Charitable Trust Program. The May 1989 issue "The Business of the Business" is fronted by a cartoon in which a custodian with mop and broom in hand stands before the lectern in a large, crowded lecture class. The custodian reports to the class that "your professor is at her publisher's. The T.A. is doing research, and before he left for the Today Show, the chair asked me to lead today's class on the Divine Comedy." The catalogue of contemporary collegiate ills is then described as follows:

- Too seldom is collegiate teaching viewed for what it is: The business of the business—the activity that is central to all colleges and universities.
- Too many institutions attempt to be all things to potential customers: Too few define their missions with precision or limit the scope of their enterprise to what they do best.

- Too often teaching is seen as private, protected by academic freedom, and conducted in the classroom behind closed doors.
- Too many professors still stand as tellers of truth, inculcating knowledge in students; too many students sit and listen passively—or not at all.
- Too many faculty, pursuing narrow specializations, teach at the periphery of their disciplines, resulting in curricula that are increasingly fragmented and atomized.
- Too often teaching is an "open loop system," leaving faculty without feedback on what or how well their students are learning.
- Too often junior faculty are sent into the classroom untrained, ill-prepared, and without a sense of what it means to be scholar mentor [Pew Higher Education Research Program, 1989, p. 1].

The authors then offer this advice: "We believe American colleges and universities must make a fundamental investment in quality control—not to provide scorecards to satisfy the whims of public inquiry, but rather to develop the context within which faculty can both singularly and collectively assess the quality of learning in their classrooms" (1989, p. 3). This comment furnishes a transitional signal for engaging now the principal purpose of the chapter, the development of a strategic vision of quality.

A Strategic Vision of Quality

All labels have liabilities. The shorthand advantage of labels can prevent us from entering into deeper understandings—of people, organizations, and concepts. In this chapter, we are interested in developing a strategic vision of quality. What exactly do we mean by the term *strategic*? Let us examine the meaning first by looking at its application in both planning and quality assurance contexts.

In the December 1984 issue of *Quality Progress*, Hagan described the basic elements of a strategic approach to quality as follows:

- It is not those who offer the product but those whom it serves—the customers, users, and those who influence or represent them—who have the final word on how well a product fulfills needs and expectations.
- Satisfaction is related to competitive offerings.
- Satisfaction, as related to competitive offerings, is formed over the product lifetime, not just at the time of purchase.
- A composite of attributes is needed to provide the most satisfaction to those whom the product serves [Hagan, 1984, p. 21].

Customer judgment of fitness for use, long-term time frame, multiple dimensions of judgment: Here are concepts that we can put to use.

Hearn has developed an extensive review of issues related to strategic planning, and he extracts from his analysis five associated principles. There are clear relationships between strategic planning and the assurance of quality. The principles that Hearn (1988) outlines can prove informing:

1. "Principle one is that strategic planning is wholistic, in that it is focused on organizational goals, purposes, values, and mission" (p. 218).
2. "Principle two is that strategic planning is medium-term in orientation, although it is executed in the short term via priority setting, program evaluations, budget, and so forth" (p. 219).
3. "Principle three is that strategic planning is both externally and internally focused and seeks actively to be both at once" (p. 219).
4. "Principle four is that strategic planning is ongoing, not simply a one-time planning effort" (p. 220).
5. "Principle five is that strategic planning pursues a blend of qualitative and quantitative approaches" (p. 221).

Chaffee (1985) explores the concept of strategy in both corporate and collegiate organizations. She points to the military origins of the concept and then outlines three models of strategy that help us understand the ways in which organizations relate to their environment: linear, adaptive, and interpretive. The first is concerned with ways in which to compete, the second with ways in which to adapt, and the third with ways in which to motivate. Chaffee suggests that sophistication in the understanding and application of strategy is more apparent in corporate than in collegiate settings, a criticism somewhat parallel to Seymour's commentary on quality perceptions in corporate and collegiate settings.

It occurs to us, however, that the presence of sophistication may be judged not just in intellectual terms (What has been written and conceptualized?) but in applied terms (Did the writing and the conceptualization do any good?). On the basis of several variables—competitiveness, market share, balance of payments, technology transfer success—there is at least some basis to ask about the success of strategic thinking in the corporate sector. And on the basis of current conversations swirling about higher education—cost containment, management integrity, educational responsibility—there is equally good reason to ask about the impact of strategic thinking in the collegiate sector as well.

Fincher is another higher education scholar who has written frequently on the concept of strategy and its application in planning and evaluation (1982, 1988). He is guarded, however, in the persuasion that strategic thinking will enjoy a useful transfer to collegiate life. In his 1982 commentary, for example, Fincher suggests that if the term *strategic planning* is to provide any conceptual or applied advantage in higher education "a considerable refurbishing is in order" (Fincher, 1982, p. 375). In the 1988 paper, Fincher points to possible negative outcomes from strategic planning and assessment: "Unfortunately for many institutions in the 1990s, the dominant strategies for change may continue to be strategic planning and the assessment of educational outcomes. The former will continue to foster a competitiveness among institutions that should seek better ways of cooperation, and the latter may easily become compliant practices that will satisfy public demand but produce no significant or enduring changes in institutional programs and student services" (Fincher, 1988, p. 275).

In one of the earlier texts on strategic planning for higher education, Merson and Qualls (1979) emphasized the development of a management intelligence system that would enable an institution to be more sensitive to changing environmental conditions in such areas as market demand, governance, student financial aid, consumer behavior, staff relations and collective bargaining, charitable giving, and management talent. Some of the language associated with strategic discussion can, unfortunately, constitute further evidence, in the perspective of some faculty, that the term *management intelligence* is an oxymoron. What Merson and Qualls have in mind, however, is an information base of external indicators (demographic and economic trends, technological and educational trends, for example) and internal indicators (enrollment profiles, faculty and staff characteristics, academic program and student service profiles, for example). Merson and Qualls develop a four-stage strategic planning and evaluation process: (1) diagnosis—What is our present position?, (2) planning—What should be our mission?, (3) resource allocation—What steps will we take during the next five years?, and (4) evaluation—Have our goals been attained? To their credit, Merson and Qualls insist that this four-step process include the discipline of asking: "How effective are our educational programs?" (p. 26). Strategy, then, not only reflects a sensitivity to environment but encourages attention to how goals will be attained and whether they have been attained.

These commentaries draw our attention to several points pertinent to this closing chapter. They remind us first that no organization—corporate or collegiate—can ignore its environment and expect to have success in responding to and shaping its future. Any sensible vision of quality, then, must involve sensitivity to some of these environmental forces. Second, strategy embraces those assumptions and values that guide our approach to the future.

What do we mean, then, when we urge the development of a strategic and unifying vision of quality? Such a vision opens with the realization that there is no policy, no behavior, no practice, no value that does not have a direct impact on the condition of quality on a college or university campus. In addition to environmental sensitivity, a strategic and unifying vision of quality, then, is one in which these perspectives are honored:

1. A philosophical perspective: The qualitative concerns of a campus constitute a philosophical window into its commitments and values.
2. A definitional perspective: The definition of quality embraces both technical and ethical performance questions.
3. A commitment perspective: The commitment to quality is one in which there is an awareness of and allegiance to quality that penetrates to the heart of the institution, constituting a premier call on administrative and faculty values.
4. A client perspective: The judgments of quality attend first to the interests and developmental needs of our students and then to the interests of civic accountability.
5. A time perspective: The time frame for evaluating quality is both short term and long term.
6. A funding perspective: The linkage of quality to funding does not assume that quality always associates with funding in a linear relationship.
7. A systems perspective: There is a coherent and logical system of interactions among the various institutional approaches to quality assurance, and this system is clearly linked to institutional purpose and decision needs.
8. A proactive perspective: There is no waiting for the stimulus of agencies external to the campus—boards, legislatures, accrediting agencies, and so on. The campus demonstrates an aggressive and offensive initiative.

A Philosophical Perspective

In his 1991 book *Assessment for Excellence,* to which we earlier referred, Alexander Astin emphasizes that assessment practices in an institution are a reflection of its values. We entirely agree and enlarge the conviction to embrace the scope of quality assurance policy and practice. In our opening and closing reflections, we want to accent the roles of both intellect and passion, of head and heart, in the construction of an effective quality assurance system.

The acquisition of college readiness data via SAT or ACT scores, the acquisition of basic skills placement data, the acquisition of student career interests and values dispositions, the acquisition of biographical data: This extensive display of diagnostic activity when students enter our academic portals testifies to our caring about their readiness and about the quality of their preparation for successful college work. The nature of the screening and the use of the information also testify to our philosophy of admissions and the role of the institution.

What can be learned about the level and limit of caring if one looks past the entering portal? Do our quality assurance efforts tell us whether we listen to our students as they move through the education program? Do they tell us whether we show concern for demonstrated progress, or are we content that they amass only courses and credit hours? Does our system of quality assurance yield any information on whether differences in knowledge, skill, and value have been realized? Does our quality assurance system indicate that we listen to other clients, such as those of our public service programs? And does it reveal that we do more than simply count research dollars and publications in the evaluation of our research mission?

Can any campus make a claim to quality when there are only islands of caring represented in isolated scholars or academic units? Are we educating more than a physicist or a psychologist, more than a manager or mathematician? Are we attending to matters of mind, heart, and spirit? The answers to these questions can be found in the structure of our programs of quality assurance, and the operational answers will be found in the behavior of our graduates as well.

Every policy, practice, and personality on a campus tells us something about the philosophic heart of that campus. Is it selective or developmental in spirit? Is it arrogant or servant in spirit? Is it closed or open in spirit? Is it caring or callous in spirit? Is it challenging or mediocre in spirit? Is it daring or cowering in spirit? Is it responsible or apathetic in spirit? The concern for quality is a window into the institutional heart of a campus.

One of the authors recently taught a seminar with a small

number of doctoral students. One of these students appeared angry and frustrated one day. When questioned about her disposition, the problem turned on the fact that she had submitted a major paper to another graduate professor in the institution and had received no feedback whatsoever on her work. The paper simply disappeared into the creative disarray of materials in this faculty office. Will the department chair, the dean, the college senate, or the university senate engage this question of teaching responsibility? Is there a statement of teaching responsibilities in the university? Has there been any discussion among the faculty on this campus about "good practices in teaching," to which we referred in Chapter Four? And what will the answers to these questions tell us about the quality commitment of this campus?

On a newly designated public doctoral university campus, an associate professor of economics is drawing a nationally competitive, state-supported salary for the academic year. During the last academic year for which he has drawn this salary, he has not taught a single course in either of the two regular semesters. Why is this? Perhaps he has been assigned to other research or public service duties or is on temporary assignment to some administrative project. No. This associate professor has neglected his research/publication responsibilities and has failed to gain admission to the graduate faculty. Rather than face this performance and personal challenge directly, the chair of the department has in effect isolated and ignored the associate professor, leaving him to stew in this indignity while graduate students and other faculty in the department look on in both amazement and concern. Regrettably, the chair is also ignoring her responsibilities for candor and courage and for responsible application of public funds. Standing off in grand detachment is the dean of the college, who refuses to insist that the chair deal with this problem. Are leadership, stewardship, and quality related? Does this illustration (not hypothetical) support the earlier cited cost-containment concerns? Will this leadership and quality neglect eventually invite external curiosity?

Colleges and universities ought to conduct quality audits, as well as financial audits. We might be more surprised with the "exception" outcomes of the former than the latter.

A Definitional Perspective

A second foundation on which to build a strategic vision of quality takes us back to the heart of Chapter One and its definition of quality. That definition, readers may remember, embraced both technical and ethical tests for quality.

May's 1990 book *Ethics and Higher Education* is an indicator of contemporary interests in values and the role of higher education in forming values. In his introduction, May notes: "Lead articles in the national press concerning falsification of scientific research data, renewed racism on campus, violations of free speech by student publications, a seemingly endless chain of sanctions by the NCAA for major rules violations, tuition and price fixing, allegation of admissions quotas for Asian-Americans, actual or perceived abuse of institutional resources by presidents for personal gain, collusion of setting limits on financial aid, and a host of other issues have put higher education in the spotlight" (May, 1990, p. 1).

These comments, the citations offered in the opening comments of this chapter, and the illustrations that can be found in almost any issue of the *Chronicle of Higher Education* surely indicate that the ethical standards of our faculty and collegiate leadership are open to serious question. Can we expect potential students, their parents, and other civic supporters to place trust in the quality of the enterprise when they find so little to trust in our operational integrity?

Another reason to conclude that quality cannot coexist with duplicity rests within our own mission statements. How many catalogue statements include aspirations for the development of the student's intellectual skill and affective values? How many of those institutions ascertain their impact in the affective domain? And is the affective development of our students an appropriate goal? Certainly, that question has been answered by the State University System of Florida, as we reported its statewide goals in Chapter Seven.

The opinions of scholars differ. In our opening chapter, we discussed the attitudes of Lewis Mayhew and his coauthors (1990) that colleges could do little to influence character traits. Honesty, tolerance, social responsibility, and other affective outcomes: Can it be, then, that college has little impact on the formation of these values? Opinion in contrast to Mayhew, Ford, and Hubbard is offered by Alexander Astin. Astin indicates that current trends "suggest that the notion that liberal education ought to be 'value free' is no longer tenable; indeed, our political and educational leaders seem to be suggesting that social responsibility and concern for others is one of the qualities that higher education institutions should try to foster in their students" (Astin, 1991, p. 58).

And what is happening to the values of our students? The truth is we really have an incomplete picture. We know more, for example, about student values on entry, and the news, according to Astin, is not encouraging: "I have been involved in monitoring the values of incoming freshmen through the cooperative institutional research program (CIRP) for some twenty-three years now, and what I see happening is unsettling. During the past two decades, students have become markedly more materialistic and concerned with having power and status. They are increasingly coming to see an undergraduate education as a means to make more money and less as a way to get a general education" (Astin, 1991, p. 57).

In *How College Affects Students* (1991), by contrast, Pascarella and Terenzini furnish a somewhat optimistic report about changes in attitudes and values: "Indeed, as one looks across the areas of consistent change, it seems clear that colleges, as their founders and supporters might hope, appear to have a generally liberating influence on students' attitudes and values. Without exception, the nature and direction of the observed changes involve greater breadth, expansion, inclusiveness, complexity, and appreciation for the new and different. In all cases, the movement is toward greater individual freedom: artistic, cultural, intellectual, political, social, racial, educational, occupational, personal, and behavioral. These changes are eminently consistent with the values of a liberal education, and the evidence for their presence is compelling" (Pascarella and Terenzini, 1991, p. 326).

An encouraging report is also made by Pascarella and Terenzini on the moral development of students, although the strength and magnitude of gains are apparently not as clear. If we were really serious about quality—if we held a strategic view—we would know as much about the knowledge *and values* of students on exit as we did on entry, at every one of our colleges and universities.

In an essay entitled "Does Anyone Know Reality?" that is now a quarter of a century past, John F. Wharton reflected on this question. Here is a keynote idea: "The more I thought about it, the more extraordinary it all became. It is not facts but our beliefs about facts which control our actions. It also occurred to me that once an unscientific hypothesis is accepted—for example, personal immortality—the true believer will support it with a devotion and sacrifice seldom accorded to any scientific thesis. Galileo bowed to the Pope; St. Peter did not bow to Caesar" (Wharton, 1966, p. 313). What we know will always be a slave to what we believe, and what we teach through our actions will always deliver a more powerful lesson than our didactic classroom exercises. A strategic view of quality, then, attends to matters of both concept and value, to matters both technical and ethical.

Arrogance, prejudice, and jealousy are enemies of quality. Any behavior in our colleges and universities that subtracts from human dignity—whether embodied in the acts of faculty and staff or in the policies of the institution—is a behavior that diminishes quality. A president who prostitutes the principles of honesty to obtain a few extra dollars from a donor, a professor who unfairly appropriates the research work of one of her doctoral students, a staff member who changes a grade for dollars or favors: These acts diminish quality.

Can any college that does not lead its students to understand the reality of goodness, the reality of evil, and the necessity for moral choice be a quality college? Can any college be a quality college if it does not lead its students to appreciate the physically and emotionally wrenching trials that come in engaging those moral choices where the limits of black and white turn to gray, where computer algorithms fail, where friends can advise but not decide, where honor and justice call but their guide is uncertain? Can any college be a quality campus if it does not lead its students to understand that there is a difference between knowing what is right and doing what is right? Not a day will pass on any campus in this nation where we will not have the opportunity to engage these ethical lessons and demonstrate that the college has, indeed, a strategic vision of quality—one embracing technical competence and ethical responsibility.

A Commitment Perspective

Surely, one of the more serious and sustained concerns today centers on the extent to which all of the pressure and activity for quality, evaluation, and assessment has and will penetrate to the heart of the institution. As we remarked in Chapter One, American business is trying to promote the idea that, in the words of Ford Motor Company, quality is job number one. Here is a commitment to quality where corporate and collegiate enterprise can be legitimately joined in challenge.

It is hard to see that a quality educational climate can exist or that a quality graduate will emerge from that climate unless every member of the faculty and staff has an active allegiance to quality. An active allegiance will not necessarily be forthcoming through the simple act of appointing a director of quality assurance, a director of assessment, or a director of planning and evaluation. Nor may we expect this allegiance to be built in short-term motions. Those campuses in this country that have earned reputations for having strategic visions of quality—visions that permeate the entire institution—did not develop overnight. As we noted in earlier chapters, these institutions have taken an extended journey and earned their reputations through daring and perseverance.

One of the authors recently visited three different institutions: a community college, a state university, and a private university, all in different stages of a quality journey. As a consequence of accreditation requirements, the community college had adopted the policy of administering the ACT Comp test to its students. When queried about the use being made of the test results, however, it was apparent that the institution was just "going through the motions." No one had examined or evaluated the test results, even though the institution had five years of data on hand. This failure to take the results and put them to work had earned the institution a "red flag" from its most recent accrediting visit. Another discovery obvious from these findings was that the faculty was little engaged.

Here, however, was an opportunity for good work on several fronts. The president appointed a standing committee of faculty and staff to review and evaluate the general education component of the college. The first order of business for the new committee was to review the data from the ACT Comp administrations to ascertain what lessons could be learned. The second challenge was to ascertain whether the institution found the ACT Comp a good match to its general education program, and the third was to make recommendations for changes to the general education curriculum. If this institution is lucky, the deliberations will be informed by more than the political and self-interests of the college's various academic departments. And if the institution is fortunate, the appointment of this committee will serve as an instrument to build ownership in the quality efforts of the institution—to build a strategic and unifying vision of quality.

In the state university, an exciting journey toward quality had been set in motion through the requirements of the ten-year accreditation self-study exercise. Hutchins once noted "that the university gained its unity and its vitality from a perpetual argument that touched the lives of every one of its members" (Hutchins, 1966, p. 183). This institution had indeed created a ferment, a perpetual argument, on planning and evaluation and quality assurance that had touched every person on the campus. And it showed.

There were friendly cynics and new believers. A new general education program was in birth stages, with all of the pain that attends thereto. A standing committee was arguing over the value of the college base exam to assess the outcomes of the general education program. A representative and participatory planning and budgeting system had brought institutional priorities to the fore and made more faculty and staff aware that advancing the legitimate financial need of the library or some other program could be realized only at the expense of scholarships, travel funds, equipment, or other institutional needs. The campus president had begun a lively dialogue that generates a comprehensive allegiance to quality. There were grins and smiles of excitement, curiosity, and commitment evident all over this campus. And, yes, there were pockets of dissent and suspicion as well. The pervasive momentum, however, favored the probability that this campus would develop a strategic and unifying vision of quality—a vision that enjoys a community of ownership.

The third institution, a private university, was struggling also with an accreditation challenge—demonstrating the quality of an extensive off-campus program. The university offered local and far-flung off-campus programs at both the undergraduate and master's levels, but the home campus faculty had evidenced little quality control over these programs. For the most part, they were products of what the institution's president had described as "academic entrepreneurship." Of course, there is nothing wrong with entrepreneurship in academia; we just need to harness our imagination to quality standards, which this campus had sadly neglected.

(Let us comment, parenthetically, that one book on entrepreneurship that can be read with profit by folks in colleges and universities is Peter Drucker's 1985 *Innovation and Entrepreneurship: Practice and Principles,* a work rich in ideas and illustration. He comments, for example, that "what really made universal schooling possible—more so than the popular commitment to the value of education, the systematic training of teachers in schools of education, or pedagogic theory—was that lowly innovation, the textbook" (Drucker, 1985, p. 31). Although we are not sure that Drucker has a total grip on the truth here, the point is a good one. Might the rapid development of computer and communication technology and a spirit of entrepreneurship bring American colleges and universities more direct competition on both cost and quality from the proprietary sector? The 1987 Carnegie Foundation technical report, *A Classification of Institutions of Higher Education,* indicated that there were twenty-two corporately sponsored institutions accredited in the United States. Recall, also, Friedman's (Spencer, 1991) call for taxable colleges cited earlier. Let us return to the quality challenges of the private university under scrutiny.

Students receiving undergraduate degrees in off-campus centers did not take the Educational Testing Service (ETS) Academic Profile assessment of general education outcomes, which students on the main campus had to pass as a graduation requirement. Nor did home campus faculty ever see or read the written comprehensive examinations taken by master's graduates in several graduate centers, even though the home campus departments were nominally responsible for these graduate programs. Here was no penetrating allegiance to quality. The imminent arrival of the accrediting association visiting team and the equally imminent possibility of having to remove the accreditation flag from the flagpoles of its off-campus centers had set in motion a frenetic activity. A strategic commitment to quality would have prevented this frenzy. More important, it might have guaranteed the presence of higher expectations for students in the off-campus programs. What a simple qualitative expedient it would have been to have undergraduates in off-campus centers also take the ETS Academic Profile and to have graduates in off-campus centers have their comprehensive exams read by at least one home campus faculty member. Caring is a simple but essential passion for excellence.

A Client Perspective

There is a tendency well known to scholars of organizational behavior for organizations to evolve in their service attitudes, neglecting over time the interests of those whom the organization was designed to serve, clients and customers, and attending instead to the interests of those within the organization. This creeping shift from a servant to a self-interest perspective can affect colleges and universities as well. A strategic vision of quality reminds us that we serve to promote first the development and growth of our students and then the advance of truth and the welfare of the society and community furnishing the financial nurture of the university.

The previously cited examples of three institutions in their pursuits of quality give evidence of what can happen when institutions lose sight of those whom they serve. In the case of the private university, the "entrepreneurial" spirit of the campus had less to do with serving the needs of students than with increasing the number of students. This preoccupation with numbers and with their immediacy is a national liability of some note, no less a problem in collegiate than corporate settings. The matter of time perspective is one to which we will turn in a moment.

If the needs and welfare of its students had been foremost in its conscience, would the community college just cited have kept five years of performance data on the shelf? If the performance of students had been really important, would the private university have ignored the quality standards of its off-campus programs? The seductive ring of the tuition cash register unfortunately kept the campus from attending to the quality of services offered.

Consider other policy debates that swirl within collegiate walls. How many of those debates on admissions, retention, and graduation policies are built on consideration for the welfare of students rather than the political and economic interests of facilities and departments? Years ago one of the authors was placed in the discomforting leadership position of having to oppose his own faculty in a critical matter of curriculum requirements. For the doctoral program in this college, students were required to complete a third of their work in supportive disciplines outside the college. When, however, enrollments in the college began to slump, the college faculty recommended eliminating the outside requirement and bringing all those credit hours back to the college. This was not a recommendation made with a strategic vision of quality in mind; indeed, quality was not even the issue, nor were the interests and welfare of the doctoral students entrusted to the care of this faculty. Convincing the faculty to place the interests of students ahead of their own interests was difficult and unpopular. The issue was the self-interest of the faculty. Such self-serving attitudes are no less transparent to civic friends who support our colleges and universities than the self-serving moves of other professions are to educators. Since we hold in trust the development of leadership for our nation, it may be argued, however, that the public has a premier right to expect nobility of motive and performance from colleges and universities.

A strategic vision of quality will cause us to consider all policy matters primarily from the perspective of student welfare, although of course there are other clients. In a paper entitled "The Quest for Excellence: Underlying Policy Issues" Morgan and Mitchell (1987) suggest that there are six perspectives on excellence, including a *political economy* perspective, in which the quality of colleges and universities is determined by how well they enhance the political and economic strength of the nation. A *productivity* perspective asks how well higher education utilizes its resources— a "bang for the buck" test. The *value-added* perspective concerns the question of how well colleges contribute to the development of student knowledge, skills, and values. The *producer-consumer* perspective turns on the qualifications of faculty (proportion of Ph.D.'s and so forth) and students (admissions selectivity and so forth). A *content* perspective is one in which quality is judged by the comprehensiveness of programs offered. And the *eclectic* perspective is a multidimensioned approach in which all of the above come into play.

This multidimensioned approach to quality is one we emphasized in Chapter One. There can be little doubt that there are many "customers" of higher education. We would add to the above list a *public service* perspective in which the test of quality concerns the extent to which colleges and universities serve the long-range, continuing education, and personal and professional development needs of its citizens.

At the origin of each of these views of quality there is, however, a student: a researcher being prepared for science and industry, a new teacher for our secondary schools, a city manager completing a master's program in public administration, an attorney returning to learn about computers, or a farmer or plant manager being served by an agricultural or manufacturing extension service. A strategic vision of quality evaluates program and policy first and foremost in terms of impact on students.

A Time Perspective

Another variable that often drives our behavior in both corporate and collegiate settings is the tendency to look at short-term pressures and goals rather than to take a long-term perspective. An April 21, 1991, presentation of the television program "60 Minutes" examined the technological competitiveness of American industry and concluded that Americans were becoming more dependent on Japanese sources, especially in the critical field of electronics. This, according to the program, portended an unhealthy shift of power, when one looked at both consumer products and military preparedness. Although the technological superiority of the American military might has been demonstrated recently in Operation Desert Storm, a vulnerability hides beneath the surface. Many of the fundamental components of the sophisticated weaponry depend on Japanese manufacturers.

The "60 Minutes" program pointed out that Americans were not short on developing new ideas and technologies but were negligent in translating these into new products. Among the reasons cited for this manufacturing liability were the tendencies for American industry to take short-term views on profitability and to shun risk-taking ventures because of that short-term view. A major trend usually cited for the future is a shift from a manufacturing economy to an information economy, a change well discussed in Toffler's new book *Power Shift* (1990). It is, however, difficult to believe that there will be much information to be shared if the majority of this nation's manufacturing capacity moves overseas—to say nothing of the economic, political, and military risks that associate with that shift.

Colleges and universities are not built primarily for short-run outcomes, and they should not be. Institutions that race willy-nilly to meet current pressures and fads do not have a strategic vision of quality. We are not suggesting here some encrusted and resistant mode of thought where tradition and inertia are the only guides to behavior and policy. What we are suggesting is the avoidance of Roman-candle-type behavior in which the energy and resources of an institution are expended in one grand display of flame and color with an empty and dark shell remaining as the only evidence of institutional performance.

Building a quality faculty, a quality program, and a quality environment is not an occupation of the moment, not a product of a three-to-five-year presidency, not a result of a one-year funding surge. Nor is quality the outcome of any other quick-fix action. A strategic vision of quality is built on long-term perspectives and commitments.

There is, however, a contrasting perspective. Although administrators and faculty can take justifiable pleasure in their engagement of long-range master-planning exercises, it pays to remember that quality is established in decisions of the moment as well. Every course approved or deleted; every faculty member appointed, promoted, or terminated; every new program of service begun—each of these actions sets a brick in the wall of quality. Shaping and responding to the future require a long-range vision, but reaching the future is a journey built on those single steps of policy, program, and personal decision undertaken every day. There are no unimportant time frames in building a strategic vision of quality.

A Funding Perspective

Was the economist Ernest Schumaker right when he wrote his provocative economic treatise entitled *Small Is Beautiful*? How many college presidents—even those who are economists—believe this relationship? And how many behave as though they believe it? The relationship between funding levels and quality is one that illustrates the observation that there is no subject so complex that careful examination and study will not make it more complex.

Is quality positively and directly related to funding levels? If the answer is yes, then our arguments for additional support and revenue make sense because any diminution of funding portends a decline in quality. There are mines in this attractive field, however. College presidents and campus lobbyists who passionately argue that quality will slip and suffer if there is less money for equipment, libraries, scholarships, and salaries are loathe to turn to graduates and friends on graduation day and say that the quality of the institution's educational credentials is less because the campus received a smaller state appropriation or suffered other revenue indignities.

We repeat: Is quality positively and directly related to funding levels? The answer can be yes or no. There are obviously limits to revenue squeezes—levels of support where even the best intentioned and most servant-spirited faculty and staff can no longer carry the load and deliver a decent educational program. Indeed, most mobile faculty would have long before departed the institution, which is one signal that quality may be slipping. When one-half of the accounting department of a research state university left the campus in one year to take positions at a younger urban university for significantly higher salaries, it is safe to say that a red flag concerning quality was an appropriate signal of distress.

On the other hand, if the campus has to make difficult priority decisions to retrench programs as a means of furnishing salary increases and other support for the accounting program, or any other program it decides to retain, then quality is diminished only if we define it in terms of bigness and comprehensiveness. We will return to this issue in a moment.

It would be hard to find any national or state report on higher education today that did not contain at least one recommendation for colleges and universities to more carefully define their mission, to do what they do best, not to try to be everything to everyone, to capitalize on their strengths, and to create a sense of distinctiveness. These are worthy goals for any campus, but often the policymakers use these lofty statements as euphemisms for "tighten up and get smaller." To borrow a corporate expression, the intent behind the mission advice is to downsize or, in military parlance, to "advance to the rear." These urgings for a more distinctive mission are often associated with other patently good advice to make differential cuts rather than fair-share or across-the-board cuts, which are suggested as cowardly strategies unworthy of real leadership. Such advice may be more often lofted at presidents by scholars and arm-chair administrators who have the advantage of dispassion and detachment than by academic administrators who have looked affected colleagues in the eye when delivering the news on how quality is to be improved with their termination.

The pressure on campus presidents and faculties to grow and to add programs and services is truly great. This is the easiest performance signal—one that is most understandable and acceptable to both internal colleagues and external supporters, whether financial or political. A few institutions in this nation, perhaps the military academies and some private institutions, enjoy a stable sense of size and mission and a reputation for quality. The pressure on public institutions to look more like their larger and more mature counterparts is significant, however. A public college or university that deliberately chooses a moderate or small enrollment in association with a carefully chosen and constrained program profile can be subject to a double liability. The budgeting formulas of most states associate increased funding with enrollment growth—not an unreasonable linkage. In difficult financial times, however, the linkage can make life miserable for institutions electing or experiencing stable enrollments. Further, the spend-or-lose-it features of public budgeting policy do not encourage realistic priority settings.

The dilemma is described in the February 1991 issue of *Policy Perspectives*, "The Other Side of the Mountain":

> To ask for a reassignment of budget lines in this environment runs counter to all instincts of institutional self preservation, for such a request is tantamount to admitting that an existing line was not necessary in the first place. Equally important is the fact that these budget lines are usually perceived as entitlements by departments and administrative units within the institution. It is far safer for a public institution to express its ambition in terms of new budget lines, seeking to expand the whole, rather than shifting resources away from ineffective units toward activities that show greater promise in effectively realizing the educational mission. Such colleges and universities know that accepting less from their state government implicitly gives power to other claims on public resources with which higher education competes for funding, such as roads, prisons, and public assistance programs [Pew Higher Education Research Program, 1991, p. 3A].

The second liability is that any president or faculty who deliberately approaches the budgeting process content to settle for the same or less support grants an advantage to other institutions that might not share the "small is beautiful" definition of quality. Indeed, they might be prone to body-count mentalities and turf-building definitions of "big is better." This is a leadership dilemma of majestic proportion.

Perhaps we may even cite a third political liability, both internal and external. Consider this hypothetical illustration in which fiction is not stranger than the truth. Faced with a multiyear budget scenario where the campus has experienced several years of significant midyear budget cuts, ranging from 3 to 7 percent, and relatively stable or smaller state appropriations, the president of a state research university might suggest that it makes no sense to continue revenue starvation for the entire campus. She then suggests termination of the veterinary medicine school, on the theory that the needs for additional veterinarians are modest to questionable in the state, that over time large dollars will be freed for reallocation by this action, and that the educational heart of the campus might be less damaged by this action than by any other program deletion.

This president might be described as a courageous leader by those who campaign for the "small-is-beautiful" definition of quality and those who cheer for a more carefully drawn mission statement. These folks should be invited, however, to sit with the president as she receives sharply worded memos, phone calls, and personal visits accusing her of threatening the quality of the state's great flagship university, of diminishing the "comprehensive nature" of the university (another phrase meaning a diminution in quality). They might also find interesting the contacts from legislators and others who want their horses and dogs served, the graduates of the veterinary school who are distressed at the possibility of losing their alma mater, and the practicing veterinarians who see the loss of a power base. Even members of the university's governing board accuse the president of undermining the university's regional and national status. Dire economic and status consequences are predicted. A short tenure for her presidency is predicted and promised. Is it not easier to be an academic hero by dashing up the legislative hill asking for more money?

Of course, this hypothetical scenario could be played out for the proposed reduction or termination of any program or service. The conversation would include observations something like this: What reputable college or university could make a claim to quality without a program in (you fill in the name) field? What are the limits to comprehensiveness? As we noted in an earlier chapter, no college or university—no matter its size or history—can hope to be completely comprehensive. All institutions will inevitably have limited missions.

Thus, a strategic vision of quality does not automatically assume that quality is immediately and linearly linked to swings, either positive or negative, in revenue and/or financial support. This vision does assume, however, that an effective retrenchment of programs and services is a priority exercise that must involve every partner in the higher education enterprise—the faculty and staff within and the governing and coordinating boards and legislature without. A strategic vision further assumes that quality is best served by stability and long-term commitment to funding support, funding that is reasonably predictable and not subject to the wild swings of boom-to-bust roller coaster rides. This perspective is built on the simple realization that what takes a generation to build in a faculty can often be lost in a year or two. A strategic view of quality is also built on some sense of historical perspective. For example, institutions and states experiencing challenging financial moments would find sobering a review of financial-support patterns for higher education in most states during the Depression and World War II decade from 1935 to 1945. The history of faculty and staff devotion during those years might also prove inspiring and informing.

A System Perspective

We suggest that a strategic vision of quality will be one in which a campus has an integrated and systematic approach to quality assurance. First there will be in this system perspective an allegiance to the principles set forth in Chapter Nine. All quality assurance efforts will be tied to the heart of the enterprise: the daily contact and interactions between those who teach and those who learn. The prime motivating force behind quality assurance efforts will be the desire to improve the impact of both instructional programs and administrative services. The style of these efforts will be relatively unobtrusive and woven into the daily fabric of practice and decision. Assessments and evaluation exercises will recognize and respect varieties of excellence for both individual talent and institutional mission and will shun pecking orders of prestige and status based on narrow notions of human and organizational promise. And expectations of quality will be impatient with shoddy and shallow work, whether personal or organizational.

A recognition of the power of diversity will call us to acquire multiple evidences of both personal and program performance, and we will try those evidences on standards involving internal and external judgments—on the experience and values of peers within and without. We will be willing to learn by doing, modeling risk taking and discovery behavior before our students and our supporters. We will inform all management and educational decisions—personal, policy, and program—with information derived from our quality assurance efforts. And we will share the results of the journey in public forum as another expression of the spirit of the academy.

These principles will be put to work in a systematic approach to quality assurance in which every person, every program, and every service—educational and administrative—of the campus continuously asks these three questions:

1. What is it that we hope to achieve?
2. How good a job are we doing and how do we know?
3. What improvements can be supported by the performance results?

The loop is closed by linking performance results to improvement.

Second, a systematic approach to quality will be characterized by communities of partnership involvement so that performance issues reaching across program and organizational lines are thoughtfully engaged. Communications and publications of the institution will furnish a conceptual and philosophical map of the quality assurance program so that both the logic and the elements of the program will be apparent. These policy statements and/or other communication vehicles will outline the elements and evidences, the planning and decision purposes, the timing of assessments and evaluations, and the responsibilities for execution of the quality assurance program.

A Proactive Perspective

Nothing is clearer from our review of the history of quality assurance initiatives in American higher education than this. The impetus for action has often come from outside the academy. This phenomenon, however, is not unique to higher education. A decent argument could be advanced that corporate America did not get serious about quality until all those foreign-built automobiles and electronics goods starting showing up on our shores—and Americans started buying them.

There are, however, happy examples of more proactive collegiate histories in the country, at all levels. Northeast Missouri State University, for example, started its value-added program over two decades ago. Alverno College has been developing its competency-based program over many years. The Tennessee performance funding project was an initiative emerging from the state's higher education system and not driven by legislative or executive threat. Many of the state incentive programs described in Chapter Eight are examples of proactive postures.

A strategic vision of quality is one in which campuses and other higher education partners attempt to stay in front of the curve. We are not so naive as to believe that any organized enterprise, corporate or collegiate, might arrive at the point when it would not need and benefit from the stimulus of external review or competition. We are saying, however, that a campus with a strategic vision of quality will be one with an aggressive and imaginative program of quality assurance, attempting to lead and demonstrate initiative of thought and action, rather than follow and react.

In a 1989 book entitled *Head First: The Biology of Hope*, Norman Cousins explores the scientific relationships among human attitudes, the presence of hope, and our physiological well-being and health. Nestled midway into the book is this comment: "Life is the ultimate prize and it takes on ultimate value when suddenly we discover how tentative and fragile it can be. The essential art of living is to recognize and savor its preciousness when it is free of imminent threat of jeopardy" (p. 107). This is an attitude with transfer potential. The work of collegiate educators is a precious work, and the essential mark of the true educator is a caring and compassion for students that emerges without the necessity of external threat. A strategic vision of quality, then, is characterized by an active caring, a "heart first" attitude, to which we turn now in our conclusion to this chapter and this book.

Quality: The Premier Leadership Call

The promise of quality can be realized in our colleges and universities with a strategic and unifying vision of quality, as operationally expressed in this chapter. The vision begins with "head first" matters of knowledge. We need to know about the strengths and limitations of contemporary approaches to quality assurance, and we hope that this book has made some contribution to that goal. We need to know and to debate various definitions of quality, including those outlined in these chapters and the main definition offered in this book: Quality is conformance to mission specification and goal achievement within publicly accepted standards of accountability and integrity. We need to know about the kinds of evidences and indicators necessary to circumscribe quality and to understand that both individual and institutional performance is too complex to be captured in a single data point. We need to know about the standards that might be used to judge quality, and we need some understanding about who the legitimate judges of collegiate quality might be. We need to know about the kinds of decisions—whether improvement or accountability oriented—that furnish the motivating force for quality assurance exercises. We need to know about ways in which campus professionals and community and civic friends can fashion effective partnerships in the quest for quality, and we hope that the book has made some contribution to the concept of partnership. Finally, we need to know that our quest for quality is a powerful instrument of decision and discovery—a reflection of our commitment to curiosity. A compulsive curiosity is the first mark of an educated man or woman, and a willingness to learn is an important signal of campus health and spirit as well.

But the final guarantor in realizing the promise of quality is a "heart first" attitude in which a concern for quality constitutes the premier leadership call on the attitudes and actions of every person on the campus—from professor to president, from custodian to counselor, from director to dean. What we know will always be a servant to what we believe, and if we believe in the promise of quality, every action of the campus, whether educational or administrative, will serve that promise and be measured by that standard. Every policy, every personality, every practice, and every performance will stand muster before the call of quality. The technical competence and the ethical commitment of the people who give life and meaning to a campus will be linked to its quality and will either build or diminish it. A strategic and unifying vision of quality, then, will emerge when assessment is built not so much on the process and resource indicators that constitute conventional wisdom but on indicators that are results oriented. What difference have we made in the knowledge, skills, and values of those students entrusted to our care and in the communities that trust us with their support and expectations? Quality reflects not just our curiosity but our caring.

The promise of quality resides, then, in the plain of our passions. Do we care enough for truth, do we care enough for service, and do we care enough for human growth and dignity that our vision of quality permeates and penetrates the entire campus and touches the mind and the heart of every person who serves there? Will that vision yield standards and encouragement that call our students and our colleagues from the poverty of the commonplace, that salute the promise of each one on the campus (whether student or staff), and that launch each person to the far reaches of his or her potential? Will that vision reveal a happy curiosity and active compassion? Will that vision marry a respect for diversity or mission and talent with a scorn for shoddy work, whether individual or institutional? And will that vision respond not just to the intellectual call to advance the truth but also to the ethical call of justice, dignity, integrity, and nobility? The promise can only be realized in a community of caring, which ought to be an accurate descriptor of a quality college or university.

References

Abernathy, W., Clark, K., and Kantrow, A. *Industrial Renaissance: Producing a Competitive Future for America.* New York: Basic Books, 1983.

Adelman, C. *The Standardized Test Scores of College Graduates 1964–1982.* Washington, D.C.: National Institute of Education and American Association for Higher Education, 1985.

Adelman, C. (ed.). "Difficulty Levels and the Selection of 'General Education' Subject Examinations." In *Performance and Judgment: Essays on Principles and Practice in the Assessment of College Student Learning.* Washington, D.C.: Office of Educational Research and Improvement, U.S. Department of Education, n.d.

Advisory Committee to the Colleges Outcome Evaluation Program. Report to the New Jersey Board of Higher Education. Trenton, N.J.: Oct. 23, 1987.

Alinsky, S. *Rules for Radicals.* New York: Vintage Books, 1971.

American Association of State Colleges and Universities. *To Secure the Blessings of Liberty: Report of the National Commission on the Role and Future of State Colleges and Universities.* Washington, D.C.: American Association of State Colleges and Universities, 1986.

American Assembly. *The Integrity of Higher Education*. Final report of the 56th American Assembly. Harriman, N.Y.: Arden House, 1979.

American College Testing Program. ACT Evaluation/Survey Service, specimen set (instruments). Iowa City, Iowa: American College Testing Program, n.d.

"America's Best College Buys." *Money Guide*, Fall 1990 (entire issue).

"America's Best Colleges." *U.S. News and World Report*, Nov. 25, 1985, pp. 46-60.

"America's Best Colleges." *U.S. News and World Report*, Oct. 26, 1987, pp. 49-87.

"America's Best Colleges." *U.S. News and World Report*, Oct. 10, 1988, pp. C3-C32.

"America's Best Colleges." *U.S. News and World Report*, Oct. 16, 1989, pp. 53-82.

"America's Best Colleges." *U.S. News and World Report*, Oct. 15, 1990, pp. 103-134.

"America's Best Graduate Schools." *U.S. News and World Report*, Mar. 19, 1990, pp. 46-78.

Anderson, S., and Ball, S. *The Profession and Practice of Program Evaluation*. San Francisco: Jossey-Bass, 1980.

Annotated Code of Maryland: Education. Charlottesville: Michie Company, 1989, p. 271.

Astin, A. *Four Critical Years: Effects of College on Beliefs, Attitudes, and Knowledge*. San Francisco: Jossey-Bass, 1977.

Astin, A. *Achieving Educational Excellence: A Critical Assessment of Priorities and Practices in Higher Education*. San Francisco: Jossey-Bass, 1985a.

Astin, A. "The Value-Added Debate . . . Continued." *American Association of Higher Education Bulletin*, 1985b, *37*(8), 11-13.

Astin, A. *Assessment for Excellence*. New York: Macmillan, 1991.

Astin, A., Panos, R., and Creager, J. *National Norms for Entering College Freshman—Fall 1966*. Washington, D.C.: American Council on Education, 1967.

Atwell, R. *President's Letter.* Washington, D.C.: American Council on Education, Mar. 26, 1990.

Augstyn, N. *Interview with Task Force on Teacher Certification.* Washington, D.C.: American Association of Colleges for Teacher Education, 1985.

Bailey, S. "People Planning in Postsecondary Education: Human Resource Development in a World of Decremental Budgets." In J. N. Nesmith (ed.), *More for Less: Academic Planning with Faculty Without New Dollars.* Papers presented at a conference sponsored by the Society for College and University Planning, Nordic Hills, Itsasca, Ill., Apr. 17-19, 1974.

Baird, L. "Value Added: Using Student Gains as Yardsticks of Learning." In C. Adelman (ed.), *Performance and Judgment: Essays on Principles and Practice in the Assessment of College Student Learning.* Washington, D.C.: Office of Educational Research and Improvement, U.S. Department of Education, n.d.

Baker, E. "Critical Validity Issues in the Methodology of Higher Education Assessment." In *Assessing the Outcomes of Higher Education:* Proceedings of the 1986 ETS Invitational Conference. Princeton, n.d.: Educational Testing Service, 1986.

Banta, T. "Major Field Assessment for Seniors: Institutional Learning and Resulting Changes." Paper presented at the 76th annual meeting of the Association of American Colleges, San Francisco, Jan. 10, 1990a.

Banta, T. "Assessment in the Major: Response to a State Initiative." *Assessment Update,* 1990b, 2(1), 5, 6.

Banta, T., and Fisher, H. "Utilizing Research on Postsecondary Outcomes: Evidence of Effectiveness." Paper presented at the annual meeting of the American Educational Research Association, Mar. 1989.

Banta, T., and Moffett, M. "Performance Funding in Tennessee: Stimulus for Program Improvement." In D. F. Halpern (ed.), *Student Outcomes Assessment: What Institutions Stand to Gain.* New Directions for Higher Education, no. 59. San Francisco: Jossey-Bass, 1987.

Barak, R. *Program Review in Higher Education: Within and Without.* Boulder, Colo.: National Center for Higher Education Management Systems, 1982.

Barak, R., and Breier, B. *Successful Program Review: A Practical Guide to Evaluating Programs in Academic Settings.* San Francisco: Jossey-Bass, 1990.

Barzun, J. "We Need Leaders Who Can Make Our Institutions Companies of Scholars, Not Corporations with Employees and Customers." *Chronicle of Higher Education,* 1991, *37*(27), B1.

Bateman, W. *Open to Question: The Art of Teaching and Learning by Inquiry.* San Francisco: Jossey-Bass, 1990.

Benezet, L. "Learning What?" In C. R. Pace (ed.), *Evaluating Learning and Teaching.* San Francisco: Jossey-Bass, 1973.

Benjamin, E. "Administrative Acquiescence in Assessment." *AGB Reports,* 1989, *31*(2), 14.

Benjamin, E. "The Movement to Assess Students' Learning Will Institutionalize Mediocrity in Colleges." *Chronicle of Higher Education,* July 5, 1990, pp. B1–B2.

Bernard, A. (ed.). *Rotten Rejections.* Wainscott, N.Y.: Pushcart Press, 1990.

Bloom, A. *The Closing of the American Mind.* New York: Simon & Schuster, 1987.

Bloom, B., and others. *Taxonomy of Educational Objectives: The Classification of Educational Goals, Handbook I.* New York: McKay, 1956.

Bogue, E. "State Agency Approaches to Academic Program Evaluation." In E. Craven (ed.), *Academic Program Evaluation.* San Francisco: Jossey-Bass, 1980.

Bogue, E. "Arrogance and Altruism in the Professions." *Vital Speeches,* 1, 1981, *47*(10), 302–308.

Bogue, E. *The Enemies of Leadership.* Bloomington, Ind.: Phi Delta Kappa, 1985.

Bogue, E. *A Journey of the Heart: The Call to Teaching.* Bloomington, Ind.: Phi Delta Kappa, 1991.

Bogue, E., and Brown, W. "Performance Incentives for State Colleges." *Harvard Business Review,* 1982, *60*(6).

Bogue, E., and Troutt, W. *The Performance Funding Project.* Nashville: Tennessee Higher Education Commission, 1980.

Bowen, H. *Investment in Learning: The Individual and Social Value of American Higher Education.* San Francisco: Jossey-Bass, 1978.

Boyer, C., Ewell, P., Finney, J., and Mingle, J. *Assessment and Outcomes Measurement—A View from the States: Highlights of a New ECS Survey and Individual State Profiles.* Denver, Colo.: Education Commission of the States, 1987.

Boyer, E. *College: The Undergraduate Experience in America.* New York: HarperCollins, 1987.

Boyer, E. *Scholarship Reconsidered: Priorities of the Professoriate.* Princeton, N.J.: Carnegie Foundation for the Advancement of Teaching, 1990.

Bridger, G. "Attitudinal Surveys in Institutional Effectiveness." In J. Nichols, (ed.), *Institutional Effectiveness and Outcomes Assessment Implementation on Campus: A Practitioner's Handbook.* New York: Agathon Press, 1989.

Bronowski, J. *Science and Human Values.* New York: HarperCollins, 1956.

Burke, J. "Campus Plans on Academic Assessment." Memo to Presidents, State-Operated Campuses, Presidents, Community Colleges, from Joseph C. Burke, Provost, State University of New York. Albany, N.Y.: State University of New York, Dec. 12, 1988.

Cahn, S. *Saints and Scamps: Ethics in Academia.* Totowa, N.J.: Rowman and Littlefield, 1986.

Callahan, R. *Education and the Cult of Efficiency.* Chicago: University of Chicago Press, 1962.

Caplow, T., and McGee, R. *The Academic Marketplace.* New York: Basic Books, 1958.

Carlzon, J. *Moments of Truth,* Cambridge, Mass.: Ballinger, 1987.

Carnegie Foundation for the Advancement of Teaching. A Classification of Institutions of Higher Education: 1987 Edition. Princeton, N.J: Carnegie Foundation for the Advancement of Teaching, 1987.

Carnegie Foundation for the Advancement of Teaching. *Campus Life: In Search of Community.* Special report. Princeton, N.J.: Princeton University Press, 1990.

Cartter, A. *An Assessment of Quality in Graduate Education.* Washington, D.C.: American Council on Education, 1964.

Centra, J. "Assessing General Education." In C. Adelman (ed.), *Performance and Judgment: Essays on Principles and Practice in the Assessment of College Student Learning.* Washington, D.C.:

Office of Educational Research and Development, U.S. Department of Education, n.d.

Chaffee, E. "The Concept of Strategy: From Business to Higher Education." In J. Smart (ed.), *Higher Education: Handbook of Theory and Research.* Vol. 1. New York: Agathon Press, 1985.

Chickering, A. *Education and Identity.* San Francisco: Jossey-Bass, 1969.

Clark, M., Hartnett, R., and Baird, L. *Assessing Dimensions of Quality in Doctoral Education: A Technical Report of a National Study in Three Fields.* Princeton, N.J.: Educational Testing Service, 1976.

Commission on Colleges. *Criteria for Accreditation.* Atlanta, Ga.: Commission on Colleges, Southern Association of Colleges and Schools, 1984.

Commission on Colleges. *Resource Manual on Institutional Effectiveness.* (2nd ed.) Atlanta, Ga.: Commission on Colleges, Southern Association of Colleges and Schools, 1989.

Commission on Colleges. *Criteria for Accreditation, 1991 Edition.* Atlanta, Ga.: Commission on Colleges, Southern Association of Colleges and Schools, 1991.

Commission on Higher Education, Middle States Association of Colleges and Schools. *Characteristics of Excellence in Higher Education: Standards for Accreditation.* Philadelphia: Middle States Association of Colleges and Schools, 1982.

Committee on Instruction and Professional Development. *Establishing and Maintaining Standards for the Governance of the Teaching Profession.* Washington, D.C.: National Education Association, 1987.

Conrad, C., and Wilson, R. *Academic Program Review—Institutional Approaches, Expectations and Controversies,* Report No. 5. Washington, D.C.: ASHE-ERIC Higher Education Reports, 1985.

Cordes, C. "Angry Lawmakers Grill Stanford's Kennedy on Research Costs." *Chronicle of Higher Education,* 1991a, *37*(27), 1, A27.

Cordes, C. "Stanford U. Embroiled in Angry Controversy on Overhead Charges." *Chronicle of Higher Education,* 1991b, *37*(21), 1, A20.

Corts, T. "Colleges Should be Consumer Minded." *Chronicle of Higher Education,* 1973, 7(32), 17.

Corts, T. "From One Customer to Another." Unpublished paper. Birmingham, Ala.: Samford University, February 1990.

Coulter, E. *College Life in the Old South.* Athens: University of Georgia Press, 1928.

Council for Advancement and Support of Education. *Special Advisory for College and University Presidents.* Washington, D.C.: Council for Advancement and Support of Education, National Task Force on Higher Education and the Public Interest, 1988.

Council of Chief State School Officers. *State Education Indicators.* Washington, D.C.: Council of Chief State School Officers, 1989.

Council of Higher Education for Virginia. "Funds for Excellence Program." Richmond: Council of Higher Education for Virginia, n.d.

Council on Postsecondary Accreditation. *A Guide to COPA Recognized Accrediting Bodies, 1986–88.* Washington, D.C.: Council on Postsecondary Accreditation, 1986.

Council on Postsecondary Accreditation. *Directory of Recognized Accrediting Bodies.* Washington, D.C.: Council on Postsecondary Accreditation, 1989.

Cousins, N. *Head First: The Biology of Hope.* New York: Dutton, 1989.

Craven, E. *Academic Program Evaluation.* San Francisco: Jossey-Bass, 1980.

Crosby, P. *Quality Without Tears.* New York: McGraw-Hill, 1984.

Daughdrill, J., Jr. "Assessment Is Doing More for Higher Education Than Any Other Development in Recent History." *Chronicle of Higher Education,* 1988, *34*(52), 52.

Davis, F. Memorandum to Faculty, Staff, Concerned University Officials and Students. Memphis, Tenn.: Cecil C. Humphreys School of Law, Memphis State University, Oct. 7, 1987.

Deming, W. *Out of the Crisis.* Cambridge, Mass.: MIT Press, 1986.

Diamond, E. "Testing: The Baby and the Bath Water Are Still with Us." *Testing and the Public Interest: Proceedings of the 1976 Educational Testing Service Invitational Conference.* Princeton, N.J.: Educational Testing Service, 1976.

Dolan, W. *The Ranking Game: The Power of the Academic Elite.* Lincoln: University of Nebraska Press, 1976.

Donaghy, W. *The Interview: Skills and Application.* Glenview, Ill.: Scott, Foresman, 1984.

Downs, C., Smeyak, G., and Martin, E. *Professional Interviewing.* New York: HarperCollins, 1980.

Drucker, P. *Innovation and Entrepreneurship: Practice and Principles.* New York: HarperCollins, 1985.

Durant, W. *The Story of Civilization.* Vol. 1: *Our Oriental Heritage.* New York: Simon & Schuster, 1954.

Education Commission of the States. *Transforming the State Role in Undergraduate Education.* Denver, Colo.: Education Commission of the States, 1986.

Educational Testing Service. *Program Self-Assessment Service.* Brochure. Princeton, N.J.: Educational Testing Service, n.d.

Educational Testing Service. *College and University Programs.* Brochure. Princeton, N.J.: Educational Testing Service, 1989.

Educational Testing Service. *Higher Education Assessment Newsletter.* Princeton, N.J.: Educational Testing Service, June 1990.

"Einstein and Schweitzer Chair Program 1985." Albany: State Education Department, University of New York, May 1986.

Eisenberg, R. "Higher Education's Crisis of Confidence." *AGB Reports,* no. 24. Nov./Dec., 1988, p. 5.

Eisner, E. *The Art of Educational Evaluation.* Philadelphia: Falmer Press, 1985a.

Eisner, E. *The Educational Imagination.* (2nd ed.) New York: Macmillan, 1985b.

El-Khawas, E. *Campus Trends, 1990.* Washington, D.C.: American Council on Education, 1990.

Elliott, S. *Origins, Elements, and Implications of the Cutting Edge Initiatives for Research and Academic Excellence in Higher Education.* Columbia: South Carolina Commission on Higher Education, 1988.

Emerson, R. "Compensation." In *The Complete Writings of Ralph Waldo Emerson.* New York: Wise, 1929a.

Emerson, R. "Man the Reformer." In *The Complete Writings of Ralph Waldo Emerson.* New York: Wise, 1929b.

Enarson, H. "University of Knowledge Factory." *Chronicle of Higher Education,* 1973, 7(36), 16.

Erwin, T. *Assessing Student Learning and Development.* San Francisco: Jossey-Bass, 1991.

Ewell, P. *Information on Student Outcomes: How to Get It and How to Use It.* A National Center for Higher Education Management Systems executive overview. Boulder, Colo.: National Center for Higher Education Management Systems, 1983a.

Ewell, P. *Student Outcomes Questionnaires: An Implementation Handbook.* (2nd ed.) Boulder, Colo.: National Center for Higher Education Management Systems, 1983b.

Ewell, P. *The Self-Regarding Institution: Information for Excellence.* Boulder, Colo.: National Center for Higher Education Management Systems, 1984.

Ewell, P. "Assessment: What's It All About?" *Change,* Nov./Dec., 1985a, pp. 32–36.

Ewell, P. *Using Student Outcomes Information in Program Planning and Decision Making.* 2 vols. Denver, Colo.: National Center for Higher Education Management Systems, 1985b.

Ewell, P. "Outcomes, Assessment, and Academic Improvement: In Search of Usable Knowledge." In J. Smart (ed.), *Higher Education: Handbook of Theory and Research.* Vol. 4. New York: Agathon Press, 1988.

Ewell, P. "From the States." *Assessment Update.* San Francisco: Jossey-Bass, 1989.

Ewell, P. "Assessment and the 'New Accountability': A Challenge for Higher Education's Leadership." Paper presented at the meeting of the Education Commission of the States, Boulder, Colo., 1990a.

Ewell, P. "Implementing Guidelines for Western Association of Colleges and Schools Standards." Paper presented at the meeting of the accrediting liaison officers of the Western Association of Colleges and Schools, Oakland, Calif., 1990b.

Ewell, P., and Boyer, C. "Acting Out State Mandated Assessment: Evidence from Five States." *Change,* 1988, 20(4), 47.

"Ex-President Is Indicted for Illegal Payments," *Chronicle of Higher Education,* 1991, 37(29), A2.

Fabrey, L., and Rupp, R. Interview with Task Force on Teacher

Certification. Washington, D.C.: American Association of Colleges for Teacher Education, 1985.

Farmer, D. *Enhancing Student Learning: Emphasizing Essential Competencies in Academic Programs.* Wilkes-Barre, Pa.: King's College Press, 1988.

Farnsworth, S., and Thrash, P. Memorandum to Chief Executive Officers of Commission Institutions, Commissioners, Accreditation Review Council Members, Consultant-Evaluators, and Friends of the Commission. Chicago: North Central Association of Colleges and Schools, Feb. 1, 1990.

Fincher, C. "What Is Strategic Planning?" *Research in Higher Education,* 1982, *16*(4), pp. 373–376.

Fincher, C. "Purpose, Strategy, and Paradox." *Research in Higher Education,* 1988, *29*(3), pp. 273–277.

Fisher, G. "Measuring the Unmeasurable." *World, 2,* 1990.

Flaugher, R. *Bias in Testing: A Review and Discussion.* TM report no. 36, Educational Resources Information Center Clearinghouse on Tests, Measurement, and Evaluation. Princeton, N.J.: Educational Testing Service, 1974.

Flexner, A. *Medical Education in the United States and Canada* (Bulletin No. 4). New York: Carnegie Foundation for the Advancement of Teaching, 1910.

Flexner, A. *Abraham Flexner: An Autobiography.* New York: Simon & Schuster, 1960.

Florida Board of Regents. *State University System of Florida, Master Plan 1988–89 Through 1992–93.* Tallahassee: Florida Board of Regents, 1988.

Folger, J., and Harris, J. *Assessment in Accreditation.* Atlanta, Ga.: Southern Association of Colleges and Schools, 1989.

Forum for College and University Governance. *State Incentive Funding: Leveraging Quality.* Briefings. College Park: Forum for College and University Governance, University of Maryland, 1990.

Frankl, V. *Man's Search for Meaning.* Boston: Beacon Press, 1959.

Friedman, M. *Capitalism and Freedom.* Chicago: University of Chicago Press, 1962.

Gardner, H. *Frames of Mind: The Theory of Multiple Intelligences.* New York: Basic Books, 1983.

Gardner, J. *Excellence.* New York: W. W. Norton, 1984.

Gardner, J. *On Leadership.* New York: Free Press, 1990.

Garvin, D. *Managing Quality.* New York: Free Press, 1988.

Gibran, K. *The Forerunner.* New York: Knopf, 1982.

Gilbert, J. "Money's College Value Rankings." *Money Guide,* Fall 1990, p. 72.

Goodlad, J. *Keeping the Gates.* Briefs of American Association of Colleges for Teacher Education. Washington, D.C.: Sept. 1989.

Goodlad, J., Soder, R., and Sirotnik, K. (eds.). *The Moral Dimensions of Teaching.* San Francisco: Jossey-Bass, 1990.

Gourman, J. *The Gourman Report: A Rating of American and International Universities.* Los Angeles: National Education Standards, 1983a.

Gourman, J. *The Gourman Report: A Rating of Graduate and Professional Programs in American and International Universities.* Los Angeles: National Education Standards, 1983b.

Guaspari, J. *I Know When I See It: A Modern Fable About Quality.* New York: AMACOM, 1985.

Guba, E., and Lincoln, Y. *Effective Evaluation.* San Francisco: Jossey-Bass, 1981.

Hagan, J. "The Management of Quality: Preparing for a Competitive Future." *Quality Progress,* Dec. 1984, p. 21.

Harcleroad, F. "The Context of Academic Program Evaluation." In E. Craven (ed.), *Academic Program Evaluation.* San Francisco: Jossey-Bass, 1980.

Harris, J. "Assessing Outcomes in Higher Education." *Assessment in American Higher Education.* Washington, D.C.: Office of Educational Research and Improvement, U.S. Office of Education, 1985.

Harris, J. "Key Concepts of Quality Improvement for Higher Education." Unpublished paper. Birmingham, Ala.: Samford University, July 1990.

Harris, J., Hillenmeyer, S., and Foran, J. *Quality Assurance for Private Career Schools.* Washington, D.C.: Association of Independent Colleges and Schools, 1989.

Hearn, J. "Strategy and Resources: Economic Issues in Strategic Planning and Management in Higher Education." In J. Smart (ed.), *Higher Education: Handbook of Theory and Research.* Vol. 4. New York: Agathon Press, 1988.

Helyar, J. "This Is Not Your Father's Business School." *Southpoint,* 1990, *2*(3), 38.

Hines, E. *Higher Education and State Governments: Renewed Partnership, Cooperation or Competition?* ASHE-ERIC Higher Education Report No. 5. Washington, D.C.: Association for the Study of Higher Education, 1988.

Hughes, R. *A Study of the Graduate Schools of America.* Oxford, Ohio: Miami University, 1925.

Hutchings, P. "Assessment and the Way We Work." Closing plenary address, 5th American Association for Higher Education conference on assessment. Washington, D.C.: American Association for Higher Education, June 30, 1990.

Hutchings, P., and Marchese, T. "Watching Assessment: Questions, Stories, Prospects." *Change,* 1990, *22*(5), 11–38.

Hutchins, R. "First Glimpses of a New World." In *What I Have Learned.* New York: Simon & Schuster, 1966.

Huxley, E. *The Flame Trees of Thika.* London: Chatto and Windus, 1959.

Jacobi, M., Astin, A., and Ayala, A., Jr. *College Student Outcomes Assessment: A Talent Development Perspective.* ASHE-ERIC Higher Education Report No. 7. Washington, D.C.: Association for the Study of Higher Education, 1987.

Jaschik, S. "Accrediting Agency's Focus on Campus Diversity Is Challenged by Education Department Panel." *Chronicle of Higher Education,* 1990, *37,* A21–A22.

Jastrow, R. *God and the Astronomers.* New York: W. W. Norton, 1978.

Jewett, R. *Interview with Task Force on Teacher Certification.* Washington, D.C.: American Association of Colleges for Teacher Education, 1985.

Johnson, R. "Leadership Among American Colleges." *Change,* 1978, *10*(10), 50.

Johnson Foundation. *7 Principles for Good Practice in Undergraduate Education.* Racine, Wis.: Johnson Foundation, 1989.

Jones, D. *Data and Information for Executive Decisions in Higher Education.* National Center for Higher Education Management

Systems executive overview. Boulder, Colo.: National Center for Higher Education Management Systems, 1982.

Jones, L., Lindzey, G., and Coggeshall, P. (eds.). *An Assessment of Research-Doctorate Programs in the United States.* 5 vols. Washington, D.C.: National Academy Press, 1982.

Jordan, K. *State Professional Standards/Practices Boards: A Policy Analysis Paper.* Washington, D.C.: American Association of Colleges for Teacher Education, 1988.

Kanter, R. *When Giants Learn to Dance.* New York: Simon & Schuster, 1989.

Kean, T. "Time to Deliver: Before We Forgot the Promises We Made." *Change,* 1987, *19*(5), 11.

Kells, H. *Self-Study Processes: A Guide for Postsecondary Institutions.* Washington, D.C.: American Council on Education, 1980.

Keniston, H. *Graduate Study and Research in the Arts and Sciences at the University of Pennsylvania.* Philadelphia: University of Pennsylvania Press, 1959.

Lawrence, J., and Green, A. *A Question of Quality: The Higher Education Ratings Game.* AAHE-ERIC/Higher Education Research Report No. 5, 1980. Washington, D.C.: American Association for Higher Education, 1980.

Leatherman, C. "Leaders of Regional Accrediting Agencies Voice Dissatisfaction with National Organization: Some Say Defections are Possible." *Chronicle of Higher Education,* 1991a, *37*(28), A15–A16.

Leatherman, C. "U. of South Carolina Struggles to Extricate Itself from Legacy of Its Former President, Recently Indicted by a Grand Jury." *Chronicle of Higher Education,* 1991b, *37*(32), A13–A14.

Lenning, O., Lee, Y., Micek, S., and Service, A. *A Structure for the Outcomes of Postsecondary Education.* Denver, Colo.: National Center for Higher Education Management Systems, 1977.

Lenth, C. *State Priorities in Higher Education: 1990.* Denver, Colo.: Joint project of the State Higher Education Executive Officers (SHEEO) and the Education Commission of the States (ECS), 1990.

Leviton, B. (ed.). *Licensing and Accreditation in Education: The Law and the State Interest.* Lincoln: Commission on Undergrad-

uate Education and the Education of Teachers, University of
Nebraska, 1976.

Lewis, A. *Gideon's Trumpet*. New York: Random House, 1964.

Louisiana Board of Regents. *1984 Master Plan*, chap. 9. Baton
Rouge: Louisiana State Board of Regents, 1984.

Louisiana State University in Shreveport. *Planning and Evaluation
Policy*. Policy No. L08.01, Nov. 30, 1989, pp. 4–6.

Louisiana State University in Shreveport. Catalogue, 1990–1991.
Louisiana State University in Shreveport, May 1990.

McGuire, J., and others. "The Efficient Production of Reputation
by Prestige Research Universities in the United States." *Journal
of Higher Education*, July/Aug. 1988, *59*, 367.

McMillan, J. "Beyond Value-Added Education: Improvement Alone
Is Enough." *Journal of Higher Education*, 1988, *59*(5), 567.

McMillen, L. "Increasing Productivity at Colleges Is a Hot Topic
for the 1990's." *Chronicle of Higher Education*, Mar. 6, 1991,
p. A23–A24.

Marchese, T. "Costs and Quality." *Change*, 1990, *22*(3), 4.

Marcus, L., Leone, A., and Goldberg, E. *The Path to Excellence:
Quality Assurance in Higher Education*. ASHE-ERIC higher education research report no. 1. Washington, D.C.: Association for
the Study of Higher Education, 1983.

Margulies, R., and Blau, P. "America's Leading Professional
Schools." *Change*, Nov. 1973, p. 22.

May, W. *Ethics and Higher Education*. New York: Macmillan,
1990.

Mayer, J. *Accreditation in Teacher Education—Its Influence on
Higher Education*. Washington, D.C.: National Commission on
Accrediting, 1965.

Mayhew, L., Ford, P., and Hubbard, D. *The Quest for Quality: The
Challenge for Undergraduate Education in the 1990s*. San Francisco: Jossey-Bass, 1990.

Mentkowski, M., and Doherty, A. "Abilities That Last a Lifetime:
Outcomes of the Alverno Experience." *AAHE Bulletin*, Feb.
1984, p. 514.

Merson, J., and Qualls, R. *Strategic Planning for Colleges and Universities: A System Approach to Planning and Resource Allocation*. San Antonio, Tex.: Trinity University Press, 1979.

Micek, S., and Walhaus, R. *An Introduction to the Identification and Uses of Higher Education Outcome Information.* Technical report no. 40. Boulder, Colo.: National Center for Higher Education Management Systems, 1973.

Michigan State University. *1989 Academic Program Planning and Review.* East Lansing: Michigan State University, 1989a.

Michigan State University. "The Refocusing, Rebalancing, and Refining of Michigan State University." Internal discussion paper, document version 2.0, East Lansing, Jan. 12, 1989b.

Miller, L. "Hubris in the Academy: Can Teaching Survive an Overweening Quest for Excellence?" *Change,* 1990, *22*(5), 9–11, 53.

Millman, J. "Designing a College Assessment." In C. Adelman (ed.), *Performance and Judgment: Essays on Principles and Practice in the Assessment of College Student Learning.* Washington, D.C.: Office of Educational Research and Improvement, U.S. Office of Education, n.d.

"Minn. Legislature Audits President's Expenditures." *Chronicle of Higher Education,* Mar. 9, 1988, p. A22.

Morgan, A., and Mitchell, B. "The Quest for Excellence: Underlying Policy Issues." In J. Smart (ed.), *Higher Education: Handbook of Theory and Research.* Vol. 1. New York: Agathon Press, 1987.

Mortimer, K. *Accountability in Higher Education.* Washington, D.C.: American Association for Higher Education, 1972.

Munitz, B., and Wright, D. "Institutional Approaches to Academic Program Evaluation." In E. Craven (ed.), *Academic Program Evaluation.* San Francisco: Jossey-Bass, 1980.

National Board for Professional Teaching Standards. *President's 1987/88 Annual Report.* Washington, D.C.: National Board for Professional Teaching Standards, 1989.

National Center for Higher Education Management Systems. Student Outcomes Questionnaires (instruments). Boulder, Colo.: National Center for Higher Education Management Systems, 1983.

National Council for Accreditation of Teacher Education. *Standards, Procedures and Policies for the Accreditation of Professional Education Units.* Washington, D.C.: National Council for Accreditation of Teacher Education, 1987.

National Institute of Education. *Involvement in Learning: Realiz-*

ing the Potential of American Higher Education. Washington, D.C.: National Institute of Education, 1984.

New Jersey. *Jobs, Science, and Technology Bond Act of 1984.* Public law, Chap. 99, July 25, 1984.

New Jersey. *Report to the New Jersey Board of Higher Education Advisory Committee to the College Outcomes Evaluation Program, October 23, 1987.* Trenton: Department of Higher Education, 1987.

Newman, F. *Higher Education and the American Resurgence.* Princeton, N.J.: Carnegie Foundation for the Advancement of Teaching, 1985.

Newman, F. *Choosing Quality.* Denver, Colo.: Education Commission of the States, 1987.

Newsom, W., and Hayes, C. "Are Mission Statements Worthwhile?" *Planning for Higher Education,* Winter 1990–91, *19,* 28–30.

Northeast Missouri State University. *In Pursuit of Degrees with Integrity.* Washington, D.C.: American Association of State Colleges and Universities, 1984.

Northeast Missouri State University. "Evaluation Plan." *Teacher Education Faculty Handbook.* Kirksville: Northeast Missouri State University, n.d.

Northeast Missouri State University. "Proposal for Liberal Arts Assessment: Portfolio Assessment System for Students." Unpublished presentation, Northeast Missouri State University, n.d.

Ohio Board of Regents. *Management Improvement Program.* Columbus: Ohio Board of Regents, 1973.

Ohio Board of Regents. *Developing a Process Model for Institutional and State-Level Review and Evaluation of Academic Programs.* Columbus: Ohio Board of Regents and Education and Economic Systems, 1979.

Ohio Board of Regents. *Ohio Continues Its Investment in Excellence.* Brochure. Columbus: Ohio Board of Regents, 1988.

Ornstein, R. *The Psychology of Consciousness.* New York: W. H. Freeman, 1972.

Osterlind, S. *College Base: Guide to Test Content.* Chicago: Riverside, 1989.

Pace, C. *Measuring the Quality of College Student Experiences.* Los

Angeles: Center for the Study of Evaluation, University of California, Los Angeles, 1984.

Pace, C. *College Student Experiences Questionnaire.* Los Angeles: Center for the Study of Evaluation, University of California, Los Angeles, 1990.

Pascarella, E., and Terenzini, P. *How College Affects Students.* San Francisco: Jossey-Bass, 1991.

Paskow, J. (ed.). *Assessment Programs and Projects: A Directory.* Washington, D.C.: American Association for Higher Education Assessment Forum, 1988.

Paul, R. *Critical Thinking.* Rohnert Park, Calif.: Center for Critical Thinking and Moral Critique, Sonoma State University, 1990.

Peters, T., and Austin, N. *A Passion for Excellence.* New York: Random House, 1985.

Peters, T., and Waterman, R., Jr. *In Search of Excellence.* New York: HarperCollins, 1982.

Pew Higher Education Research Program. "The Business of the Business." *Policy Perspectives,* May 1989, pp. 1, 3.

Pew Higher Education Research Program. "The Lattice and the Ratchet." *Policy Perspectives,* June 1990, p. 1.

Pew Higher Education Research Program. "The Other Side of the Mountain." *Policy Perspectives,* Feb. 1991, pp. 1, 2, 3A.

Pfnister, A. "Accreditation in the North Central Region." In *Accreditation in Higher Education.* Washington, D.C.: Office of Education, U.S. Department of Health, Education and Welfare, 1959.

Pirsig, R. *Zen and the Art of Motorcycle Maintenance.* New York: Morrow, 1974.

Public Affairs Research Council of Louisiana. *The Very Special 8(G) Money, Report No. 7, July 1989.* Baton Rouge, La.: Public Affairs Research Council of Louisiana, 1989.

"Rating the Colleges." *U.S. News and World Report,* Nov. 28, 1983, p. 41.

Rebell, M. *Licensing and Accreditation: The Law and the State Interest.* Lincoln: Commission on Undergraduate Education, University of Nebraska, 1976.

"Report of the Committee on Graduate Instruction." *Educational Record,* Apr. 1934, p. 194.

Roose, K., and Anderson, C. *A Rating of Graduate Programs.* Washington, D.C.: American Council on Education, 1970.

Rudd, M. *Candidate Certification in Law.* Paper presented at the Conference on Enhancing the Teaching Profession: Lessons from Other Professions, Racine, Wis., Johnson Foundation, October 21, 1985a.

Rudd, M. *Interview with Task Force on Teacher Certification.* Washington, D.C.: American Association of Colleges and Schools, 1985b.

Russell, B. *Authority and the Individual.* New York: Simon & Schuster, 1949.

Sandefur, J. "Historical Perspectives." In *What's Happening in Teacher Testing: An Analysis of State Teacher Testing Practices,* chap. 3. Washington, D.C.: Office of Educational Research and Improvement, U.S. Department of Education, 1988.

Saunders, R. Letters to Mary Futrelle, president, National Education Association; Albert Shanker, president, American Federation of Teachers; Richard Kunkel, executive director, National Council for the Accreditation of Teacher Education; and David Imig, executive director, American Association of Colleges for Teacher Education. Memphis, Tenn.: College of Education, Memphis State University, November 17, 1987.

Schmotter, J. "Colleges Have Themselves to Blame for the Influence of Journalistic Rankings of Their Quality." *Chronicle of Higher Education,* 1989, *35*(42), A40.

Schumacher, E. *Small Is Beautiful.* New York: HarperCollins, 1973.

Selden, W. *Accreditation: A Struggle Over Standards in Higher Education.* New York: HarperCollins, 1960.

"The Senior Year Experience Conference." Conference flier. Columbia: Division of Continuing Education, University of South Carolina, 1989.

Seymour, D. "The Changing Face of Program Approval." *AGB Reports,* Nov./Dec. 1988, p. 24.

Seymour, D. "Beyond Assessment: Managing Quality in Higher Education." *Assessment Update,* 1991, *3*(1), 1.

Skolnik, M. "How Academic Program Review Can Foster Intellectual Conformity and Stifle Diversity of Thought and Method." *Journal of Higher Education,* 1989, *60*, 6.

Skubal, J. "State-Level Review of Existing Academic Programs:

Have Resources Been Saved?" *Research in Higher Education,* 1979, *2,* 231.

Smith, P. *Killing the Spirit.* New York: Viking, 1990.

Solmon, L., and Astin, A. "Part One: Departments Without Distinguished Graduate Programs." *Change,* 1981a, *13*(6), 27.

Solmon, L., and Astin, A. "Part Two: The Quality of Undergraduate Education: Are Reputational Ratings Needed to Measure Quality?" *Change,* 1981b, *13*(7), 18–19.

South Carolina Coordinating Commission. *Guidelines for Institutional Effectiveness.* Unpublished manuscript. Columbia: South Carolina Coordinating Commission, Oct. 28, 1988.

Southern Regional Education Board. *Goals for Education: Challenge 2000.* Atlanta, Ga.: Southern Regional Education Board, 1988.

Southern Regional Education Board. 1989–90 Annual Report. Atlanta, Ga.: Southern Regional Education Board, 1990.

Spaeth, J., and Greeley, A. *Recent Alumni and Higher Education: A Survey of College Graduates.* New York: McGraw-Hill, 1970.

Spangehl, S. "The Push to Assess: Why It's Feared and How to Respond." *Change,* Jan./Feb. 1987, *19*(1), 35–36.

Spencer, L. "The Perils of Socialized Higher Education." *Forbes,* May 27, 1991, p. 304.

State University System of Florida. "Procedural Guidelines for Review of Existing Programs." *Academic Program Review in the State University System of Florida.* Unpublished manuscript. Tallahassee: State University System of Florida, n.d.

State University System of Florida. *Program Review of Psychology.* Tallahassee: State University System of Florida, 1987.

State University System of Florida Master Plan 1988-89—1992-93: Tallahassee: Florida Board of Regents, 1988.

Sternberg, R. *The Triarchic Mind: A New Theory of Human Intelligence.* New York: Viking, 1988.

Stevenson, M., Walleri, D., and Japely, S. "Designing Follow-up Studies of Graduates and Former Students." In P. T. Ewell (ed.), *Assessing Educational Outcomes.* New Directions for Institutional Research, no. 47. San Francisco: Jossey-Bass, 1985.

Storr, A. *Solitude.* New York: Free Press, 1988.

Sykes, C. *PROFSCAM.* Washington, D.C.: Regnery Gateway, 1988.

Sykes, G. "Examining the Contradictions of Licensure." *Education Week,* Mar. 29, 1989, p. 32

Tennessee. General Assembly. *Public Chapter 308 of the Acts of the 94th General Assembly of the State of Tennessee.* Nashville: Tennessee General Assembly, 1987.

Tennessee Higher Education Commission. "Centers and Chairs of Excellence." Unpublished paper. Nashville: Tennessee Higher Education Commission, n.d.

Tennessee Higher Education Commission. Alumni survey. Nashville: Tennessee Higher Education Commission, 1987.

Terenzini, P. "Assessment with Open Eyes: Pitfalls in Studying Student Outcomes." *Journal of Higher Education,* 1989, *60*(6), 645, 654.

Texas Higher Education Coordinating Board. *Texas Charter for Public Higher Education.* Adopted by the 70th Texas Legislature. Austin: Texas Higher Education Coordinating Board, 1987.

Texas Higher Education Coordinating Board. *Guidelines for Quality Review of Doctoral Programs.* Austin: Texas Higher Education Coordinating Board, 1987.

Texas Higher Education Coordinating Board. *Advanced Research Program and Advanced Technology Program: Preliminary Report.* Austin: Texas Higher Education Coordinating Board, 1988.

Thomas, L. *The Youngest Science: Notes of a Medicine Watcher.* New York: Viking, 1983.

Time, Sept. 12, 1988, pp. 72–73.

Toffler, A. *Power Shift.* New York: Bantam Books, 1990.

Toulmin, S. *Knowing and Acting: An Invitation to Philosophy.* New York: Macmillan, 1976.

Townsend, R. *Up the Organization.* New York: Knopf, 1970.

Troutt, W. "Relationships Between Regional Accrediting Association Standards and Educational Quality." In R. I. Miller (ed.), *Institutional Assessment for Self-Improvement.* New Directions for Institutional Research, no. 1. San Francisco: Jossey-Bass, 1981.

Utah Board of Regents. *Utah's Centers of Excellence: Economic Growth from Technology.* Brochure. Salt Lake City: Utah System of Higher Education, State Board of Regents, n.d.

Viadero, D. "NCATE Rejects Reaccreditation for 14 Colleges." *Education Week,* 1990, *9*(4), 1.

Virginia Plan for Higher Education 1989. Richmond: State Council of Higher Education for Virginia, 1989.

Warren, J. "The Blind Alley of Value-Added." *AAHE Bulletin,* 1984, *37*(1), 10.

Webb, E., Campbell, D., Schwartz, R., and Sechrest, L. *Unobtrusive Measures: Nonreactive Research in the Social Sciences.* Skokie, Ill.: Rand McNally, 1966.

Webster, D. "Advantages and Disadvantages of Methods of Assessing Quality." *Change,* 1981, *13*(7), 20-24.

Webster, D. "America's Highest Ranked Graduate Schools, 1925–1982." *Change,* 1983, *15*(4), 14-24.

Webster, D. "Who Is Jack Gourman and Why Is He Saying All Those Things About My College?" *Change,* 1984, *16*(8), 14-55.

Webster's Ninth New Collegiate Dictionary. Springfield: Merriam-Webster, 1983.

Weiss, S. "Southern College Group Seeking Tougher Supervision of Athletics." *New York Times,* May 19, 1991, pp. 1, 23.

"West Texas President Files Lawsuit Against 2 Professors." *Chronicle of Higher Education,* Mar. 9, 1988, p. A13.

Westling, J. "The Assessment Movement Is Based on a Misdiagnosis of the Malaise Afflicting American Higher Education." *Chronicle of Higher Education,* 1988, *35*(8), B1.

Wharton, J. *What I Have Learned.* New York: Simon & Schuster, 1966.

Whitehead, A. *The Aims of Education.* New York: Macmillan, 1929.

Wilson, L. *The Academic Man.* New York: Octagon Books, 1964.

Wolff, R. "Assessment and Accreditation: A Shotgun Marriage." Paper presented at conference of American Association for Higher Education, Washington, D.C., June 28, 1990.

Worthen, B., and Sanders, J. *Educational Evaluation: Alternative Approaches and Practical Guidelines.* New York: Longman, 1987.

Young, K., Chambers, C., Kells, H., and Associates. *Understanding Accreditation: Contemporary Perspectives on Issues and Prac-*

tices in Evaluating Educational Quality. San Francisco: Jossey-Bass, 1983.

Zemsky, R., and Massey, W. "The Rain Man Cometh." *AGB Reports,* 1990, *32*(1), 21.

Zemsky, R., and Massey W. "Cost Containment: Committing to a New Economic Reality." Pew Higher Education Research Program. Policy Perspectives, Feb. 1991, pp. 1, 2A.

Zukav, G. *The Dancing Wu Li Masters.* New York: Morrow, 1979.

Index